MASS MEDIA, PEOPLE AND POLITICS IN NIGERIA

MASS MEDIA, PEOPLE AND POLITICS IN NIGERIA

LUKE UKA UCHE
University of Lagos

CONCEPT PUBLISHING COMPANY, NEW DELHI-110059

ISBN 81-7022-232-X

First Published 1989

© L.U. Uche 1989
Luke Uka Uche (*b*. 1947-)

Published by
Ashok Kumar Mittal
Concept Publishing Company
A/15-16, Commercial Block Mohan Garden
NEW DELHI-110059 (India)

Lasertypeset by
Microtech Advance Printing System (P) Ltd.
H-13, Bali Nagar
NEW DELHI - 110015

Printed at
New Gian Offset Printers
495, Shahzada Bagh
DELHI - 110035

DEDICATION

This book is dedicated to a Nigerian patriot, nationalist and the father of Nigerian journalism, Dr. NNAMDI AZIKIWE, The Owelle of Onitsha, the first indigenous Governor General and President of Nigeria; for his immense and selfless contributions to the making of the Nigerian nation and his struggles for the Nigerian independence, through his *West African Pilot*.

FOREWORD

Nigeria's continuing quest for national identity has been indelibly marked by the character of her political history. The Nigerian case is undoubtedly a particular manifestation of the general malady which afflicts "nations" crafted by colonial administrators. Lack of consensus about the nature and goals of the postcolonial state and about the rules and modalities of political articulation among the indigenous elite who inherited the colonial burden, has made national development problematic, fostering political and economic instability.

Between those who see the development of Nigeria as an evolving process of negotiated understandings and structures, and those who accept the colonial legacy as the finished product and final destiny of the Nigerian nation, stress and struggle are inevitable. The incompatibilities of the several interest groups struggling for ascendancy on the political landscape, underlie the fragility of cultural development in Nigeria which is reflected in the behaviour of key cultural institutions such as the mass media.

In this landmark study, **Luke Uka** Uche has demonstrated the relationship between the "spirit" of recent Nigerian politics and the orientation of the Nigerian mass media. What he has described so graphically and analysed so fastidiously in fact goes beyond mere "reciprocity"; the fact that the Nigerian media are the way they are first because Nigerian society has been motivated by the forces of ethnicity and fuelled by aggressive partisanship; and the media, having imbibed of this influence, derive their character from it, and in turn become vehicles for reinforcing the ethnicity thesis.

Those who see the evils of Nigerian society as emanating from the media need to look again; if causality is possible, it is probably from the structures and values of political culture to the mass media rather than the other way.

The implications of Uche's work are that while we seek to document and critically analyse the structure and content of the media, we must be no less thorough in our critique of the structures and contents of political behaviour. Uche has demonstrated how this relationship can be productively explored in a responsible and scholarly manner. His writing is ebullient; some of his criticisms are pungent; but they are also mostly cogent.

He has not set out to write a descriptive history of the growth and development of the media, as such. Therefore, many aspects of such a task are not present in this book. What he has demonstrated here is the quality of research and analysis that makes him an obvious candidate to embark on such descriptive histories of the Nigerian mass media.

I commend this book with the expectation that others will be forthcoming.

Lagos, Nigeria
September 1986

Professor Alfred E Opubor, Ph D
Department of Mass Communication,
University of Lagos.

PREFACE

MASS MEDIA, PEOPLE AND POLITICS IN NIGERIA is a book that brings to the fore the precarious predicament of the mass media of a country whose political culture is characterised by divergent and powerful interest groups with insatiable political and economic demands on the larger political entity. My primary intention has been to demonstrate how Nigeria's development as a nation state has similarly influenced the way and manner of the organisation, administration and contents of her mass media systems.

The present volume, it must be admitted, does not pretend to be concerned with presenting the history of the Nigerian mass media, per se. Rather, the book's primary concern has been to deal with the development of radio, television, newspaper and news agency (wire service) as predicated by the various political administrations that have had to govern. The Federal Radio Corporation of Nigeria (FRCN), the Nigerian Television Authority (NTA) and the News Agency of Nigeria (NAN) are critically analysed and evaluated not only because I am quite familiar with their organisation, structure and administration as they were part of my work schedule of media parastatals during my stint with the public service, but also because they just have organisations that have made them the institutions they are. The *other* media are just harried in their organisation, administration, structure and content. They just come and you never can tell when they will disappear. The only exceptions are the *Daily Times*, *New Nigerian* and those newspapers that are owned by the various state governments of the federation. Their stability could also be attributed to Federal and State Governments' intervention in ownership, management and control.

This book contains quite a substantial amount of the original material from my doctoral thesis of 1977 from the Ohio State University, Columbus, Ohio, U.S.A., titled : "The Mass Media Systems in Nigeria : A Study in Structure, Management and Functional Roles in Crisis Situations." I have thought it appropriate to widen and update the scope of that Ph.D thesis. Also, during the 34th annual conference of the International Communication Association

(ICA) in San Francisco in May, 1984, I had not only the luck but also the honour of having a competitive research report accepted for presentation to the Political Communication Division's Star Session of the ICA. That paper on "Influence of Ethnic Politics in the Development of Broadcasting in Nigeria" forms the backbone of chapters three and four of this book. The other sources from which original materials have been drawn in putting together this volume are the *Gazette, The Third Channel,* and Zeszyty *PRASOZNA WCZE.* I am most grateful to the publishers of these journals for granting me their permissions to include in this book some of my related articles that were previously published by their respective journals.

I am also very grateful to all those who provided me with the data I needed for putting this book together. To such people I say thank you very much; especially Malam Yaya Abubakar, the Director of Network News, Nigerian Television Authority, Lagos; Mr. Vincent Maduka, former Director-General of the Nigerian Television Authority; Mr. Ayo Okesanya, former controller of the Federal Radio Corporation of Nigeria, Management Services and former General Manager of Lagos State Broadcasting Corporation; Mr. George Bako, former Director-General of the Federal Radio Corporation of Nigeria; Mr. Onuorah Nzekwu, former General Manager of News Agency of Nigeria; and Mr.Femi Adefala, former Editor-in-Chief of News Agency of Nigeria; Mr. B.Raj Bhandari, the UNESCO Administrative and Programme Officer for South and Central Asia, New Delhi, India and his staff; and Mrs.Julie Poku of the Federal Ministry of Education, National Commission for UNESCO, Lagos.

I am most indebted to Professor Alfred E. Opubor, a colleague and one of Africa's foremost scholars in the field of mass communication, whose keynote address during the final plenary session at the fifteenth biennial conference of the International Association for Mass Communication Research, (IAMCR) August, 1986, in New Delhi, India, has brought about a renewed international respect for, interest in, and recognition of African scholarship in the field of journalism and mass communication. His "FOREWORD" to this book is a very intelligent and incisive critique of what this book is all about : the Nigerian political vis-a-vis mass media environment.

Finally, I thank my wife, Joyce Chibuzo, an officer with the Youth Development Department in the Federal Ministry of Social Development, Youth and Sports. She is my closest academic and professional ally and confidant in the field of journalism and mass communication. Her intellectual insights, suggestions and criticisms have all added to strengthening this book. She and our children (Ugochukwu, Adaku, Uzodinma, and Nnanenyem) have given me the joy, happiness and conducive environment in the family for a productive and challenging scholarship. I am most grateful to her and our children for their support and encouragement.

One problem an author faces in writing a book on Nigerian mass media is the mercurial nature of the profession. Many things take place in quick successions, with the result that a researcher's data are easily rendered obsolete; especially when edicts, decrees and other laws are promulgated and enacted for purely smoothening the administrative convenience of the ruling elite, without any regard to public good, continuity and sustenance of a tradition in the system. If brutal changes are effected before this book comes out of the press or as soon as it comes out, please bear with me. It is all part of our search for a development paradigm.

Lagos, Nigeria
September, 1986

Luke Uka Uche, Ph D
Department of Mass Communication
University of Lagos.

CONTENTS

INTRODUCTION

This is a book on the evolution, growth and political influence of radio, television, newspaper and news agency media in Nigeria. But before one can understand the underlying factors behind the way mass media operate in Nigeria and their influence in the nation's political development, a background knowledge of the Nigerian society, with all the attendant cultural variables embedded in the philosophy of the national media set-up, becomes imperative. As long as this book focuses on the media's development and impact on Nigeria's political evolution, it then becomes essential to examine the cultural, historical, social, religious, political and educational structures of the nation. The reason for such an anatomy of the society is that Nigeria's political development in which the political influence of the media is being studied, can be traced to the various cultural entities existing in the society. Also, differing cultural patterns may affect people's perception of the media functions in ethnic conflicts that had in the past led to major national crises.

The task of describing the cultural, linguistic and ethnic differences existing among the leading ethnic groups in Nigeria makes this book as comprehensive as possible for one who is unfamiliar with the Nigerian politics of ethnicity and the role of the mass media in such a political set-up.

The establishments of the mass media in Nigeria were along ethnic lines and their ethnic orientation has somewhat affected their functionalism. Also, the mass media played the leading role of promoting the political, social and economic aspirations of their tribesmen. In essence, a basic understanding of the economy, history, politics and other major characteristics that contrast the major tribes of Nigeria is necessary to an understanding of this book. It is also by an understanding of the peculiarities of the Nigerian society that one is able to trace the origins and patterns of the mass media establishment in Nigeria; as well as the genesis of the political crises in which the roles of the mass media became quite pronounced and pervasive. Chapters one and two are therefore devoted to an overview of Nigeria, her economy, education, major ethnic groups, history and politics.

The respective chapters on radio and television have attempted to critically examine the structure and evolution of radio and television broadcasting in Nigeria. In the process of tracing their historical evolution, the impact on the national political system is also analysed. The basic analyses in chapters three and four have been to show how the radio and television mass media evolved along regional lines with the result that they became integrated with the partisan politics of each of the major ethnic groups vying for national political leadership.

Prior to her independence in 1960, the Nigerian Broadcasting Service (NBS) was under the administration of the colonial government. When Nigeria became independent, the Federal government inherited the control of the NBS and, together with the regions, all the ministries of information as colonial legacies from Great Britain. But it was the regions that established their own radio and television broadcasting systems. The Federal government, somewhat reluctantly and belatedly, did join the race in the establishment of the television system.

The transition to modern mass communication systems in Nigeria was completed in October, 1959, when the Western Nigeria Television (WNTV) began its operation in Ibadan. It became the first television ever to go on the air in Africa, and as a result no announcer of the WNTV ever forgot to say "The First in Africa" during station identification. The former Eastern Region did not want to be left behind. One year later, it started its own television system. Its own announcers also used to boast of "Second to None". In 1962, both the Federal government and the Northern Region began operating their own television stations in Lagos and Kaduna, respectively.

What we are now noticing is a trend towards regionalisation of radio and television mass media in Nigeria. This pattern was bolstered by one of the numerous pre-independence constitutional amendments in Britain that granted each of the former three regions of Nigeria (North, East, and West) power to make its own laws within its region. The Federal Government was granted an Exclusive Legislative List of subjects that gave it the monopoly to make laws on those subjects on the list.[1] However, radio, television and the press were not included in that Exclusive List; hence the regional governments were able to establish competitive organs of mass communications in their respective regions.

During the regional administrative set-up, each region of Nigeria was once dominated by a single political party that was usually formed by the dominant ethnic group of the region.

There was no national political party that appealed to national as opposed to regional audiences. The result was that the mass media of the regions became the megaphones of political interest articulation of each of the regions within the federation. The then Nigerian Broadcasting Corporation (NBC) was assumed to be neutral in sectional politics, with its statewide affiliates in the whole country.

The establishment of radio and television was thus based along regional and ethnic lines. This was to be the pattern of mass media structure and control in Nigeria, and a potential breeding ground for political irresponsibility that would inevitably culminate in ghastly national accidents (coups and a civil war). The quest for the regionalisation of the mass media with the attendant concurrent integration with the political structure of each region, is aptly demonstrated by the following reservation the former Northern Region Government expressed against the NBC:

> The Northern Regional Government wishes to express its serious concern about the presentation of news from the Lagos studio of the Nigerian Broadcasting Corporation (NBC). Despite its continued representations to the NBC about its handling of news items concerning the Northern Regional Government, in which facts favourable to the Northern Regional Government are omitted, while those damaging to the Northern Region are given considerable prominence, the NBC have (sic) continued to present unbalanced news programmes from their Lagos studio. This discriminatory handling of news came to a head yesterday when the Regional news service in Kaduna included M. Ahidjo's criticism of Alhaji Ibrahim Imam and his threats to sue the Leader of the Opposition in the court for his statements about the Cameroun. Yet M.Ahidjo's criticism of Alhaji Ibrahim Imam was cut out from the Lagos report of Ahidjo's statement.
>
> The Northern Regional Government has now lost faith in the NBC news service from Lagos and intends to go ahead without further delay with its own sound broadcasting service.
>
> News programmes from the Lagos studio of the NBC have, in the opinion of the Northern Regional Government, failed to take into account the interest of the Northern Region and have forfeited the Northern Government's confidence in the NBC's ability to present news fairly and objectively on their national programme.
>
> It is hoped to form a company to operate both sound broadcasting and television services as soon as negotiations are completed with experienced and established overseas firms. When this service comes into operation, it will be broadcasting its own news bulletin which will be completely independent of the NBC.[2]

Military dictatorship (democracy?) has become part of Nigeria's political culture. The past three decades in Nigeria have been characterised by military rule. The coups that led to the military regimes have also scored the importance the ruling elite attaches to the radio mass medium in the nation. Instead of the military armoury, the Federal Radio Corporation of Nigeria's (FRCN) studios in Lagos have always been the prime targets. During the February 13, 1976, abortive military coup d'état, the fight for the control of the government of the country began at the FRCN headquarters in Lagos, and it was also there that it ended. The following account of the fight for the control of the FRCN studios in Lagos during the attempted coup, as reported in the *Washington Post*, is indicative of the importance of radio when a struggle for power occurs:

The coup announcement was made from the radio Nigeria's studio, just 300 yards from where .... shooting was said to have taken place.

Sources close to the radio said Lt. Col. Dimka entered the studios in civilian clothes surrounded by armed soldiers, and changed into uniform before taking the microphone to address the nation.

The troops remained at the station until units loyal to the Muhammed government counter-attacked in mid-afternoon, recapturing the radio after about ten minutes of firing, the sources said. They did not mention any deaths in this action.

Rebel troops were rounded up and taken away .... Soon after the recovery of the radio station, broadcasting resumed with light music until the collapse of the coup has (sic) officially announced.[3]

This is a further evidence of how radio and other national mass media systems have always been used in leadership struggles in the nation. The way the military administrations have used the radio is not very different from that of their civilian predecessors. Various chapters will vindicate the validity of this claim.

The establishment of the press in Nigeria followed exactly the same pattern (along regional and ethnic lines) as that of radio and television, discussed in chapters three and four. Both the Federal and regional governments maintained (and still maintain) their own newspapers. One striking difference was that private ownership of the press had existed in Nigeria prior to independence in 1960. But at present, privately-owned newspapers are in the minority.

In Nigeria, it is accurate to suggest that the tribally-based politics of the past also affected the national press system. The important question thus becomes what happened in Nigeria when independence was won from Great Britain on October 1, 1960? Surprisingly, the oppositional mentality of the press that characterised it during the colonial era still prevailed - a condition that is generally good for any open society. However, the Nigerian press became more and more region-based (or tribal in their orientation and appeal). Each region aspired for the interest and supremacy of its tribesmen. One is not far from the mark to suggest that the type of structure of, and controls exerted over the entire mass media systems in Nigeria were the precursors of Nigeria's devastating Civil War. Each of the former regions had its own press, and all the media joined their regional governments to engage in bitter political polemics.

One can only grasp the realities of the ramifications of the politico-tribal structures and controls of the pre - and post-independence Nigerian press by reading the following by-line a foreign correspondent dispatched from Lagos during the "weti e"[4] period that stigmatised an overt parliamentary elections rigging in Nigeria's history. This happened during the 1964 general elections in the Western Region of Nigeria.

In the populous Eastern Region, whose political powers are aligned with the opposition Action Group in the West, key city councils adopted ordinances banning papers that stayed neutral or actively backed the Western Government's return to power.

This group includes the Federal Government-owned *Morning Post*, the Western Government-owned *Daily Sketch* and the independent *Daily Express* and the *Daily Times* - Nigeria's most widely read paper. The net effect of the ordinances has been to block the entrance of these papers into the Eastern Region by either air or road.

In retaliation, city councils in the West have made it a crime not only to read pro-opposition *Pilot*, *Telegraph* and *Daily Tribune* but also to tune in the Eastern Region radio. If caught errant newspaper readers and radio listeners are subject to a year's imprisonment.

The East has imposed no such penalties. But purple-uniformed political thugs have set up road blocks, searched cars for the "wrong" papers, and beaten the occupants who possessed them.[5]

It was in the midst of this political atmosphere that Nigeria's five years' attempt at parliamentary democracy became a shambles, and she plunged into one of the world's bloodiest civil wars ever fought - the Biafran war. The political parties vying for the country's leadership extensively used both the press and other mass media as battle grounds.

Chapter six, among other things, examines the evolution of the press in Nigeria and the manner the press system has affected the political philosophy of the nation. It also analyzes the problem of control, ownership and responsibility in the mass media. Chapter seven treats the laws of the nation as they relate to the press. It also presents an interpretative analyses of various Acts of the defunct parliament of the First Republic and military decrees and their implications on the freedom of the mass media. The chapter is concluded with factors, the author believes, that do influence the degree of press freedom in Nigeria.

FOOTNOTES

1. Ian K. MacKay. "Concepts of Nigerian Broadcasting".
    European Broadcasting Union Review, No. 788, March 1963, pp. 12-20.
2. Federal Ministry of Information (Lagos), "News From Nigeria," No. 5, Section 10, January 18, 1961.
3. *Washington Post*, February 14, 1976.
4. Weti e is a Yoruba expression that was the rioters' slogan during the 1965 post-election crisis in the former Western Region. It means wet with petrol and set it ablaze.
5. *New York Times*, November 20, 1965.

ONE

NIGERIA: BACKGROUND TO THE STUDY

Nigeria, often referred to as "The Giant of Africa," lies along the Gulf of Guinea in the West Coast of Africa. Nigeria occupies an area land mass of 356,669 sq. miles (or 923,773 sq.km.). When the States of Texas, Michigan and South Carolina, and the District of Columbia are combined, that will equal the size of Nigeria.

Nigeria shares a common boundary with the Republic of Cameroun on the east, Republic of Benin on the west, Chad Republic on the north-west and Niger Republic on the north. She is bordered on the north-east by Lake Chad, and the Atlantic Ocean on the south. She extends from 2° 30' to 14° 30' E. and from 4° 30' to 14° 17'.[1]

There are two principal seasons in Nigeria: the rainy season and the dry (harmattan) season; and they, in turn, affect the climatic conditions of the country. The rainy season starts from April and lasts till October, with an August dry spell that lasts three weeks in-between this period. The average annual rainfall is around 70" in the West, 170" in many parts of the East; 50" in the most central part of the country, and 20" in the extreme north of the country[2] where the Sahara desert encroaches.

The dry season (popularly known as the "harmattan" locally) commences in November and ends in March. During this period, dust-laden wind currents from the Sahara desert enter the northern part of the country, and drift into the South of the country. Their effects are those of high temperatures during the day, and cool temperatures at night; and the human skins are generally dry at this time.

Nigeria is characterised by four main vegetations: swamp forest, rain forest, savanna and mountain grassland. The two major seasons - rain and dry - are influential factors in the variations of vegetations that exist in Nigeria. The swamp forest is located along the coastal and riverine areas of the country and is characterised by mangrove trees: palm trees, abra, mahogany, etc. The rain forest lies north of the swamp and extends between 75 to 150 kilometers in width. Its principal trees are the iroko, mahogany, walnut, timbers, obeche, etc. etc. As one goes farther inland, the vegetation changes to savanna and woodland. The savanna is characterised by tall grasses, small deciduous trees, and these are the areas of the country where cattle are ranched in the north.

Nigeria is neither a mountainous nor a flat land nation. In the north-east of the country is located the highest elevation - the Adamawa highlands (about 2050 meters), and in the central region in the North is the famous Jos Plateau where four hydro-electric power stations are built; in the eastern portion of the south is the Udi Hill, where the rich coal mining is located. The longest distance in the country, from the East to West, is about 1,120 km, and about 1,040 km from North to South.[3] The River Niger, the third largest river in Africa, traverses the entire length of the country. It takes its sources from the Futa Jallon Mountains in Senegal, and enters into Nigeria through the north-west of the country. It joins with River Benue, the second largest river in Nigeria, at Lokoja, and their Lokoja confluence has become one of the most attractive geographic scenes in national tourism. From Lokoja, the two rivers flow down southward and empty into the Atlantic Ocean.

A gigantic dam has been built on the River Niger at the town of Kainji. The Kainji dam supplies the nation most of its electricity as well as some neighbouring West African nations. The Kainji dam, when it was initially commissioned, was producing about 880,000 kwh per annum.[4] Other important power stations are located at the Oji River, Afam Sapele and Egbin.

Economy

The backbone of the Nigerian economy is oil. During the 1970's the lucrative market for oil, with the high foreign exchange it once generated into the nation's coffers, made it overshadow the agricultural sector which is the mainstay of the Nigerian population. Before oil became the major source of income in Nigeria, agriculture used to account for the main source of the nation's foreign exchange earnings. In 1960, 90% of Nigeria's foreign exchange earnings depended on agricultural produce; it fell to 61% in 1965, and by 1974, oil revenue had pushed it to 8% position![5] The major agricultural products in Nigeria are: cocoa, coffee, tea, groundnut (peanut), soya beans, beniseed, shea nut, ginger, cotton, kenaf, palm oil, palm kernel, copra, rubber, cassava, yams, manioc, guinea corn, millet, corn, rice, cocoyams, cowpeas, etc.

The importance of agriculture to the Nigerian economy can only be appreciated when it is seen that locally consumed items account for about 80% of agricultural production; over 80% of the population live on farming villages, and agriculture once accounted for about 63% of the gross domestic product.[6]

Nigeria has realised that some day her oil reserves will eventually exhaust and, in order not to depend solely on oil, she has started paying great attention to agriculture. Following the footsteps of the People's Republic of China in her "Green Revolution", Nigeria launched a similar massive nation-wide agrarian programme with the aim of mobilising human and material resources to achieve self-sufficiency in food production. The government established the Nigerian Agricultural Development Bank where farmers can now go for loans for developing agricultural projects. In most parts of the country, several river basin authorities have been developed. Despite this revolutionary trend in the agricultural sector, farming in Nigeria is still traditional; it is not mechanised. Mechanised farms only exist in isolated special government-owned demonstration centres and those of retired millionaire military officers who invested the wealth they amassed in farming. The majority of the farmers in the country still rely on shifting cultivation.

Nigeria was once the world's largest exporter of peanut, palm oil, and palm kernel - providing about 50% of international trade in palm kernel, 30% in palm oil, and 30% in groundnut (peanut); she was once the world's second largest producer of cocoa.[7] Cotton and rubber are the other two major agricultural commodities Nigeria exports to other nations.

Animal husbandry, fishery and forestry are also important contributors to the Nigerian economy. It was believed that in 1965 there were about seven million cattle, 14 million goats, 4.5 million sheep;[8] this made Nigeria to be an important exporter of hides and skins. There are about 500,000 pigs, and poultry exists everywhere in the country. There are about 150 varieties of fish that can be found in Nigerian waters, and fishing contributes to about 2.5% of the gross national product. The Nigerian high forests are known for their production of timbers which are exported abroad and widely used locally. There are plywood and veneer industries at Sapele and Warri.

In recent years, the agricultural sector has been getting priority budgetary allocations. But in reality, the huge budget allocations being made to the agricultural sector are yet to make any significant impact, besides political and military rhetorics, in the feeding of Nigerians as significant amount of food is still being imported. This has had adverse effect in draining the nation's foreign reserve. Also, some erstwhile politicians and other public office holders capitalised on importation of rice and other essential (food) commodities to enrich themselves and become millionaires. The presidential Task Force on Rice, a committee appointed to see to the importation and distribution of rice to stave off imminent hunger and scarcity of the commodity during the Shagari presidency, became scandalous as its members became instant millionaires. It was headed by Umaru Dikko, who took refuge in the United Kingdom when the Shagari administration was overthrown. He was kidnapped in a London street and crated to be flown to Nigeria to face trial for corrupt practices. But the whole attempt botched.

The greatest revolution in Nigeria's national economy has been in the sphere of her mineral oil. In 1965 oil export accounted for only 26% of the total value of exports.[9] But during the 1970's oil emerged as the dominant factor in the Nigerian economy. Oil now accounts for 90% of the nation's annual revenue.[10] Between 1963/64 and 1972/73, oil sector contributed to 44.5% of Nigeria's total exchange in real gross domestic product. It is estimated that when current figures are computed and released, oil will contribute about 80% of the nation's gross domestic product.

Nigeria is the world's fifth largest producer of oil and a member of the Organisation of Petroleum Exporting Countries (OPEC). She was producing a little over two million barrels of crude oil daily before the oil glut that led to quota allocation by OPEC to its members. Her current oil reserve is put at 20 billion barrels of crude, and 40 trillion cubic capacity of natural gas.[11]

The United States is the single largest importer of the Nigerian oil - she purchases 31.9% of Nigeria's oil. Other leading customers of the Nigerian oil are the Netherlands, France (10%), Japan and Brazil.[12]

Nigeria's oil wells are located mostly in the Eastern States of Rivers, Imo and Cross River in the South, and the rest are in the Bendel state, also in the South. In recent years Nigeria has developed a very aggressive and pragmatic oil policy which allows her to participate actively in her oil industry, through the Nigerian National Petroleum Corporation, NNPC. The nationalisation of the BP in 1979, as Britain, under Margaret Thatcher, dragged her feet over Zimbabwean independence during the Lancaster House Constitutional conferences, epitomised the aggressive and pragmatic oil policy that formed the bedrock of Nigeria's foreign policy in the 1970's.

Besides oil, Nigeria has the largest deposit of coal in Africa, and is the only West African country that produces it. Nigeria's coal is mostly used for internal needs, although a reasonable amount is exported; export reached its peak in 1957 when 102,000 tons were shipped abroad.[13] But it has declined in recent years due to world's switch to fuel and the environmental problems associated with coal.

Nigeria is also the world's largest producer of columbite; she accounts for 90% of the world's supply.[14] Nigeria also produces tin and exports it in large quantities to foreign markets.

There are hundreds of small and medium-scale industries in Nigeria. The government owns the giant corporations; otherwise it is a laissez-faire type of economy. However, government has recently indicated its willingness to privatise some of its industries and parastatals. The Nigerian government has been placing emphasis on the development of industries to make her less vulnerable to foreign manufactured goods. In her 1975/80 National Development Plan, $10 billion were earmarked for the development of industries.[15] In 1982, a multi-million dollar iron and steel industry went into production at Ajaokuta.[16]

Nigeria is an associate member of the European Economic Community (EEC). She ships about one-third of her goods to members of the community. But back home in Africa, in May 1975, at her initiative and that of the Republic of Togo, a treaty formally establishing the Economic Community of West African States (ECOWAS) was signed and ratified by the 15 member states. The basic objective of this community is to bring together these fifteen West African states in a wide range of economic cooperation with a market for over 200 million people, as well as "economic emancipation of the continent" and encouragement of growing as economic units among smaller African nations without being "appendages to Western economies."[17] The ECOWAS encourages free movement of citizens of member nations. In 1986, ECOWAS heads of government approved a brown card scheme for motor vehicle insurance purposes in the West African sub-region. Once in a while, the issue of introducing common currency among the member nations of ECOWAS generates exciting debates.

Education

When Britain colonised Nigeria, British missionaries followed it up with a massive introduction of Western-styled education in the South of the country. The missionaries were only allowed to get into those areas of the North where the Moslem rulers permitted them. This injunction stemmed from an agreement Britain and the Northern traditional rulers reached in which Britain was not to interfere with the Moslem religion which is diametrically different from the religion of the missionaries. Also, it must be noted that prior to the advent of the Western missionaries, the North was the only literate area of Nigeria due to Koranic studies. The concentration of missionary activities in the South only led to the concentration of educated Nigerians in the South. This created problems that are thoroughly discussed in the next chapter.

The only type of education Nigerians knew of before the missionaries came into their midst was learning the basic cultural skills of their society and its economy. However, "...since the missionaries were not prepared to modify their educational programmes to suit African needs, academic rather than technical education was given to children."[18] As a result of British-styled education, the English language, more or less, became the *lingua franca* in Nigeria. This enabled people from the various autonomous tribes that speak different tongues to communicate with one another in a neutral language everybody understands, as it was the official language of the former imperial masters who were rapidly introducing western civilisation in all its ramifications.

There is no society that can aspire to develop in the contemporary world without education. Western education has radicalised social, economic and political thought in modern Nigeria. After more than one half century of colonial rule, Britain left Nigeria with only one university, at Ibadan. But since attaining independence on October, 1,1960, Nigeria has established thirty additional universities in all parts of the nation, irrespective of religious bigotry.

In 1976, Nigeria introduced a very ambitious educational scheme: the Universal Primary Education (UPE) which increased elementary school enrolment from four million to eight million.[19] The scheme made elementary school education compulsory for Nigerian children who were of grade school age at the time it was introduced.

Nigeria's educational system is fundamentally patterned after the British model. But with the increasing needs of a developing society, the basic question becomes that of evolving the best educational philosophy that is suitable for her so as to meet her manpower need in all spheres of life. The urgent need to integrate Nigeria's immediate needs with the educational curriculum that will meet these national needs is now a problem confronting policy-makers in the nation's educational establishment. One of the nation's experts in educational administration, Ukaonu Uche, makes the following observations:

> Nigeria's growing economy requires an education programme that prepares all of its people to be active... participants. Nigerian economy needs skilled personnel for different management.... In most Western societies, the total educational process is ... tied to the work required by their societies.... The educational system inherited from the colonial government contains a serious drawback, and may hold up any educational system introduced to serve the political, economic, social and cultural needs of contemporary Nigeria.... Nigeria's present educational organization does not allow education to assume its role as it should in a modern democracy.... The present system has failed to adapt to the present conditions and life of the Nigerian society.[20]

The top priority successive administrations accorded education eventually paved the way for the redesigning of the whole national educational apparatus so as to meet the nation's needs and aspirations for social justice and equality, bearing in mind that educational imbalance among the Nigerian tribes was a catalyst in the national crises the country experienced. With the inception of the 1984/85 school calender year, a new education policy was introduced in the nation's school system. It is the 6-3-3-4; that is: six years of primary (grade) school, three years of junior high school, three years of senior high school, and four years of university education.

PEOPLE OF NIGERIA

Nigeria has the largest diversified set of people in the whole of Africa. There are multiplicities of cultures within the country, numbering well over 250 autonomous ethnic groups. And each of them has its own unique language and cultural patterns. Nigeria's 1963 census gave a population of 55 million people. A 1973 census figure that listed a population of about 80 million was abandoned due to the national controversy it generated and its inability to "command national respect." The controversy notwithstanding, the present population has been projected to be over 100 million.

But the Hausa-Fulani, Yoruba and Igbo constitute the three largest single dominant ethnic groups in Nigeria. The political and economic domains of the country have been virtually dictated by them. One is not far from the mark to state that the political history of modern Nigeria is the history of inter-tribal schism, open rivalry and manoeuvring among the Hausa-Fulani of the North, the Yoruba of the South-west, and the Igbo of the South-east. It is thus necessary to look into the cultural backgrounds of these three dominant ethnic groups, and to see how cultural differences have transcended the social, political and economic development of the country, and their implications on the mass media development in Nigeria. Also, as long as this book is on the development and political implications of the mass media establishments in Nigeria, it becomes increasingly imperative to recapitulate how ethnicity has influenced the history of Nigeria and the structure of her mass media system.

The Hausa-Fulani

The Hausa and Fulani live in the savanna belt of Northern Nigeria. Prior to the advent of the British conquest of the North and the subsequent colonial rule, the Hausa and Fulani had excelled all other people around them in literacy through Islamic studies. The Hausas had long established trans-Saharan trade routes with the people of North Africa and the Middle East. These trans-Saharan contacts with the Arab world consisted of trades in gold, salt, hides and skins and slaves. As a result of this contact, they became easy converts of the Moslem religion and ultra conservative adherents of the Moslem laws and faith.

The Hausas and Fulanis form the bulk of the Nigerian population, about 27 million. The Hausa language is not only a *lingua franca* in Northern Nigeria, but also in most of West Africa where the Hausa-Fulani had had lasting historical contacts. Not very much is known about the early history of the original Hausa but scholars of the Hausa culture have generally agreed that well established Hausa settlements preceded the advent of Islam which slowly diffused into their culture and immensely affected their social and political organisations.[21] And Islamic laws and doctrines became inseparable from their political institutions.

In the 13th century, the Fulanis, who were mostly nomads, began to infiltrate into Hausaland. The infiltration had far-reaching consequences. Under their leadership, powerful kingdoms and highly sophisticated political administrative networks became established in the North. When the Fulanis migrated to Hausaland from the Futa Toro area of Senegal, they were not social isolates, but intermingled with the Hausa people, inter-married with them and adopted their Moslem faith and language; although some scholars say they brought the Moslem faith. By virtue of their superior intelligence, they occupied positions of high integrity and political importance.[22] However, before the Fulani infiltration into Hausaland in which they came along with "books on Divinity and Etymology"[23] the Hausas had been the dominant political figures in their land.

They had established successful city-states in Kano and Katsina, monopolised the trans-Saharan trade with Arabia, and Leo Africanus is said to have described them as "rich merchants and most civic people."[24] This Hausa commercial ingenuity, and the weaving of religion with the political structure have had a tremendous social influence of detaching them from people of other ethnic groups. But it also strengthened their cohesiveness and cultural consciousness, as well as easy political administration within their midst. The impact of such cultural variables as religion, commerce and politics, on the Hausa, is aptly summed up by Kalu Ezera:

> Possessing a highly developed skill in trading, Hausa traders have settled in almost all urban towns throughout West Africa and Central Africa. In most of these places they tend to live together in exclusive Hausa "colonies" separate from the peoples of the other tribes and thereby keeping intact their traditional culture. By virtue of their religion and their theocentric government, the Hausas have become a well disciplined people, one of whose characteristic features is unquestioning obedience to constituted authority.[25]

Sometime in the early 19th century, Usman Dan Fodio, a Fulani scholar of a proud descent, and his followers, unleashed the Jihad (Moslem Holy War) against the urbanised Hausas to divorce Islam from pagan culture and to restore purity in the religion because they depended on it for their value systems, ambitions and sense of security.[26] What triggered off the Jihad was a long dispute between Usman Dan Fodio and the Sultan of Gobir in which the latter unsuccessfully tried to kill the former when their relations became strained as a result of certain religious restrictions the Sultan promulgated aimed at curbing the influence of Usman Dan Fodio and his followers.[27]

The Jihad was very successful and this led to the establishment of Fulani empires: Bornu and Kanem empires became outstanding examples. Some areas of northern Yorubaland (Kwara) that shared a common border with the North were systematically conquered and converted to Islam.

During one of the bitter constitutional conferences, in the 1950's, that heralded the Nigerian independence, the Yorubas demanded that those northern Yoruba areas that had forcibly become integrated with the North as a result of the 19th century Jihad be integrated with their kith and kin in the Western Region. To this demand the North responded that those Yorubas could move if they so wished, but the land could not be integrated or "moved" to any region outside of the North.[28]

The administrative skill that the leaders of the Jihad developed was the emirate (or county) system of government in which the emir's allegiance is to the sultan. But the emirs have their own subordinates at the district and village levels who, in turn, pay allegiance to them. Although Richard L. Sklar and C.S. Whitaker, Jr. have observed that there are certain distinctive features in each of the political systems of the emirates, they do admit that there are certain basic universal principles that govern the application of emirate rule in Northern Nigeria. These are their assessments:

> ...emirate rule is theocratic in the sense that an emir is thought to personify the Islamic fusion of political and religious authority ... it is dynastic: emirs are chosen from the membership of royal dynasties by traditional electors, subject to the special customary procedures of particular states ... emirs govern their domains through ranks of titled officials. Some traditional offices are restricted to men of royal birth and some to men of noble birth; others are within the emir's unrestricted power of appointment. Among those eligible for office, competition is keen, and its intensity is reinforced by the participation of those who stand to gain by the advancement of a prospectively more powerful patron.[29]

Another important aspect of the emirate rule that has pervaded the structure is the clientage system. And M.G. Smith describes it as "an exclusive relation of mutual benefit which holds between two persons defined as socially and politically unequal, which stresses their solidarity."[30]

More than any other factor, Moslem religion united the vast areas of the North to the extent that Southerners erroneously refer to all Northerners as Hausas and Fulanis, without regard for other minority tribes that have been eclipsed by the Hausa-Fulani majority. These other tribes include the Jukun, Igbirra, Tiv, Gwarri, Idoma, Igala, Nupe, Kanuri, and many others.

The North was well organised administratively before the British colonised Nigeria. The result was that Britain introduced complete "Indirect Rule" system in the North as opposed to its partial success in the South. Also, the British agreed neither to interfere with the religion of the North nor to impose Western educational ideals because of the North's sensitivity to its Moslem religion. And the cultural pride of the North that stemmed from the Jihad and the conquest of other empires, led to the rejection of Western ideals. The result was that while the South aspired for modern technology and innovations through education, the North was vacillating and reminiscing on the past greatness and glories of its forefathers, and aspired to return to such a period. Also, when the British decided to grant self-rule to the then three regions of Nigeria: North, West and East, the North said it was too soon and decided not to opt for self-rule at the same time the West and East did. The North increasingly became the laggard in modern education in Nigeria due to its pride in cultural accomplishments of the past.

When independence became imminent for Nigeria, the North was caught unprepared and feared Southern domination in political and economic control of the country. At times the North clamoured for secession and publicly emphasised the "irreconcilable" cultural differences between it and the South.

The Northern fear of Southern domination, as a result of its modern educational handicap, is validated by the following editorial that appeared in the Northern vernacular newspaper, *Gaskiya Ta Fi Kwabo* :

Southerners will take the place of Europeans in the North. What is there to stop them ...? There are Europeans but, undoubtedly, it is the Southerner who has the power in the North.[31]

If one detaches himself from the bias and prejudices of Western education and technology, it cannot be fairly said that the North was backward, per se. In fact, it was the Hausa-Fulani group who became the first literates in Nigeria as a result of Moslem influence; they excelled in Islamic studies. It was also in the central portion of the North, that, perhaps, one of the oldest and highest advanced civilisations in Africa and the world in iron-using technique during the Iron Age, reached its height around 900 B.C. and 200 A.D.[32] This civilisation, popularly known as "Nok culture", existed in the Nok region of central Nigeria, and the people excelled in making fine figurine head portraits in terra cotta around the plateau region of Northern Nigeria.

The problem of the North was that it did not know how to reconcile modernity with a proud traditionalism. The North tried to hang on to its past heritage in political, social and economic matters without realising how modern skills have rendered such enviable heritage obsolete. The unequal pace and speed with which the North and the South accepted modern ways of life created a great disparity in the distribution of national intelligentsia cadre. This resulted in political catastrophies that plunged the nation into a series of crises, in which the mass media became integral parts of the nation's political development process.

The Yoruba

The Yoruba-speaking people of Nigeria number about twenty million. They live in the South-West (often referred to as the West) of Nigeria. The Yorubas claim a common ancestral descent from the legendary *Oduduwa* that has been epitomised in their history. The Yorubas are the most urbanised group of people in Nigeria and Africa. Ibadan, a city in Yoruba heartland, is among the most populous in tropical Africa. The desire to lead urban life is natural among the Yorubas as Robert Collis notes that "the Yorubas like to live together, so that they do not inhabit individual hamlets but prefer to dwell in villages or collections of villages which in the end form a town."[33]

Just like the Hausa-Fulani of Nigeria, the Yorubas also have a proud tradition. During the 17th century, the Yorubas established highly powerful kingdoms at Ibadan, Oyo, Abeokuta, Ife, Egba, Egbado, Ketu, Benin and many other areas within the Yorubaland. Although African historians have down-played it, the Yoruba empire of Oyo was so powerful that, in 1730, it colonised the sovereign kingdom of Dahomey (now Republic of Benin), and the cultural impact of that colonisation still exists there till this day: Yoruba language is not only widely spoken in Benin,[34] but also, many cultural practices of the Yorubas, especially the worship of ancestral spirits, are widely practised. A vivid account of the power of the Yoruba empire of Oyo and its conquest and rule over the kingdom of Dahomey is given by I.A. Akinjogbin:

> Politically, Dahomey remained a tributary state within the Oyo empire. The attempt made towards the end of Agaja (the king of Dahomey) and the beginning of the reign of Tegbesu... to throw off the Oyo Yoke resulted in very heavy punishment of Dahomey. After 1748, Dahomey did not again neglect to pay the annual tribute for the rest of the 18th century. Indeed from 1740 onwards until the end of the century the court of Dahomey increasingly imbibed both cultural and religious ideas from the Yoruba.[35]

But the powerful and successful Moslem Jihad of the 19th century had its impact on the Yoruba kingdoms. As the Oyo empire began to show signs of weakness, Dahomey eventually freed itself, and the Oba (king) of Ilorin, a northern Yoruba city, invited the powerful army of the Fulanis to help hi n declare freedom from his fellow tribesmen at Oyo. When this was accomplished, a Moslem emirate was set up in Ilorin and the traditional Yoruba Oba was deposed and his subjects converted to Islam. This forcible annexation of a Yoruba area as part of Fulani empire raised eyebrows in

Yorubaland, and as John E. Flint notes: "It seemed as if the conquest of Ilorin was but the preliminary to the collapse of the entire Yoruba power-system, indeed the nearby capital of the Yoruba empire, Old Oyo, had to be evacuated and a new city built farther south. The Yorubas were saved by the emergence of the new state of Ibadan on the northern frontiers facing Ilorin. The Ibadans first checked, then defied the Ilorins, in a permanent war punctuated only by periods of uneasy truce."[36]

The Yorubas, especially those of the Egba clan, were the first set of people in Nigeria to be exposed to Western contact. And soon afterwards, Western education and other value systems diffused within the Yoruba cul-ture. The reason for this early exposure was due to the location of Lagos, Nigeria's principal port, through which the early European missionaries and traders entered into Nigeria and established trading posts along the coast; also Lagos became the first Nigerian city to be annexed by the British Crown.

The Yorubas are wealthy and middle class people, highly educated in the Western tradition. Kalu Ezera attributes the wealth of the Yorubas to the fact that Lagos, being the nation's capital city[37] and seaport, and located in Yorubaland, meant that a large proportion of the nation's exports and im-ports had to travel through Yorubaland with the economic consequence that "the Yorubas... relatively enjoyed a much higher *per capita* income than the peoples of the other regions of the country."[38] Ezera further observes that their early contact with the Europeans "aroused in them an interest in West-ern education... coupled with a marked propensity for commercial activity... enabled them to occupy leading positions not only in government services but also in the professional and commercial life of the country."[39]

The Yorubas are both Christians and Moslems due to their contacts with these two religions. But the Yoruba Moslems are not as conservative in Mos-lem faith as the Northern Moslems are. Among the Yoruba Moslems, many of the Moslem laws are not strictly practised. Some Yorubas still adhere to the religion of their forefathers in which there is a hierarchy of gods.

The overwhelming evidence of eastern influence on Yoruba culture, espe-cially in religion and arts that are cast in bronze and brass, have made scholars believe that the Yorubas might have migrated from the Upper Nile Valley. This is a result of archaeological discoveries of meticulous artistic carvings of Yoruba national god, Shango, in which appears a ram's mask, and Shango is equally the god of storm and thunder.[40] This kind of artistic design for the god with a ram's mask is said to be reminiscent of Kushite or old Egyptian origin.[41]

In the modern Yoruba culture, constitutional monarchy is still prevailing, although the institution is now more of a cultural pride than that of a political power as the nation state has become very powerful under a strong central government for the rest of the nation. However, some of the Yoruba obas still wield political powers in their localities because there are some monarchies whose thrones are more prestigious, due to historical achievements, than others. There is hardly a Yoruba monarch who is as powerful in political influence as a Northern Nigeria Sultan or Emir because of the impact of the Western culture on the Yorubas, whereby people became less dependent on the oba for divine guidance as modern education became a powerful weapon for individualism.

In the traditional Yoruba political structure, which is based on patrilineage, functional roles are differentiated among three gerontocratic institutions of exogamous descent groups: the lineage head, the chief and the oba (king). P.C. Lloyd has noted that in the Yoruba political system:

The head of the descent group is concerned primarily with matters affecting the group; the chief is concerned with the government of the town.[42]

And Sklar and Whitaker, Jr. go further to make the following addition:

In many cases, specific titles of chieftaincy are vested in particular lineages. When a vacancy occurs, every adult male member is eligible for election by the members at large, with due regard for the principle of rotation among the several segments or kinship divisions of the lineage. Similarly, candidates for the office of oba are nominated by the royal descent group for selection by the "kingmakers," or council of senior chiefs. Rarely is the oba regarded as the head of his accession, and such wealth as may accrue to him by virtue of his office belongs to the state.[43]

One of the best outstanding features of the Yoruba culture is the talking drum. A stranger in Yoruba culture is astonished to see how the Yoruba understands what note a drummer is communicating to him through the rhythm of the drum. Just by beating the drum, the drummer can be communicating many ideas to someone, such ideas as "the oba wants you to get cola for the visitor;" or "what is your name?" or "Where do you come from?" The Yorubas are ingenious in their culture, and they enjoy a proud tradition.

One unique factor that separates the Yoruba region from all the other regions in Nigeria is that it enjoys cultural homogeneity; since the Mid-west region, now Bendel state, was carved out in 1963, the West of Nigeria is wholly Yoruba, other than those Nigerians from other states in the country who have come to work there. There is no minority tribe, although certain petty jealousies and differences do exist among the numerous Yoruba clans.

In their social relations, Collis is not too far from the truth in noting that:

Yorubas are easy-going, some will say too easy-going, but in a world with so many obsessionalists perhaps this is a virtue rather than a failing. They are certainly loveable people and it is always a great pleasure to drive again through their forest country and see their smiling faces and blue, blue garments.[44]

The Igbo

The Igbo ethnic group of Nigeria is located in the Eastern thick forest portion of Nigeria. It is often said that the thickness of their vegetation and its impenetrability by outsiders afforded them a natural protection to beat off a large-scale invasion from the outside.[45] This shielded them from being routed during the Jihad, and perhaps, from subsequent conversion to Islam. Also, the inaccessibility of their region not only retarded internal mobility, but also delayed contact with early European explorers, traders and missionaries.

The Igbos number about twenty million. However, this figure precludes almost one million Igbos who do not live in the eastern states of Nigeria, but are located West of the River Niger in the Bendel state of Nigeria.

The Igbos, unlike the Hausas and Yorubas, did not develop any form of political hierarchical kingdom under which past achievements could be glorified. They were very republican in nature, lived in small communities where the manners in which the affairs of these communities were administered have caused them to be referred to as village democracies.

F.C. Anene's account of political and social administration among the Igbos during the 19th century is, perhaps, the most vivid:

The institution of age-groups... played an important part in the performance of services carried out in other societies by the executive organ of government. The senior age was concerned with peace and war and provided the leadership needed by the community to meet the exigencies of external danger. The junior age grade of young men were charged with social services, such as sanitation and related matters. There were lower grades for music, recreation and for other agencies of socialisation. Generally speaking, the Igbo communities were democracies in the sense that the government of the communities was the concern of all. The manner in which these democracies operated was subtle and complex.[46]

The Igbo belief of a common ancestral descent, more than any other factor, bound them together in this political unit of village group. It consisted of lineage segments[47] which primarily functioned to see to their corporate existence and the formulation of social regulations governing behaviour.[48] To the Igbo, religion was *la raison d'etre* of life. And because of this pervasive universal acceptance of the supernatural world in their midst, "religion, law, justice and politics were inextricably bound up. No Igbo community was complete without a shrine of the god of the land. There was indeed a hierarchy of gods. Law and custom were believed to have been handed down from the spiritual world from time immemorial from ancestor to ancestor."[49]

Within the Igbo culture, there is nothing like prescribed status. The Igbos are temperamentally competitive, and high emphasis is placed on achieved status. And also, non-existence of recognised social and political organisation, contrary to what the Hausas and Yorubas had developed, has created in the Igbo what Ezera calls egalitarian "belief that there are no social or class barriers to self-advancement and, thus, excites in him a spirit of aggressive competition. Because of this highly competitive nature of their society and ultra-democratic attitude to, and intense dislike and suspicion of, any form of external government or authority, the Igbo people have ... proven to be the most difficult to govern in Nigeria ... they have equally earned the antagonism of most of the other tribal groups in the country."[50] And the reason for this seeming antagonism and hatred against the Igbos could be attributed to their tradition of republicanism and individualism as opposed to developing political appendages to any form of government with a pyramidal type of authority. Because of their democratic orientation in which individual participation is highly encouraged in any affairs relating to the majority, disagreement with the Hausa-Fulani and the Yoruba in national policy seemed inevitable. Another source of this antagonism against the Igbo is further explained by Collis who notes that the Igbos:

Being more hard working and energetic than the other Nigerians... tended to despise the other tribes. They gradually acquired a feeling of superiority towards the other more easy going peoples. This made them think they had more drive, efficiency and intelligence than the other Nigerians and therefore had heaven sent right to overlordship.[51]

But the same writer does contradict his above assessment of the Igbos, and faces the realism of the Igbo drive for a better life through self-determination and labour thus making them unique from the other tribes in Nigeria when he admits:

...there is no doubt that the Igbo men are the hardest workers in Nigeria, and their women among the most charming and the most intelligent. They are neither mentally nor physically lazy,[52] and have shown themselves to have IQ's as high as any race or group anywhere in the world.... Many expatriates (foreigners) have found the Igbos easier to work with than the men of other tribes in Nigeria.... I found them very pleasant work companions. They had a greater capacity for had work than most and could grasp the significance of what they were doing very quickly. They often made first class research workers....[53]

Before 1900 the Igbo area of Nigeria was the most backward due to lack of contact with the outside world and early European explorers and missionaries. But once this contact was eventually made, the Igbos accepted *in toto* Western ideals, especially Western education. Millions were converted to Christianity. In their eagerness for the education of their children, villages contributed cash by engaging into cooperatives to send their sons and daughters to the white man's land to learn the "wonders" of his culture. Within Nigeria itself, the Igbos demonstrated their projective personality - they became very mobile and adapted to the various cultures in those areas of Nigeria where they migrated to live.

Soon afterwards, they had all of a sudden acquired the Western know-how. When a large number of them started returning from abroad, this created an imbalance in the spectrum of educated Nigerians. Their traders began to form the nomenclature and nucleus of the Nigerian economy outside the East. They began to acquire lands and to build schools for their children and those of the indigenous culture they adapted. The Igbo total assimilation into the Yoruba culture in the West was such that "they lived on the same streets as the Yoruba," observes Fredrick Forsyth, "mixed with them on all social occasions, and their children shared the same schools."[54]

Another insight into the Igbo personality is put forward by John Gunther who observes that the Igbos are:

...a mobile, vividly industrious people sometimes they are called the "Jews of Africa" and they are spread all over Nigeria as traders and small merchants.... Most Igbos have a lively sense of humour; they are clannish despite their individualism and hold together in non-Igbo communities; they are often unpopular because they push hard to make money.... But the Igbos... are so effervescent politically that the British sometimes differentiate between the "good East" and the "disruptive East", meaning by the latter the radical Igbo strongholds.[55]

There are, however, other vocal minority tribes in the East who share the area with the Igbos, such as the Ibibio, Efik, Annang, Ekoi, Ijaw and numerous others.

FOOTNOTES

1. *Worldmark, Enclyclopedia of the Nations: AFRICA*. New York: Worldmark Press, Harper & Row. 1967, p. 205.
2. *Ibid.*
3. *U.S. Army Area Handbook: NIGERIA.* Prepared by Foreign Studies Division, American University. Washington, D.C.: Government Printing Office, 1972.
4. *Worldmark Encyclopedia of the Nations: AFRICA,* p. 211.
5. *Federal Nigeria,* Vol. 1, No.1 Embassy of Nigeria, Washington, D.C. October-December, 1976. p. 15.
6. *Worldmark: AFRICA* p. 210.

7. *Ibid.*
8. *Ibid.*
9. *Ibid.*
10. *Federal NIGERIA,* Vol. 1, No. 1, p. 15.
11. *Federal NIGERIA,* Vol. 11, No. 11, p. 9.
12. *Ibid.,* Vol. 1, No. 1, p. 12.
13. *Worlmark Encyclopedia: AFRICA.* p. 211.
14. *Ibid.*.
15. *Federal NIGERIA,* Vol. 1, No. 1, p. 19.
16. *Ibid.,* p. 20.
17. *Ibid.,* Vol. 11, No. 11, p. 6.
18. Michael Crowder, *The Story of NIGERIA.* London: Faber & Faber, 1962, 1966. p. 238.
19. *Federal NIGERIA.* Vol. 11, No. 1, p. 2.
20. Ukaonu W. Uche, *Education in Nigeria Today: A Critical Analysis and a Proposal for Change.* Greensboro: Piednont Press. 1975. pp.26, 27,a, 36.
21. Kalu Ezera, *Constitutional Developments in Nigeria* Cambridge: University Press 1963. p. 4.
22. *Ibid.*
23. Frederick A.D. Schwartz, Jr., *NIGERIA: The Tribes, the Nation, or the Race - The Politics of Independence.* Cambridge, Mass: 1965. p. 12.
24. *Ibid.*
25. Kalu Ezera, *Constitutional Developments in Nigeria,* p. 5.
26. Joseph C. Anene & Godfrey Brown, editors, *AFRICA in the Nineteenth and Twentieth Centuries.* Ibadan: University of Ibadan Press, 1966. p. 294.
27. *Ibid.*
28. This was one of the issues deliberated by the leaders of Nigeria during the 1950 Ibadan General Conference on review of a new national constitution. See Kalu Ezera's book, p. 115, for a further analysis of this issue.
29. Richard L. Sklar & C.S. Whitaker, Jr. "The Federal Republic of Nigeria." In *National Unity and Regionalism in Eight African States.* Edited by Gwendolyn M. Carter. Ithaca, New York: Cornell University Press. 1966. p. 12.
30. This is quoted from Gwendolyn Carter's book, opp. citation, p. 12. The original source of this quotation is M.G. Smith's *Government in Zazzau.* London: Oxford University Press. 1960. p. 8.
31. *Gaskiya Ta Fi Kwabo.* Kaduna. February 18, 1960.
32. Basil Davidson, *The Lost Cities of Africa.* Boston/Toronto: Little Brown & Co. 1959. p. 58.
33. Robert Collis, *Nigeria in Conflict,* London: Secker and Warbung Ltd.1970. p.92.
34. Dahomey has changed its name to Benin.
35. *AFRICA in the Nineteenth & Twentieth Centuries.* pp. 258-59.
36. John E. Flint, *Sir George Goldie and the Making of NIGERIA.* London: Oxford University Press 1960. pp. 232-233.
37. A military decree was promulgated in February 1976 in which a new Federal capital would be built at Abuja, and Lagos would cease to be a Federal capital.
38. Ezera, *Constitutional Developments in Nigeria,* p. 7.
39. Ibid., pp. 7-8.
40. Davidson, *The Lost Cities of Africa,* p. 51.
41. Ibid., p. 141.
42. This quotation is culled from Gwendolyn Carter's edited book, opp. citation, p. 14. The original source is P.C. Lloyd, *Yorubaland Law.* London: Oxford University Press. 1962.
43. Carter, edited, *National Unity and Regionalism in Eight African States,* p. 14.
44. Robert Collis, *Nigeria in Conflict,* p. 92.
45. Anene & Brown, editors, *AFRICA in the Nineteenth & Twentieth Centuries,* p. 281.
46. *Ibid.,* pp. 281-282.
47. *Ibid.,* p. 281.
48. *Ibid.*
49. *Ibid.*
50. Ezera, *Constitutional Developments in Nigeria,* p. 10.
51. Robert Collis, *Nigeria in Conflict,* p. 94.

18

Mass Media, People and Politics in Nigeria

52. Robert Collis says the Hausa and Yoruba men are mentally and physically lazy, respectively, on pages 88 and 90 of his book. I consider this observation Collis makes to be a derogatory remark which has no foundation whatsoever. Also, the civilisations the Hausas and Yorubas developed do not portray the image of lazy people.
53. Robert Collis, *Nigeria in Conflict,* pp. 93-94.
54. Frederick Forsyth, *The Biafra Story.* Baltimore, Maryland: Penguin Books Ltd. 1969. p. 17.
55. This has been culled from Kalu Ezera's book, opposite citation, p. 10. The original source is John Gunther, *Inside Africa.* Harpers, New York. 1955, p. 760.

TWO

HISTORY AND POLITICS

Nigeria had not become a single political entity until 1914 when a shrewd and enterprising British imperialist, Lord Frederick Lugard, amalgamated both the Southern and Northern Nigeria into one British colony to be known as Nigeria. To this individual accomplishment of an almost impossible feat on the part of Lord Lugard, Frederick Forsyth describes him as forming "the bridge between the haphazard trail-breaking of the merchants and missionaries and bona fide imperialism."[1] And W.E.F. Ward also states that "Lugard forms the bridge between the old humanitarian and the new imperialism. Lugard's race against the French to plant boundary posts along Nigeria's western border was part of the new imperialistic world."[2] The primary question that needs answered is how the British were able to unify all the various autonomous people and their diametrically opposed cultures, tribal temperaments and past heritages to form a nation to be known as Nigeria.

Along the West coast of Africa, the Portuguese explorers had established the first contact with African kingdoms in the 15th century. This initial contact led to trade in African ivory, gold and clothes; it later developed into slave trade in the early part of the 17th century. But soon after the beginning of the 17th century the Dutch, through their naval superiority, wrested the West African coast trade monopoly from the Portuguese, took away Portuguese trading stations, and gradually assumed "the leadership as a source (supplier) of slaves for Spanish and English plantations in the North and South American colonies."[3] But the English and the French challenged the Dutch by the 18th century. The English eventually established effective slave and other commodity trading stations along the Guinea coast. The most notorious slave outposts were at Lagos, Benin and Old Calabar.

Domestic slavery had existed as an institution among the tribes before the white man came. What gave it an added impetus was when the external demand for people to be bought and shipped across the Atlantic to the New World was introduced. The slave trade was so lucrative that new and powerful kingdoms evolved in which their economy solely depended on the slave trade. Many towns suddenly became rich at the expense of poor villages that were ravaged and destroyed in the wake of inter-tribal and communal wars that were waged to capture slaves for the trans-Atlantic journey to the New World. It has been conservatively estimated that by the middle of the 18th century about 100,000[4] slaves had been shipped from West Africa every year, and that the total number of slaves who departed West Africa was 6.3 million.[5]

In 1807 Britain and America abolished the slave trade due to humanitarian voices and anti-slavery sentiment that arose, especially in Britain. Despite this abolition, slavery continued along the West African coast and between 1819 and 1869, the British had permanently deployed along West African waters a British West African Squadron which was empowered to stop any ship or vessel and inspect its cargo to see if it carried slaves. This practice was so successful that many slaves were instantaneously liberated and shipped to Sierra - Leone or other areas they chose to lead a free life.

When the slave trade had been successfully contained, the European merchants turned their attention to other commodities in palm produce, cotton, cocoa, tobacco, gold, diamond, etc., that mostly came from the West African hinterland. It has always been said that the white Europeans came to Africa to civilise the African who became the white man's burden. But a group of American scholars have had to refute this claim, asserting that:

> Contemporary evidence suggests that the European traders were anything but civilizing agents. Many of them had adopted legal trade only as a last resort when their original slave-trading occupation had grown too hazardous. Brutal and disreputable as many of them were, they often suffered greatly from the precariousness of their position at the mercy of unpredictable coastal rulers.[6]

However, in order to ensure effective legal trading in these new commodities, the British trading merchants employed gun-boat diplomacy: Lagos was annexed in 1861 and its ruler, Oba Kosoko, was deposed and his nephew was hand-picked by the British to replace him. Further inland, the powerful kingdom of Benin was overthrown by the British in 1897 in a special punitive expedition in retaliation for Benin's ambushing and liquidation of a party of British emissaries who were on their way to pay a homage to the court of the Oba of Benin in 1897. However, the Benin empire was notorious for its defiance of the abolition of slave trade and other inhuman practices. But it was one of the greatest centres of civilisation in West Africa. In the Niger Delta areas, the powerful king Jaja of Opobo, whose Niger City States were founded and had prospered on the lucrative slave trade, was deported to the West Indies in 1897 after his city-states had become part of the British Oil

Rivers Protectorate that extended from Lagos to some parts of the Camerouns. These areas were amalgamated to form the Southern Nigeria Protectorate after all the powerful empires, city-states and kingdoms had been subdued and treaties concluded with the rulers and village elders. The policy of these British merchants was: "Open up the country, push the trade, hoist the flag; Philanthropy is good, especially if it pays five per cent dividends."[7]

It was Sir George Goldie's Royal Niger Company, which was granted a royal charter by the British government in 1886, that was responsible for these gun-boat diplomacies of seek, disunite and destroy in these areas. The charter authorised the company "to administer the law in territories where the British had commercial interests."[8] These British traders did not want to deal with the African middle men in the new trade; they wanted to get to the source of the trade themselves. This resulted in bitter wars.

As the volume of trade increased, the British government appointed John Beecroft to become its Consul-General for the Bights of Benin and Biafra. This action was taken at the request of British merchants who wanted some form of political support and protection from their home government; especially when some military clashes among the French, German and English seemed inevitable, not to talk of hostility from the indigenes

In 1884, under the leadership of Bismark of Germany, European powers were summoned to Berlin for the purpose of partitioning Africa among themselves. The reason was to avert war among the major European powers in the scramble for commercial bridgeheads over Africa. At the Berlin conference any European power that was able to prove that it had a predominant interest in any region in Africa was accepted as the sole administering power in the region, *provided it could show that its administration was a reality*. The British delegation to the Berlin conference did not have a hard time proving the reality of its presence in many regions of Nigeria.

In 1906 Lagos colony and the Oil Rivers Protectorates were amalgamated to form the Southern Nigeria Protectorate of Great Britain. Earlier on December 31, 1899, the Royal Niger Company had had its charter revoked by the British Crown government, and the British government assumed direct administration under a governor-general, Lord Frederick Lugard. Lugard quickly embarked upon the conquest of the Hausa-Fulani empires of the North so as to bring them under the British sphere of influence and control. It took Lugard three years to subdue the North. The North offered stiff resistance and demonstrated its military might - an experience acquired during the Jihad. But the British superior weapons did eventually prevail over the North. The North was subsequently colonised and declared a Northern Protectorate of the British. During the British campaign against the North, the Hausas did not support their Fulani colleagues; this could be attributed to vengeance for the Fulani-led Jihad against the Hausas and the subsequent imposition of Fulani overlordship. But this did not deter the British from keeping the Fulani ruling class (the Sultans and Emirs) in power with the British controlling the North through them. This was the beginning of in-direct rule - the governing of the people through their traditional rulers with the latter being answerable to the foreign colonisers. Why did Lugard opt for indirect rule in the North or decide to keep the emirs in power? Frederick Forsyth has this to say:

...he had no choice; his forces were small, the attitude of London indif-ferent, the area to be ruled was vast and would have required hundreds of administrators. By contrast, the emirs had a nation-wide administrative, judicial and fiscal structure already in place. Lugard chose to permit the Emirs to continue to rule as before (subject to certain reforms) and main-tained for himself only a remote over-lordship.[9]

But this sort of arrangement had its own disadvantages which outweighed whatever apparent advantages it had. According to Forsyth: "Indirect rule... fossilized the feudal structure, confirmed the repression by the privileged Emirs and their appointees, prolonged the inability of the North to graduate into the modern world, and stultified future efforts to introduce parliamen-tary democracy."[10]

When Lord Lugard discovered the success of Indirect Rule in the North, he quickly introduced it to the South. It was not a complete success in Yorubaland because of the nature of their constitutional monarchy - the Oba (king) must consult with his chiefs in all affairs pertaining to the Yorubas, or else he would be deposed. But indirect rule arrogated ultimate powers to the Oba alone. Among the Igbos of the East, indirect rule was a complete failure; it led to a fiasco in 1929 when the unpredictable Igbo women of proud Ngwa clan challenged the authority of a British appointed "warrant" chief who had planned to introduce universal taxation in which women would be included. The women sacked the British military posts in Aba and its environ, kid-napped the chief, who was later released with his chieftaincy title gone, and the concept of indirect rule was eliminated in the East. Forsyth makes the following evaluation of the concept of indirect rule in the East and its reper-cursion:

The British were so concerned with the idea of regional chiefs that where there were not any they tried to impose them. The Aba Riots of 1929... were caused by resentment against the 'warrant chiefs', men imposed as chiefs by the British but whom the people refused to accept. It was not difficult to impose measures on the Northerners, accustomed to implicit obedience, but it did not work in the East. The whole traditional structure of the East makes it virtually immune to dictatorship - Easterners insist on being consulted in everything that concerns them. This assertiveness was hardly to endear itself to the colonial administrators and is one of the reasons why the Easterners came to be referred to as 'uppity'.[11]

On January 1, 1914, the two British (Northern and Southern) Protectorates were amalgamated to form the nation of Nigeria. The reason for the amalgamation, according to Michael Crowder, was primarily economic expediency. The Northern Protectorate was being subsidised by funds from the Southern Protectorate and the Imperial Grant-In-Aid from Britain in the sum of about three hundred thousand pounds annually.[12] This type of assistance was in conflict with the British established colonial policy of each territory being self subsisting[13] and maintaining its administration without outside financial bail out.

The Emergence of Nigerian Nationalism

It is an accepted fact that "at first Nigerian nationalism was largely promoted by non-Nigerians..."[14] The road to Nigerian nationalism was paved by freed slaves from the West Indies and the United States: men like Blyden, Garvey, DuBois, etc., "who sought the cultural emancipation of the Negro" and whose concern "was on Africa as a whole, rather than the seemingly artificial units drawn up by the European colonial powers".[15] However, in the 1920's, Herbert Macaulay emerged as the father of the Nigerian nationalism and with his *Lagos Daily News*, started unleashing nationalist attacks against the British.

In the 1930's there was nothing yet to be regarded as a political party in Nigeria. The only thing near to that was the formation of the Nigerian Youth Movement in 1936 which "was geared up into a genuine national movement with a broad representation... when Nnamdi Azikiwe became a member and an effective leader of the movement."[16] But it was World War II, more than any other factor, that spurred the cause of Nigerian nationalism. As many Nigerian soldiers who fought on the Allied side returned home, having been exposed to new cultures, and having fought as equals in the war, and many times excelled their European counterparts, the myth of the invincibility of the white man began to erode rapidly. The British order of things in Nigeria began to be challenged by these veteran soldiers. Added to this was the newly educated Nigerian elite class who had graduated from British and American universities, and had returned home as victims of racism. They waged total war of opposition against British rule. They exploited a clause in the Atlantic Charter that guaranteed "'the right of all peoples to choose the form of government" suitable to them as a major case against foreign rule. But the British Prime Minister at that time, the late Sir Winston Churchill, quickly countered by denying that the Atlantic Charter ever applied to the overseas colonies. Michael Crowder has noted the significance of the World War II as one of the main factors that influenced the effectiveness of Nigerian nationalism:

...the outbreak of war in Europe in 1939...acted as an immense stimulus to nationalist activity. The World War projected Nigerians out of a colonial backwater into a modern world in which ... Nigeria became suddenly important...as a strategic link in allied defenses, as a producer of primary goods essential to feed the starved allied nations, and as a provider of indispensable troops for the Burma Campaigns.[17]

It was this type of situation that led to the emergence of the most anti-colonial militant newspapers in Nigeria.

Realisation of independence seemed obvious due to the emergence of an educated elite class of nationalists, the favourable climate the World War II had created, and Britain reluctantly but positively responding to nationalist demands as a result of the American disdain for colonialism and the pressure she exerted on Britain to grant independence to her African colonies, and for participation in their country's government.

In 1944, at the instigation of the powerful Nigerian Youth Movement, Herbert Macaulay and Nnamdi Azikiwe formed the first political party, National Council of Nigeria and Camerouns (NCNC). The NCNC was not a tribal party, but a national one. But when tribal animosity reached its peak between the Yorubas and Igbos of the Nigerian Youth Movement - the parent body of the political party, NCNC - Azikiwe broke away from the Movement. And another blow to the party came when its first president Macaulay, a Yoruba, died. But the NCNC still retained its national outlook.

But in early 1951, Late Obafemi Awolowo, a Yoruba, formed the Action Group (AG) political party from a Yoruba cultural organisation - *Egbe Omo Oduduwa* (Society of the Children of Oduduwa) that came into being in 1945. The aim of the party was to control the West - the Yoruba homeland - when elections were held. It thus became the first exclusive ethnic political party in Nigeria. The Igbo Pan-Union was forced to back up the NCNC, then under the leadership of their fellow tribesman after the death of Macaulay. The party was forced to seek support within its own non-politically committed other Igbos of the East. It soon began to represent the sectional interests of the East dominated by the Igbos.

While the nationalist struggle had gained momentum in the South, among the Igbos, Yorubas and other minority tribes for over twenty-five years, the North was still aloof of nationalism. As one British political expert on Nigeria observes, "the North was largely isolated from the South, and since its traditional form of government had largely been preserved there was little opportunity for Western-style politics."[18]

But in December 1949, a handful of about twelve realistic Northerners (who had seen that the trend in Nigerian politics, with the introduction of the

McPherson Constitution, was leading towards nationalist rule) formed a cultural organisation to be known as *"Jam'iyyar Mutanen Arewa"* (the Northern People's Congress). The children of the Northern aristocrats who had the privilege of going to school, formed this organisation. They had to be cautious and pretentious; daring not to call it a political party or else they would be seen as threatening the Northern status quo and emirate system of government. The penalty could be harsh labour in the prison camps. They would be accused of being subversive and trying to usurp the powers of the autocratic traditional rulers. Being aware of this precarious and delicate situation, and the sensitivity of the Northern traditional rulers to their throne, the so-called cultural organisation had to be prudently modest and its members had to be tactful so as to allay any fears and suspicions of the ruling class. They declared the aim and intention of their organisation, thus:

> Jam'iyyar (NPC) does not intend to usurp the authority of our Natural rulers; on the contrary, it is our ardent desire to enhance such authority whenever and wherever possible. We want to help our Natural rulers in the proper discharge of their duties .... We want to help them in enlightening the Talakawa[19] (the common people).

But with rapid political changes taking place, and the McPherson draft Constitution calling for a federal structure for Nigeria, and the representation of each region in the central government, and with the emergence of a more radical political party in the North - the Northern Elements Progressive Union (NEPU) - whose leader (Aminu Kano, now deceased) broke away from the Jam'iyyar and allied himself and the party (NEPU) with the NCNC, political awareness began to develop in the North. The leader of the NEPU professed to fight ignorance, illiteracy and backwardness in the North. Indeed he did live up to his declared objectives up to the time of his death in 1983. With the new radical party (NEPU) winning primaries in the North in preparation for the 1951-52 general elections, the Jam'iyyar cultural organisation was forced to accept the political realities of the time; it was converted into a political party to be known as the Northern People's Congress (NPC). Its membership was confined to people of Northern descent who were moslems. When the elections were held in 1951-52 in accordance with the provisions of the McPherson draft Constitution, the NPC won the whole seats in the North; the Action Group won the majority of the seats in the West; and the NCNC won overwhelming majority in the East. From thenceforth, Nigerian politics developed along ethnic lines and in 1954, the country became a federation of the North (Hausa-Fulani majority), the East (Igbo majority), and the West (Yoruba majority). Within the North, East and West, the minority tribes formed their own minority political parties. But among the minorities, most of their powerful opinion leaders joined the political parties of the dominant majority tribe in their areas.

In 1959, after a series of painstaking negotiation and agonising and divisive constitutional conferences for independence in 1960, general elections were held all over Nigeria for an independent nation. The NPC swept the North, and the NCNC and the AG also swept the East and West, respectively. Although the NPC was assigned the largest number of seats in the Federal House, it did not command the necessary majority required by the constitution. It thus entered into an alliance with the NCNC to form a coalition government.

Post-Independence Politics

On October 1, 1960, Britain granted independence to Nigeria and the most powerful political office of a Prime Minister went to the NPC; the NCNC'S, former leader, Nnamdi Azikiwe, was appointed the Governor-General (later changed to President in 1963 when Nigeria became a republic). The Prime Minister was Sir Abubakar Tafawa Balewa, now deceased. The leader of the Action Group, Obafemi Awolowo, (now deceased) resigned as the premier of the Western Region, and chose to become the leader of the opposition in the Federal Parliament. His lieutenant, Late Samuel L. Akintola, became the premier of the West.

But due to differences in political and economic ideologies between Awolowo and Akintola of the Action Group party, the two leaders eventually fell apart. The rift between the two men was so great that political scandals within the AG party were publicly disclosed. In 1963 a fight broke out in the Western House of Assembly; some members were hospitalised. The Federal government suspended the Western Region government and declared a state of emergency in the Region and appointed a Yoruba administrator for the Region. The rank and file of the Action Group party met and decided to dismiss Akintola from the party. Akintola and his supporters quickly formed their own political party - Nigerian National Democratic Party (NNDP). The Federal government started an extensive investigation into the affairs of the Action Group. The inquiry turned out a preponderance of evidence of a plot to overthrow the Federal government by Obafemi Awolowo, the Action Group leader, and other ranking members of his party, with the aid of the communist world. They were accordingly charged with treason. The sensational trial lasted for months and at the end, Awolowo was sentenced to ten years imprisonment; some others charged along with him received varying sentences while others were found innocent. When tranquility returned to the West, the state of emergency was lifted and Akintola was reinstated as the premier.

Meanwhile, the Federal House was dissolved in late 1964 and general elections were slated for December 1964. The NPC formed the Nigerian National Alliance (NNA) with the NNDP in the West, and the Mid-West Democratic Front; while the NCNC formed its own alliance: United Progressive Grand Alliance (UPGA) with the battered Action Group in the West, the NEPU in the North and the United Middle Belt Congress (UMBC), also in the North. But it thus seemed that the West was in such a political disarray that the North and East seemed vying for a political trophy there. During the ensuing campaign for the 1964 general elections, members of the UPGA were not allowed to campaign freely in the North, and neither were the members of the NNA allowed to campaign freely in the UPGA strongholds in the South. When the UPGA saw that it was going to lose the elections under the prevailing non-democratic atmosphere, it boycotted the election.

The election results were so rigged in the West that Political riotings ensued. Houses, cars and other valuables belonging to people of opposite political parties and views were set ablaze by political thugs. People were kidnapped and killed during the 1965 post-election riotings in the Region in protest against alleged overt election riggings by the ruling NNDP.

National political crisis seemed imminent when the figure head President, Azikiwe, hesitated to reappoint the Prime Minister from the winning party, the NPC in alliance with the NNDP, due to accusations of election riggings in the West and other parts of the country.[20] But Azikiwe rescinded, and a political crisis was temporarily averted when Nigeria's constitutional experts advised the President that it was unconstitutional on his part not to appoint Balewa to the office of the Prime Minister despite allegations of election fraud.

The East that had boycotted the election then held its own in the East and Lagos in March, 1965.

But the political riotings continued in the West unabated. It assumed a new dimension with increased death toll and increased loss of properties. The Prime Minister refused to declare another state of emergency in the Region. Instead, he convened an emergency conference of Commonwealth Prime Ministers in Lagos to deal with the white minority rebels' unilateral declaration of independence in Zimbabwe (Rhodesia), while political uncertainty and upheaval prevailed in Nigeria.

The Military Coups and Civil War

On January 15, 1966, a group of young army officers who were mostly of Igbo origin from the Mid-West and the Eastern Regions staged a military coup d'état in which the premier of the Northern Region and the Sarduana of Sokoto, Ahmadu Bello, the most powerful political figure in Nigeria, was murdered by the soldiers during the operation of the coup in the North. The Prime Minister, Balewa, also a Northerner, was murdered. In the West, the controversial premier, Akintola, was killed. And in Lagos, the Federal Minister of Finance, Festus Okotie-Eboh, was killed in his residence. Also the coup leaders killed some leading **Northern Army** officers from the Hausa-Fulani tribe, as well as a few **Igbo army officers** who refused to cooperate with them.

The coup was not a complete success. In Lagos it was thwarted and the Federal Council of Ministers handed over power to the Commander of the Nigerian Armed Forces, Aguiyi Ironsi, who suspended the Republican Constitution of the country, and began to rule by military decrees. The leaders of the coup were rounded up and imprisoned.

Ironsi was an Igbo. He introduced a unitary government that granted greater power to the central government so as to curtail the autonomy and power of the four dominant regions that led to constant political bickerings and skirmishes in the country. The concept of unitary government displeased the North.

On July 29, 1966, army officers from the North staged a successful counter-coup in retaliation for the first coup that had liquidated the most prominent Northern politicians and leaders in the country. The leaders of the counter-coup claimed the first coup was aimed at perpetuating the Igbo domination of the political and economic systems of the country. The Igbo army Commander of the nation's Armed Forces and the head of the military government that came to power in the January 15 coup, Aguiyi Ironsi, was kidnapped and killed by the Northern leaders of the July counter-coup. The July coup resulted in an indiscriminate massacre of Igbo army officers, privates and civilians in apparent vengeance for the first coup's killing of the Northern leaders. More than 30,000[21] Igbo men, women and children living in Lagos and in the Northern cities were killed and the survivors fled to their Igbo region of the East.

Meanwhile, the Northern army officers who carried out the counter-coup had decided to pull out the North from the Nigerian federation. But the British and American ambassadors[22] intervened and told them that it would not only be suicidal, but it would also be an unwise decision since the North was economically dependent for survival under one Nigeria. For more than three days confusion ensued among the leaders of the coup as to whether to secede from the rest of the nation or to remain an integral part of it. The result was that Nigeria did not have a head of government for the three days this period of uncertainty lasted. Eventually, the leaders of the coup decided not to pull out the North from the Federation.

The Igbos and some sections of the South began to accuse the North of Hausa-Fulani domination over the rest of Nigeria. In order to allay the fears of these Southerners, the leaders of the coup chose Yakubu Gowon to be the new head of state for Nigeria. Gowon became the only compromise because of his christian religious background and also he hails from a minority tribe in the Middle-Belt region of the North. Gowon's military government suspended Aguiyi Ironsi's decree that established a unitary form of government. In his maiden address to a bewildered nation, Gowon stated that there was no basis for national unity - a statement the East was to exploit in its fullest in its clamour for secession.

There was a massive exodus of the Igbos from the other regions of Nigeria to their Eastern homeland. Their exodus threatened the nation's economy. The Igbos' economic and political aggressiveness undeniably caused them to be disliked by the other tribes who considered them as threats to their own well being. They made rapid progress in education, their entrepreneurship was enviable, and they dominated high social, economic and administrative posts in the nation. Their traders and merchants formed the nucleus of the Nigerian economy, and it was in their Eastern Region that most of the nation's crude oil wells were being drilled. This made their incentive for secession from the rest of Nigeria high and attractive; even though they have the highest population density in Nigeria within their region, and in fact one of the highest in the world. There are 639 persons per square mile.[23]

The head of state, Gowon, freed many political prisoners that included Awolowo, the leader of the Action Group opposition political party, who had been sent to jail three years earlier for treason. Observers then believed that this was done to please the Yorubas and to buy their support in the event of any showdown with the East.

The East, homeland of the Igbos, refused to recognise the federal authority. Peace overtures were made and agreement for reconciliation to end the political stalemate in the nation was reached at a peace conference in Aburi, Ghana. But when Lagos authorities learned of the legal implications of that agreement, and how Ojukwu had outwitted Gowon and his Federal delegation to the conference, the Aburi accord was never implemented. The East blamed Lagos for dishonouring the accord. The East began to confiscate Federal properties in its territory in protest against the non-payment of salaries of Federal employees who had fled to their home tribe in the wake of Igbo massacre in the North and Lagos.

On May 28, 1967, the Nigerian head of state, Gowon, in a military decree, created twelve states in the country and abolished the four region structure - the North, East, West and the Mid-West (the Mid-west Region was created out of the West in 1963). Three of these twelve states were created in the East. The Federal Government claimed to have created the states to forestall imminent secession by the East.

On May 30, 1967, two days after the creation of the new states, Emeka Ojukwu, in a dawn broadcast, announced the secession of the East from the Nigerian federation to form a nation of Biafra. The reason for the secession, as claimed by the broadcast, was what the East called a calculated massacre of the Igbos whom, it felt, Nigerians did no longer want. Ironically, it was the same East that had in the past been the strongest proponent of one united Nigeria. On several occasions the North had threatened to secede, and during one of the constitutional conferences for Nigerian independence, the Yorubas of the West had insisted for the addition of a secession clause that would permit a region to break away from the federation.[24]

The secession of the East led to the launching of full-scale military assault by the North. Initially the Yorubas and the Mid-West refused to join in the war. But when tides of war started to favour the Federal side, with the Russians competing with Great Britain for the supply of military hardwares to the Federal forces, the Yorubas entered the war on the Federal side; although Awolowo, the Yoruba leader, had threatened to pull out the West from the rest of Nigeria if the East was forced to secede. Apparently, the early Yoruba indecision not to immediately join any of the warring sides was to see which of the two sides was most likely to win. The Russian and British military hardwares to the Federal side made them decide to go with the winning side.

A fratricidal war raged between the East (Biafra) and the rest of Nigeria from July 6, 1967 to January 12, 1970. The war led to Biafra's defeat and her extinction as a nation when her leader, Ojukwu, fled into exile with his top advisers. When the war ended, there was no wide-spread acrimony or vendetta against the Igbos and those minority tribes in the East that joined forces with them to fight for Biafra's brief existence. Everybody accepted the blame and the slogan that emerged was "neither a conqueror nor a vanquished".

On July 29, 1975, a third military coup d'état was staged in Nigeria against Gowon's leadership. Exactly nine years after Gowon had ruled Nigeria, his personal bodyguard and the commander of the Federal Brigade of Guards, Joseph Garba, acting in concert with his other colleagues in the Armed Forces, deposed him in what apparently appeared to be a bloodless coup. Gowon was away in Kampala, Uganda, attending the annual conference of the Organisation of African Unity (OAU). He thus became the first African head of state to be overthrown while attending the OAU conference since its founding in May, 1963.

Mu:tala Muhammed became the head of state after Gowon's downfall. In his maiden broadcast to Nigerians, he said:

.... Events of the past few years have indicated that despite our great human and material resources the government (under Gowon) has not been able to fulfill the legitimate expectations of our people. Nigeria has been left to drift. After the Civil War, the affairs of the State, hitherto a collective responsibility, became characterised by lack of consultation, indecision, indiscipline, and even neglect .... The public ... became disillusioned and disappointed by these developments ....[25]

Government and court records have shown that Gowon's administration was characterised by open scandals and corruption on the part of high government officials. There were indications that majority in the inner circle of the government became rich and those who felt cheated went to courts to swear affidavits attesting to the illegal ways their colleagues had acquired ill-gotten wealth. A classic example was the Aper Aku versus Joseph Gomwalk episode.

After only seven months in office as Nigeria's third military head of state, Muhammed was assassinated in a Lagos traffic jam by a group of relatively unknown army officers who were led by D.S. Dimka in Nigeria's fourth military coup d'état on February 13, 1976. Dimka succeeded in seizing the national radio headquarters and used the NBC (now FRCN) radio facilities to announce his ascent to power as the new head of state. After the nation had recovered from the initial shock of the coup announcement, troops loyal to the Muhammed regime stormed the FRCN studios and eventually put down the coup after some hours of fighting with the rebel troops.

Prior to his assassination, Muhammed had become the most nationally admired leader Nigeria had ever known due to the efficiency of his leadership in dealing with the basic political, social and economic problems of Nigeria. His seven-month-term in office accomplished what Nigerians generally believed no other regime had been able to accomplish since their independence. He changed the political map of Nigeria and created seven additional states. He appointed a panel to determine the people's demand for statehood, the economic and political viability of such states, if created; and to advise the government the areas of the country where such states should be created. As a result of the findings and recommendations of the panel, Nigeria became a federation of nineteen states, with a powerful central government, the structure of which has almost, but not quite, broken the ethnic (or tribal) loyalties. There is no longer a particular geographical region where the Yoruba, the Hausa-Fulani, and the Igbo enjoy an exclusive dominance over other minority tribes due to the way the nineteen states are structured. However, Nigerian politics and economy are still under the control of the Hausa-Fulani, and the Igbo and the Yoruba because of their human majority when compared with the rest of the country. Nonetheless, the vertical ethnic schism and intrigues that led to all these crises when the regions had such sweeping autonomy are being neutralised by the nineteen-state structure. (The following four maps illustrate the political passages of Nigeria from three dominant regions, made up of the North, East and West; to four regions - the fourth being the Mid-West that was created from the Western Region in 1963; and then to the twelve states; finally, to the nineteen states, for the time being). *Stop Press*:Nigeria is now made up of twenty-one states, with the creation of Akwa Ibom and Katsina states.

After the abortive coup of February 1976, those people the military tribunal found guilty were executed. The leaders of the coup confessed that their aim was to restore Gowon back to power in Nigeria, and that he knew of their plot. Nigerian authorities demanded that Great Britain extradite Gowon to Nigeria to defend himself. But Great Britain refused, fearful that Gowon would not be granted a fair trial despite assurances to the contrary by the Nigerian authorities. Nigeria then declared Gowon a wanted man; he was dishonourably discharged from the Nigerian army. But the Shagari administration granted him and Ojukwu state pardon. Both men are now back in Nigeria from their political exiles. The Babangida administration, in 1987, restored to Gowon his army rank of a general.

The military government under Olusegun Obasanjo's leadership, (Obasanjo succeeded late Muhammed) eventually relinquished military rule on October 1, 1979, to a democratically elected civilian administration under the check and balance system of government. This was in fact the first commitment of the Muhammed regime when it took office. In preparation for the new civilian administration, a new constitution, patterned after the American check and balance system, was drafted, debated and approved by a Constituent Assembly regarding its suitability and practicability to a society such as Nigeria. Also, local government elections were held all over Nigeria to elect members into local government area councils in preparation for the new presidential system of government.

On December 31, 1983, a military coup d'état overthrew the Shagari administration. Gross mismanagement of the economy that was infested by worldwide recession was highly pronounced. Corruption, rather than a vice, became a virtue during the Second Republic; and sheer ineptitude in ruling a complex society provoked the coup d'état. Also, on August 27, 1985, Nigeria's Army Chief of Staff staged his own coup. He accused the Buhari military administration of extreme dictatorship and abuse of human rights. He preferred to be addressed as president as he did not like to be called the traditional and conventional head of state to which former military rulers had been addressed. He also abolished the term "Supreme Military Council" for the highest decision-making military body. He preferred the term "Armed Forces Ruling Council". The Babangida administration favours panels and their reports for political administration. Barely three months in office, it uncovered a plot for a bloody coup against it. The coup plotters, led by Major-General Mamman Vatsa, were rounded up, tried by a military panel, and executed. Some others were acquitted and discharged from the Armed Forces.

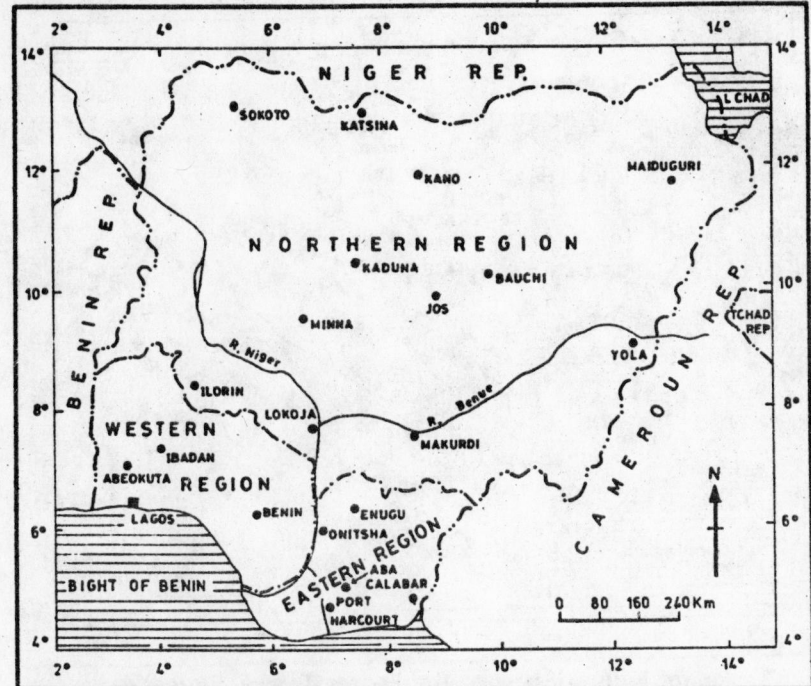

Fig. 1 : Map of Nigeria Showing the Former Three Regions
SOURCE : ADAPTED FROM JAMES S COLEMAN.

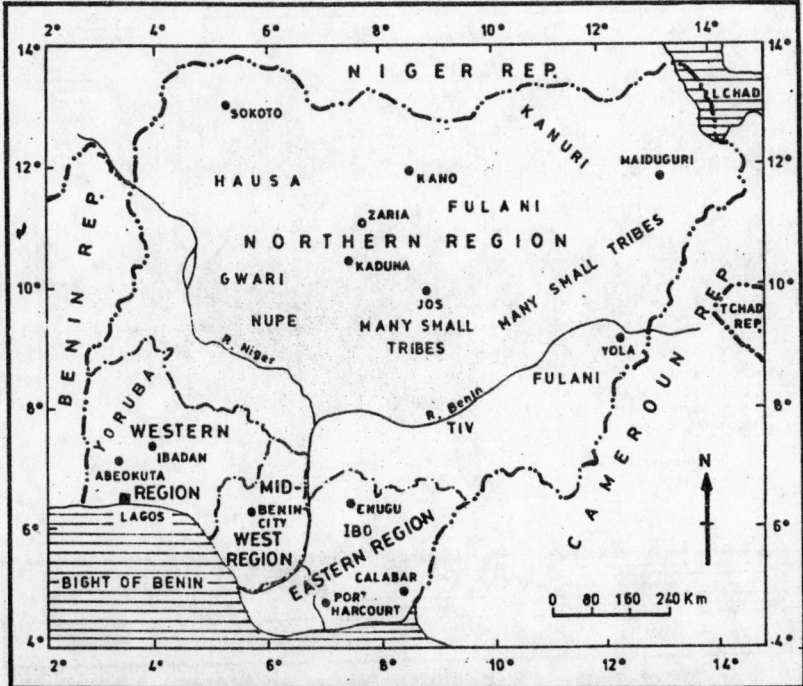

Fig. 2 : Map of Nigeria Showing the Former Four Regions
SOURCE : ADAPTED FROM REX NIVEN.

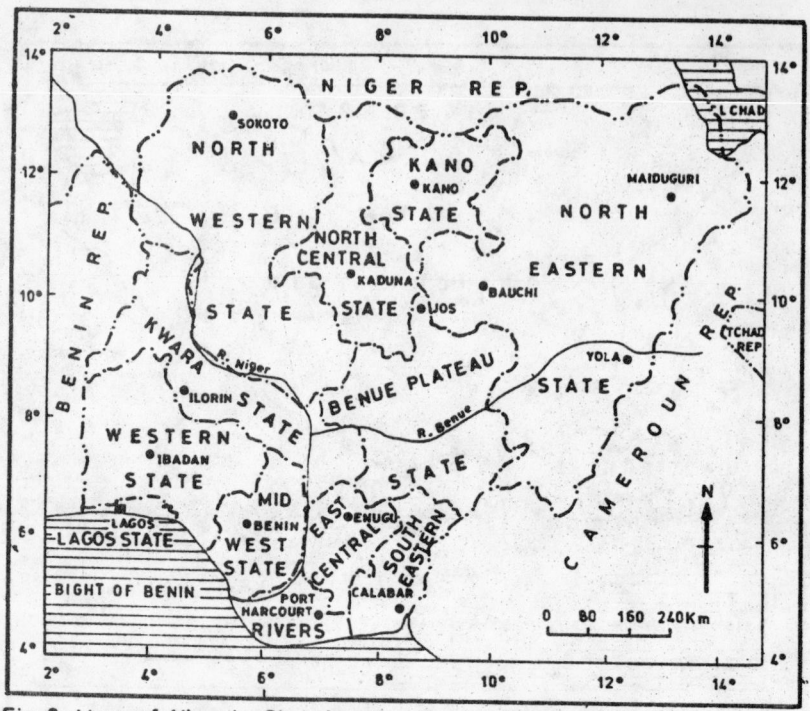

Fig. 3 : Map of Nigeria Showing the Former Twelve States
SOURCE : ADAPTED FROM A.H.M. KIRK— GREENE.

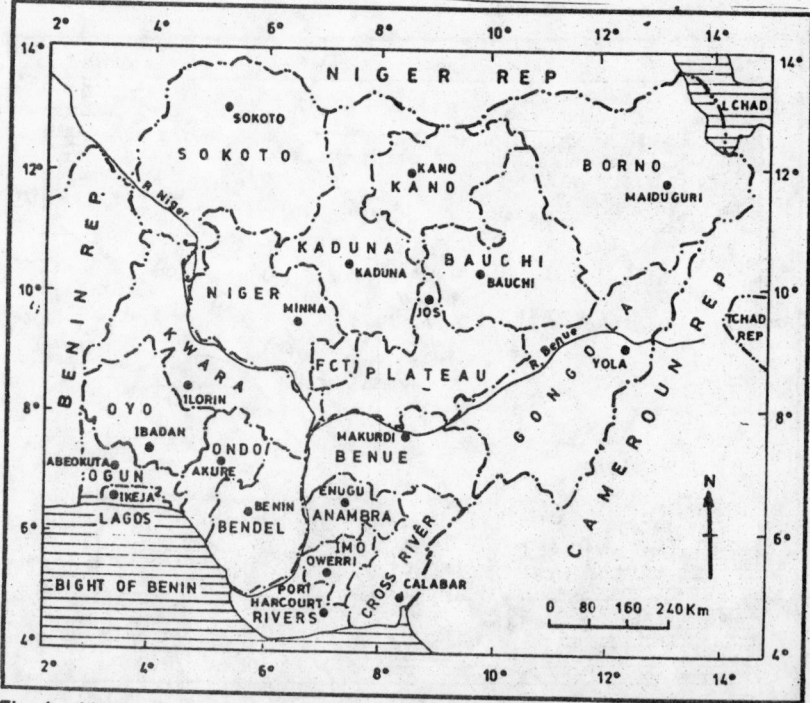

Fig. 4 : Map of Nigeria Showing the Nineteen States
SOURCE: ADAPTED FROM FEDERAL NIGERIA VOL. I № 1, 1977.

At this stage it is appropriate to reflect on Coleman's observation that "traditional political systems have largely shaped the political perspectives, orientations to politics and attitudes towards authority of all but a small fraction ... of Africans involved in modern political activity."[26] This observation aptly describes the Nigerian situation. Modern political orientations in Nigeria have always revolved along contrasting cultural patterns of tribal and regional governments that had existed prior to the British unification of the autonomous cultural entities to form the federation of Nigeria. This can be easily discerned when reference is made to the preceding pages that have analysed the different political institutions of the Hausa-Fulani, Igbo and Yoruba and the premises under which each of them was founded.

FOOTNOTES

1. Forsyth, *The Biafra Story*, p. 14. Earlier citation.
2. Anene & Brown, edited, *AFRICA in the Nineteenth & Twentieth Centuries*. pp. 313 - 314.
3. *U.S. Army Area Handbook: NIGERIA*, p. 47. Earlier citation.
4. *African Encyclopedia*. London W. I., Ely House: Oxford University Press. 1974, p. 369.
5. *U.S. Army Area Handbook: NIGERIA*, p. 48.
6. *Ibid.*, p. 49.
7. Anene & Brown, *AFRICA in the Nineteenth & Twentieth Centuries*, (edited), p. 313.
8. *African Encyclopedia*, p. 369.
9. Forsyth, *The Biafra Story*, p. 15.
10. *Ibid.*.
11. Ibid., pp. 16 - 17.
12. Crowder, *The Story of NIGERIA*, P. 240, Earlier citation.
13. *Ibid.*
14. *Ibid.*, p. 254.
15. *Ibid.*
16. *Ibid.*, p. 266.
17. *Ibid.*, pp. 267 - 269.
18. *Ibid.*, p. 279.
19. *Daily Comet*, December 29, 1949. The quotation is culled from James S. Coleman, *NIGERIA: Background to Nationalism*. Berkeley & Los Angeles: University of California Press, 1958, p. 358.
20. A reference to major Nigerian newspapers, such as the *Daily Times, West African Pilot, Daily Sketch, Outlook Nigerian Citizen,* published during this period, December 1964 to February 1965, will give more information on the election riggings and the president's initial hesitation to appoint the prime minister.
21. This was the figure released by the commission of inquiry the former Eastern Nigerian government appointed during the 1966 crisis in the wake of Igbo massacre.
22. Frederick Forsyth discusses this in more detail in his book, *The Biafra Story*, pp. 58 & 144. And Kirk-Greene and St. Jorre also discuss this diplomatic manoeuvre by the British and American ambassadors to dissuade the North from secession on pp. 54 & 72 of their respective books: *Crisis and Conflict in Nigeria* Vol. I. January 1966 - July 1977, (Kirk-Greene), and *The Nigerian Civil War* (St. Jorre).
23. Paxton, *The Statesman's Yearbook*, p. 461. Earlier citation.
24. Ezera discusses this in greater detail throughout his book, opposite citation.
25. This was the text of Murtala Muhammed's maiden radio-television address to the people of Nigeria as contained in the *Daily Times* of July 31, 1975, p. 3.
26. Coleman, *The Politics of the Developing Areas*. Princeton: Princeton University Press. 1966. pp. 247 - 368.

THREE

RADIO BROADCASTING

Early History

Broadcasting age came to Nigeria in 1932 when Lagos began to relay the British Empire Service from Daventry, England. Soon after that year, the Lagos station began to experiment with rediffusion service. The Nigerian Posts and Telegraphs Department was given the authority to work out a plan for the distribution of programmes to subscribers in Lagos, Kano and Ibadan. This was to "operate in conjunction with the Empire Broadcasting Service."[1] In 1936, radio finally made its debut when the first Radio Distribution Service (rediffusion) was opened in Lagos as a means of distributing programmes originating from the British Broadcasting Corporation (BBC) in London, as part of its Overseas Services.

In the late 1940's through the mid-1950's, rediffusion became the principal mode of broadcasting in Nigeria; many people subscribed to the programmes. This was how rediffusion was technically developed when it was introduced in Nigeria:

The programmes in this system are distributed by land lines from the studio to the various listening boxes for which the subscribers pay a small fee. Amplification is needed at some locations and was provided ... by a makeshift and homebuilt apparatus. This system caught the interest of Nigeria and was expanded to include stations at Ibadan, Abeokuta, Ijebu-Ode, Calabar, Port Harcourt, Enugu, Kano, Kaduna, Jos, and Zaria.[2]

At first the British colonial administration thought it would be wiser and more economical to establish a common West African broadcasting system that would embrace all its West African colonies. It hired the firms of Mr. F.A.W. Byron of the Crown Agents and Mr. L.W. Turner of the BBC as its chief consultants to advise it on the feasibility of this ambitious project. The Turner-Byron Report indicated that "a West African Broadcasting System was not feasible due to the multiplicity of languages and geographical demarcations among territories."[3] It rather recommended that the Nigerian situation could be improved by introducing the following broadcasting facilities in the Federal and Regional capitals:

Lagos: 20 KW, short-wave: for national coverage and Western Regional programmes;
Kaduna: 10 KW, short-wave: for northern coverage.
Enugu: 5 KW, short-wave: for eastern coverage.
Ibadan: 5 KW, medium-wave: for local coverage.
Kano: 5 KW, medium-wave: for local coverage.[4]

The Nigerian Broadcasting Service (NBS) was formally formed on April 1, 1951, after the Federal Government, following the Turner-Byron report, had decided to convert the major existing rediffusion stations into fully operative radio stations. So, in 1952, all the Radio Distribution Services formed the nuclei of the NBS. The BBC, London, was awarded a contract for the establishment of the Federal Government broadcasting service due to its involvement in the development of the broadcasting scheme in Nigeria since 1932. The BBC sent two of its experts who laid the foundation stone of major broadcasting in Nigeria. The BBC provided all the training and technical equipment. In fact BBC's T.W. Charmers became NBS's first director-general while his counterpart, J.W. Murray, became the chief engineer.

It has been often speculated that the location of the NBS in Lagos was a political rather than a technical decision.[5] Lagos was technically considered not feasible for the location of NBS transmitters because the impact of the Atlantic Ocean would be so powerful that it would dissipate the signal strength of the station.[6] The middle-belt region, an area around the Jos plateau, was preferred. But Lagos was chosen because of its political clout as the Federal capital. A one-time British-born director-general of the NBS recollects that the first large studio of the NBS used to be a hostel for seamen; and that the land in Ikoyi, Lagos, where Broadcasting House is located, had originally been reserved as a cemetery for the American war dead of World War II. But eventually, the land was no longer needed, and Broadcasting House was erected there in 1954.[7]

Converting NBS to NBC

The Nigerian Broadcasting Service (NBS) was severely attacked by the Nigerian public and press for being a government tool. The nation wanted the NBS to be impartial and to reflect divergent views and the cultural set-up of the nation. In order to restore public confidence in the services the NBS provided, a member of the Federal House of Parliament, the late Alhaji D.S. Adegbenro, after a combined lobbying with the Eastern members of the House, introduced a motion that called on the Federal Government to disband the NBS and set up an autonomous broadcasting corporation in its place. In introducing his motion, Alhaji Adegbenro said in part:

> Mr. President, Sir, I rise to move the motion in my name. That this House calls (sic) upon Government to consider the setting up of a corporation to takeover the activities of the Nigerian Broadcasting Service in order to remove the press criticism that the Nigerian Broadcasting Service is an organ of the Nigerian Government. Nobody can deny sir, that the Nigerian Broadcasting Service has been a credit to Nigeria because it has been built on the traditions of the British Broadcasting Corporation in the United Kingdom. We in Nigeria do not want half measures. We would like to see our own broadcasting service growing from strength to strength so as to reach the very high standard that has already been attained by the British Broadcasting Corporation. That onward march, Sir, cannot be achieved excepting a corporation is set up to develop our Nigerian Broadcasting Service.[3]

This motion received a wide support. A bill to that effect was introduced on August 23, 1954.[9] The debate on the motion to pass a bill creating a broadcasting corporation lasted for almost two years. The general pattern of the debate seemed to be a Nigerian broadcasting model that was patterned after the BBC. One parliamentarian unequivocally stated:"The intention is... to form a Nigerian broadcasting corporation on the general model of the BBC but owing to the circumstances of Nigeria it is proposed to have three independent Regional set-ups with Regional autonomy subject only to the overall control of policy by the Broadcasting Corporation of the whole country."[10]

Finally, on April 1, 1957, the Nigerian Broadcasting Service, by an Act of Parliament, was converted into a statutory corporation to be thenceforth known as Nigerian Broadcasting Corporation (NBC). The reason for this change was to shield it from government interference and the propagation of the views of the ruling political party.

It was thus the 1956 Act of Parliament, assented to by Queen Elizabeth II, that formally established the NBC. The NBC thus became the first public service broadcasting corporation to have existed in any British Colonial Territory.[11] The original government proposal of the nature of the corporation stated that:

> ...the Corporation should be modelled on the British Broadcasting Corporation with a national and regional organisation and that so far as the regional organisation is concerned there should, within the lines of the Corporation's policy, be a large share of regional autonomy in deciding the content of programmes. The detailed arrangements, when they have been formulated will be subject to the approval of the House of Representatives. Among other provisions there would be laid upon the Cor-

poration the obligation of impartiality. Controversial broadcasts could be given by the corporation provided that all reasonable points of view are represented. It should be the particular care of the Corporation to ensure reasonable expression shall not be denied to minority groups, whether cultural, religious or political.[12]

The NBC was then created to allay public fear of government monopoly of the broadcasting industry. It became a public property. The interesting thing about the corporate status of the NBC was that it was acquired three years ahead of Nigeria's independence. The 1956 ordinance that created the NBC specifically detailed the Corporation's functions to include, among others, (a) provision of independent and impartial broadcasting services; (b) provision of services, when considered as a whole, reflect the unity of Nigeria as a federation and at the same time give adequate expression to the culture, characteristics, affairs and opinions of the people of each Region or part of the Federation: (c) provision to engage in unprejudicial presentation of ministerial speeches, from various political parties that seek to explain the views and policies of various political parties, speeches that express divergent views on controversial issues other than political views, and presentation of religious thought or belief within the Federation; and (d) provision of educational services.[13]

The Ordinance created both Federal and Regional boards of governors for the NBC. It made the cooporation an independent policy-making institution. The NBC board consisted of a chairman, the chairmen of the regional boards, ten others to be appointed by the President of the nation, and a director-general of the corporation who would be an ex-officio member of the Corporation's board without a voting right. The Ordinance also created the post of a secretary to the Corporation.

The functions of the regional boards were identical to those of the national board. The only differences were that while the network was supposed to portray the national cultures in their programmes, the regional affiliates of the NBC were required to pay greater attention to the cultures of the regions they served. The regional boards were specifically required to "ensure that Regional programmes designed for the use of schools or other educational institutions shall have regard to the educational policy of the Government of the Region."[14] Besides the chairman of the Corporation and his regional counterparts, the other members of the board were appointed for a three-year term. At the expiration of the three-year term, they were still eligible for reappointment, according to the provision of the Ordinance.

The Emergence of Regional Broadcasting Systems

The greatest setback to the concept of Nigerian unity occurred when each of the then three regions of the federation established its own independent broadcasting system. One would have thought that each region would have been appeased with the establishment of NBC regional affiliates in each region. In fact the 1956 Ordinance that created the NBC also established a regional board of governors for the NBC regional affiliates. But this sort of planning would not satisfy the highly autonomous regional governments that competed with the Federal Government at all levels but in foreign and defence matters.

It thus seems apparent that the idea of regionalisation of the mass media as effective organs of the regional governments was nourished in 1953 in the then Western Region. It has been widely said that the leader of the banned Action Group, and also of the banned Unity Party of Nigeria, Obafemi Awolowo, had criticised the newly introduced MacPherson Constitution for the nation. The then British Governor-General went to the NBS and made a broadcast in defence of the Constitution. During the broadcast he accused Awolowo of being unfaithful. Awolowo then demanded equal time from the NBS to offer a rebuttal over what the Governor-General had said. The NBS denied him that request.[15] This led to the agitation not only for the incorporation of the NBS as public property but also for eventual establishment of separate individual regional broadcasting systems, independent of the Federal Government control. It is also interesting to note that it was an Action Group member of the House of Parliament who moved the motion to make the NBS a statutory corporation.

The former Western Region, which became the first region to set up its own broadcasting systems in 1959, started the first television broadcasting not only in Nigeria but also in the entire continent of Africa. Seven months later, in May 1960, it initiated a radio broadcasting system over Western Nigeria Broadcasting Service (WNBS).One critic described the inception of the Western Region's broadcasting system as "bold and imaginative in planning."[16] The Western Regional Government signed a contract with the Overseas Rediffusion Company Limited to build its television and radio broadcasting systems.

The former Eastern Region quickly contracted the same Overseas Rediffusion Company to build its own radio and television broadcasting systems. On October 1, 1960, its radio and television signals went on the air to coincide with the attainment of Nigerian independence. However, the East and the West eventually assumed full control of their broadcasting systems by paying off the foreign companies that initially owned them jointly with their governments.

In 1962, after castigating the NBC, the Northern Region Government started its own broadcasting systems. It hired the Granada Group Ltd., to set up the region's radio and television systems.

The three regional governments' broadcasting organisations were wholly independent of the Federal Government control. The only thing they had to do that required action on the part of the Federal Government was to apply, through the Federal Ministry of Communications, for frequency allocation. In fact this was even considered to be automatic in granting. And frequency allocation was necessary so as to avoid interference with the already assigned frequencies to other stations.

The Western Region broadcasting system was the most successful among the three in commercial advertising. It had the heavily populated Lagos and Ibadan markets to exploit. To achieve this, it started a booster television station near Lagos so that its residents could equally switch on to the Western Region stations.

However, the purpose of regionalisation of the broadcast media, and later the print media, was not solely for commercial reasons. They were used as powerful political instruments for the integration of each region and cultivation of regional awareness more than national consciousness and integration. The emphasis was on the regional interest rather than on the national. The politicians who established them greatly exploited them for sectional politics. When political crises occurred, these regional media became more powerful than the NBC. They were used to the fullest in protecting the political, economic, cultural and social interests of the regions.

The reason given for the emergence of regional media that were independent of any Federal Government control was dissatisfaction with the NBC. Each region felt that its own views were not being properly represented by the NBC. Some accused the NBC of partiality and partisanship. Some of these allegations were both real and imagined. But still we cannot deny the fact that it was the regional integration of the media with state politics that triggered off a chain of political crises in Nigeria. Ian MacKay almost had a premonition of the end result of unnecessary regional competition in important national issues when he made the following criticism on the regional set-up of the mass media, some years before major crises erupted in Nigeria:

The sole responsibility of regional broadcasting is to radiate a Regional image and that cannot encourage the artistic endeavours of Nigeria as a nation. The setting up of regional corporations does not bring about true competition. That can only be achieved by setting up a number of corporations having national coverage and offering a range of programmes which would benefit the whole country. There is no sign of that in Nigeria.

Whatever the benefits - and there are benefits - the cost is too high and the danger exists that divided control in a developing society may promote regional feeling instead of encouraging the desire to live together and act together.[17]

It is no crime to have developed highly competitive media network in Nigeria. The only objection is how the media, both at the Federal and regional levels, were mismanaged by the politicians who established them. Otherwise, competition was wholesome for the audience and for national interest and variety, if such competition would provide balanced and objective views of events in the nation.

The 1961 Amendment to the 1956 Ordinance

When the bill that created the NBC as a statutory corporation was being debated in the House of Parliament, some of its proponents emphasised the need to free it of any government control and interference.[18] The Acting Chief Secretary said that there were three reasons for the Bill:

...the first of them was that broadcasting in Nigeria should, on the model of the BBC, be removed from political and Government control and interference. The second was that the Corporation would ... have to be dependent on its finances upon subsidy from public funds. The third principle, which followed both the pattern of constitutional development in Nigeria and the pattern of the BBC... was that there should be both a Corporation at national level and organisations at a regional level, and that so far as the regional organisations were concerned there should be, within the broadcast lines of policy laid down by the Corporation, a considerable measure of regional autonomy in deciding regional performances...[19]

Another member of the House noted that:

... it is potentially dangerous if the NBC is used to stifle criticism, to voice only the thoughts and aims of a particular group of people who, for the time being, are in political power. It may be all very well to have political control of broadcasting so long as one's party is in power. It is not so funny when one is not in power.[20]

In 1961 T.O.S. Benson, the Minister in-charge of broadcasting, introduced a motion to amend the 1956 NBC Ordinance to provide a direct government control over the NBC. In his motion he said he wanted the House to, among other things:

...amend the Nigerian Broadcasting Ordinance to enable the minister responsible for broadcasting to give general and specific directions to the Corporation on matters of policy or matters appearing to the minister to be of public interest and also to enable him, after consultation with the appropriate regional government in the case of regional boards, to make recommendations to the Governor-General in Council as to the appointment of all members of the Corporation...[21]

This motion was not only jeered but it also generated hostility in the House by many members. But Benson, the Minister of Information, had a rational and sound argument. He said that since the regions (The West and the East, and with the North concluding arrangements for establishing its own broadcasting systems) had started their own independent broadcasting, and since they were directly controlling their systems, it was also wise and appropriate for the Federal Government to assume direct control of its national network, NBC. He considered the region's actions as posing a stiff competition for the NBC. He felt that the regions had the edge over the Federal Government in the membership of the NBC board as provided by the 1956 Ordinance. He also said that this situation was all the more anomalous since the regions then had their own broadcasting systems in which there was no Federal representation. To him this would mean that the regions were indirectly controlling the broadcasting industry in the entire nation. He then wanted the 1961 amendment to provide for:

(a) "The appointment of all members of the corporation by the Governor-General in Council on the recommendation of the Minister responsible for broadcasting;

(b) The members of the Regional Boards to be similarly appointed by the Governor-General in Council on the recommendation of the Minister, who will consult the appropriate Regional Governments before making any such recommendation."[22]

The regions attacked Benson and defended the reason why they had established their own broadcasting systems. They accused the NBC of lacking "the capacity for broad vision... dominated by Lagos thinking... unsympathetic to regional requirements, and because of its indifference, it did not serve the *whole* public interest as it should. The regions were victims of NBC discrimination, there was too much emphasis on BBC foreign news and insufficient attention to Nigerian news and there was an unsupported charge that newsreaders 'go to the microphone when they are heavily drunk and cannot even read the script.'"[23]

At this stage of criticism, Benson, the Minister in-charge of broadcasting, made an analogous reference to the NBC and a woman who is married to four husbands at the same time. In his analogy, he noted that "in such a domestic situation it is unlikely that a wife would be able to satisfy the demands of each of these husbands. And so it is with the Corporation (NBC) and four demanding Governments, the Federal Government, and the three Regional Governments, all of whom expect to give priority and preference to their own items of Regional interest...."[24] The Minister even claimed that the NBC was quite objective, impartial and non-partisan in view of complaints coming from both the ruling political parties and those of the opposition. To substantiate this fact, he quoted before the House four major complaints the

NPC, the NCNC, the Action Group and the NEPU had recently made against the NBC between July 29 to August 2, all in 1961. These are some of the excerpts of these complaints the Minister quoted, as compiled by Ian MacKay.

NPC: Press release of July 29, 1961:

"The Northern People's Congress has expressed grave concern over the continued discrimination of the Nigerian Broadcasting Corporation against the government of the North as well as the NPC. It is surprising to note that the Director-General of the NBC, who is strongly biased and deliberately allows discrimination to continue, is now coming to the North to bid farewell to the people of the Northern Region."[2]

NCNC: Letter from Acting National Administrative Secretary to the NBC Director-General dated July 30, 1961

"On behalf of my party, I send you this protest drawing your special attention to the uncooperative and vexatious attitude of the News Division of the NBC towards us. This is not the first time we are protesting against the inexplicable discrimination of the NBC against the NCNC, a partner in the two-party Federal Coalition Government."

NEPU: Press release of July 31, 1961:

"If anybody is to complain against the NBC it is the Opposition parties whose releases are being shortened or abandoned in order to give full coverage to those of the NPC and the Northern Government."

Action Group: Press release of August 2, 1961:

"In the view of the Action Group, the NBC has all along been showing bias in favour of the NPC and its partner in the Federal Coalition Government...Its bias is against the Federal Opposition Party."[25]

It is this type of dissatisfaction among the major parties that led Benson to make the analogy. It appears his analogy was accurate, judging from the fact that none of these parties seemed pleased with NBC's services to their respective political views.

The Bill that sought to amend the Ordinance that created the NBC was passed on August 28, 1961, with more than half of the House members not showing up.[26] The following day the Nigerian newspapers accused Benson of "marrying" the NBC and out-manoeuvring the other three husbands. Some newspapers had banner headlines that read: "BENSON TAKES WIFE."[27] These were then the circumstances that led to a complete government takeover of the NBC. But the NBC was (and still is) theoretically regarded as a public corporation.

Administration of Radio Broadcasting

Radio broadcasting is owned and controlled by both the Federal and State Governments. The Federal and State Governments are the sole bodies that fund their individual broadcasting organisations in the country. While the various states' broadcasting organisations have been engaging in commercial broadcasting since their inception, the Federal Government did not allow those it owns to go commercial until August 1, 1987, as will be shown shortly. Formerly, every radio set owner in the country was required by law to license his radio set annually. The money paid for the licenses went to the Federal Inland Revenue Department. The main operational costs of broadcasting in the country are borne by the Federal and State Governments which appropriate reasonable annual budgets.

There was a token opposition in the Federal House of Parliament when the NBC wanted to start accepting commercial advertisements. People feared that those who would sponsor programmes would influence their contents. Moreover, the NBC had been modelled after the BBC as a public service corporation. But for the fact that the state broadcasting systems had gone commercial, NBC management argued that it too should be allowed to go commercial so as to subvent some of its huge expenses. In November, 1960, NBC began to accept advertisements when the Act of incorporation was amended.[28] However, during the Murtala/Obasanjo military administration, the NBC (FRCN) was barred from accepting advertisement and getting involved in commercial broadcasting. The military argument was that it was developed as a public utility and as such it should aid the government in its development campaigns. It was feared that permission to go commercial might affect the policies and orientation of the management. When the fourth military coup d'état occurred on December 31, 1983, the FRCN management made a series of representations to the military authorities through the Federal Minister of Information, (himself a military officer) to justify why it should be allowed to go commercial. It claimed that going commercial would enable it to generate a substantial portion of its annual subvention to augment whatever subsidy the Federal Government makes available to it. The Federal Military Government gave the FRCN's representation a serious thought. But it eventually rejected it. The ousted Shagari civilian administration also turned down a similar request by the FRCN to be allowed to go commercial. As a matter of fact, during the Onosode Commission on Federal Government Parastatals, the FRCN, through its former Director-General, George Bako, voluntarily opted to remain in the unified salary structure system of the Civil Service Commission. Its management openly admitted that it (the FRCN) could not generate 100% of its annual revenue without Federal Government bail-out. But the fact remains that millions of dollars were being lost as a result of the government policy of not permitting the FRCN to go commercial. The government was running it at a great financial deficit. That was the prize it paid for a rigid control. However, the state radio systems, as well as the Nigerian Television Authority (NTA) and the state-owned television stations, are allowed to go commercial. The Babangida administration, determined to force profit-oriented public corporations to generate their own incomes, permitted the FRCN to go commercial with effect from August 1, 1987. This departure from a rigid Federal Government control that previously forbade commercialisation will definitely lead to greater professionalism in the nation's broadcasting industry.

Nigeria's 1979 Constitution makes radio broadcasting a concurrent subject between the Federal and State Governments. The committee that drafted the Constitution categorically stated that it "decided that private persons should not own, manage or control any television or broadcasting station."[29] The Constitution reaffirms the authority of the Federal Government to allocate wave lengths for wireless broadcasting and television transmission.[30]

This, of course, has always been the order of things in the media organisation of the country - a legacy bequeathed by colonial administration. But with immense political changes that have occurred in Nigeria in recent times, and with the important contributions private businesses have made in the economic and social development of Nigeria, there was intensive lobbying for private ownership of wireless broadcasting to be embodied as a constitutional right of anybody to own a means of broadcasting if the person could afford it. But it seems the government pressure prevailed.

Ever since the dawn of broadcasting in Nigeria, as has already been noted in the previous pages, the Federal and former Regional Governments, and now the State Governments, have monopolised the broadcasting industry. The FRCN, which is owned and controlled by the Federal Government, at various times (depending upon broadcasting policies of particular regimes) has operated its own state stations in each of the states of the federation.[31] At the same time each of Nigeria's states has its own radio broadcasting station[32] that is totally independent of the FRCN affiliate in the state. For political reasons, all the radio stations are located at both the Federal and state capitals. The FRCN owns and controls twenty-two broadcasting stations - nineteen of which were formerly located in nineteen states; and one at the Federal Capital Territory, Abuja; one at its national network headquarters, Ikoyi, and an AM/FM-stereo at 45 Martins Street, Lagos.

The FRCN, in the 1970's, still maintained some provincial broadcasting stations. As at 1983, there were forty-eight radio transmitting stations in the country. Subsequent pages will show that the number of forty-eight was reduced as a result of economic recession and political expediency, during the

Buhari/Idiagbon military administration.

The Federal Radio Corporation of Nigeria (FRCN) is undoubtedly one of the most powerful political and social institutions of the Nigerian society. It has played a role that is second to none in the political leadership power struggle of the country. The military has always used it as a means of out-manoeuvring their rivals in leadership struggles in the country. This has consequently led to low credibility image perception of the system by its national audience as studies have shown. The FRCN is virtually viewed among the Nigerian public as a big "white horse" that is only answerable to any government of the day—a sort of "prostitute" whose boyfriends come and go and is ready to meet the demand of each and everyone of them.

The organisation is guided by a-nine-point objective, which, it claims, will lead it to accomplish its activities and policies so as to operate within the framework of the law that established it as a public broadcasting corporation for the Nigerian public.[33] The nine-point objectives of the Corporation are;

(1) "to provide efficient broadcasting services to the whole Federation of Nigeria, based on national objectives and aspirations; and to external audiences in accordance with Nigerian foreign policy;

(2) to provide a professional and comprehensive coverage of Nigerian culture through broadcasting; to promote cultural growth through research into indigenous culture and to disseminate the results of such research;

(3) to contribute to the development of Nigerian society, and to promote national unity by ensuring a balanced presentation of views from all parts of Nigeria;

(4) to ensure the prompt delivery of accurate information to the people;

(5) to provide opportunities for the free enlightened and responsible discussion of important issues, and to provide a two-way contact between the public and those in authority;

(6) to provide special broadcasting services in the field of education, and in all other areas where the national policy calls for special action;

(7) to promote the orderly and meaningful development of broadcasting in Nigeria through technical improvements, the training of appropriate professional staff, programme and other exchanges with other broadcasting organisations in the country;

(8) to promote research into various aspects of the communications media and their effects on the Nigerian society. (This will include audience research, the investigation of fresh methods of production, and the true indigenisation of the broadcasting media);

(9) to ensure that the facilities and techniques of broadcasting in Nigeria keep pace with developments in the world of communication (e.g. FM transmission, colour television, etc.)".[34]

It is good for any organisation, especially a powerful broadcasting medium organisation in a developing country such as Nigeria, to have some objectives which it uses as a reference dictionary in its operation for meeting public interest. But it will be much better and laudable for the FRCN to implement its nine-point objectives provided some of them can be defined. If the FRCN can operationalise and define all of its nine objectives in concrete terms, it will then have come a long way in meeting the yearnings of the Nigerian public. One good thing about some of these nine-point objectives is that they took into account the degree of the Corporation's major weaknesses based upon public criticisms and overt reaction of dissatisfaction with its services. Some of these allegations against the FRCN have been empirically supported by an audience research.[35] But the question now is the extent to which the FRCN is committed to attaining its objectives; or, are these nine-point objectives another gimmick at solving a major problem of a Corporation whose audiences are very distrustful of its services, especially during national crises?

The vast political changes Nigeria has undergone within the last two decades have equally entailed simultaneous changes within the structure and organisation of the FRCN. Events of the past two decades have proved the industry to be a political institution. When formerly there were only three regional services, the number dramatically changed to twelve, and then to nineteen, depending on the number of states created in the country; it could increase in the near future, or could stay at nineteen.

In order to achieve affective services for the nation, the quality of such services notwithstanding, the FRCN once operated a three-tier system of broadcasting. As has been noted earlier, its national headquarters is located at Ikoyi, Lagos, and is on the air at 5.30 a.m. and signs off at 12.00 midnight on week days. The programmes originating from its national studios in Lagos are national in their contents and in most cases, produced by the FRCN national headquarters. However, it does use programmes its state affliates produce, when the management at Lagos is of the view that such programmes are of particular national interest.

At the state level, the FRCN stations (do not confuse them with those of the state governments) originate their own programmes. These programmes are primarily aimed at the various cultures of the states in which they are based. Consequently, these programmes are more local in nature than national. They are targeted to the audiences of their immediate state environment. This is, of course, in accordance with the provisions of the 1956 Ordinance that created the FRCN. The FRCN state services are answerable to the FRCN headquarters in Lagos for their programme contents. The FRCN national headquarters in Lagos, zonal and state management hold a National Planning Conference during which the national programmes from the headquarters that are to be transmitted by the FRCN state services are determined by mutual agreement. But all the FRCN services, as well as the radio stations of the state governments, are required by the 1978 FRCN decree to monitor FRCN major news services.

Within the state broadcasting systems of the FRCN organisation, there existed what used to be the third tier of Provincial Broadcasting Houses (PBH) which were primarily established to serve certain large local communities considered to be of political, cultural and economic importance. They were under the supervision of the NBC state broadcasting system, rather than the national. However, they were within the overall jurisdiction of the national headquarters of the NBC, in Lagos. With the creation of more states in the country in 1975, and for economic purposes, the FRCN converted some of these Provincial Broadcasting Houses into state broadcasting systems. So, Provincial Broadcasting Houses do not any longer exist in the states. They were formerly located in the following cities and towns: Katsina, Zaria, Onitsha, Warri, Abeokuta and Ijebu-Ode. The FRCN eventually converted the station in Abeokuta into an FRCN state broadcasting system for Ogun State.[36]

The Provincial Broadcasting Houses originated their own programmes which, in turn, were supposed to reflect the cultures of their communities, and to promote a sense of belonging among their local audiences.[37] In certain instances, the PBHs sent their programmes to the NBC state broadcasting systems through which they derived their existence.[38]

The following diagram illustrates the three-tier system the FRCN formerly operated within the nation:

NBC National Services

↑

NBC State (affiliate) Broadcasting Systems

↑

NBC Provincial Broadcasting Houses

↑

Figure 6 The NBC (FRCN) Three-Tier System

The arrows indicate that the Provincial Broadcasting Houses were under the supervision of the FRCN state broadcasting systems, while the latter systems were under the control of the FRCN national network services in Lagos. Also, the following map[39] of Nigeria on the next page shows the location of the FRCN transmitters in each of the nineteen states in the federation. The Provincial Broadcasting Houses are not included. Also, for technical reasons, the national network of the FRCN has been divided into four zones. These are:

Zone A (Lagos, Ogun, Oyo, Ondo and Kwara states);
Zone B (Bendel, Anambra, Imo, Rivers, and Cross River states);
Zone C (Kaduna, Plateau, and Benue states); and
Zone D (Kano, Borno, Bauchi, Gongola, Sokoto, and Niger states).[40]

Voice of Nigeria (VON)

The Voice of Nigeria, the External Service of Radio Nigeria, is another important one that could be regarded as making up the fourth-tier of the FRCN. VON started its own operation on January 1, 1962.[41] The FRCN management policy states that the programme policy of the External Service has been "to project the personality, culture, and traditions of the people of Nigeria to the outside world, and to broadcast news of international significance in keeping with the foreign policy of the Federal Government...."[42]

The powerful role the former Voice of Biafra played during the Nigerian thirty-month-old war forced the Federal Government to embark on a gigantic development and reorganisation of Voice of Nigeria. During the Civil War, Voice of Biafra virtually shut up Voice of Nigeria. The latter's reception was extraordinarily poor. But during the execution of the third national development plan of 1975-1980, more than $12.5 million were allocated for the expansion and modernisation of the External Service. Under the plan, the External Service purchased four additional 500 K/W transmitters and modern studio equipment.[43] Also, the plan called for the expansion of the building that houses the External Service so as "to make room for studio and other equipment to be installed."[44]

The 1975-1980 Nigeria's third national development plan made a handsome budget allocation for what was then generally known as "Radio Development Project" for the entire nation. The FRCN was the sole beneficiary of over $82 million appropriated for the project during the third national development plan. Besides the refurbishment and modernisation of FRCN studios in each of the nineteen states, "Radio Development Project" envisaged building an alternative second channel in all the state headquarters in the form of FM stations. Already, an FM station, under the plan, has been operating in Lagos. It is known as Radio Nigeria Two (RN-Two). The RN-Two channel lacks originality, as its announcers and D-Js imitate the style and manner FM stations operate in the United States. Moreover, this second channel is mostly a musical station.

The third national development plan also made adequate funding for development in the following areas in the broadcast media industry:

(a) Purchasing and installation of telecommunications equipment to link the FRCN and its affiliate stations all over the nation;

(b) establishment and installation of modern equipment for monitoring services;

(c) introduction of modern facilities for remote radio broadcasting and recording for all the FRCN stations in all the nineteen states;

(d) construction of a modern complex to house research and development unit... and for researches to be conducted on the adaptation of local material for the needs of the FRCN;

(e) building a new FRCN training school to be equipped with studios, classrooms, laboratories and equipment;

(f) ordering and providing new transmitters and studio equipment for the FRCN and its affiliates in all the state capitals; and

(g) completing FRCN studio buildings in all the state capitals.[45]

The other projects included in the third development plan were buildings for the FRCN staff accommodation, welfare services, offices, and land acquisitions for projects in all the states. Already some of these projects have been completed. There is no doubt that such a huge investment, in an effort to modernise the FRCN, will herald a new era of broadcasting in Nigeria. However, the primary question still remains the contributions of the FRCN towards national development and integration through its programmes.

An Evaluation of the FRCN Programmes and Policy

The FRCN, through a variety of some ingeniously conceived local programmes, is perhaps the only institution in the country that, at least, presents and perpetuates a certain degree of feeling of common national identity and belonging. It has an array of diversified cultural programmes that can appeal to any group of people.

The English language is the official language the FRCN uses in most of its programmes. The FRCN news programme is rigidly patterned after the BBC format. The major news that used to last ten minutes but now 15 minutes is read first in English at 7.00 a.m., 10.00 a.m., 1 p.m., 4.00 p.m., 7.00 p.m., and 10.00 p.m. There is the news summary in English on every hour from the Broadcasting House, Ikoyi, Lagos. At the FRCN zones, news summaries are either in English or languages of the respective linguistic zones. Prior to the 1978 reorganisation, there used to be news translation and other magazine programmes in nine major Nigerian languages, (out of 252 languages) in Hausa, Igbo, Yoruba, Edo, Efik, Fulfude, Kanuri, Ijaw, and Tiv. The fifteen minutes major news in English is edited and abridged to last between three to five minutes in each of these nine Nigerian languages. One often wonders why the FRCN news services could not exceed fifteen minutes in English as well as giving it equal time treatment in the major Nigerian languages that the English version gets. Why cannot the news last at least twenty or twenty-five minutes? And why does it not deserve equal treatment in more Nigerian vernaculars besides these nine?

Educational broadcasting is among the leading services the FRCN provides. About 11% of its weekly hours used to be devoted to the broadcasting of school subjects "to supplement classroom teaching of syllabus-oriented subjects."[46] There is also a limited programme on adult education. But recently, a new channel that is entirely devoted to educational broadcasting was inaugurated. It has been functioning effectively. The suspended National Open University utilised it for a series of its inaugural lectures. This channel was then on the air from 5.30 a.m. to 12.00 midnight.

The FRCN management makes an important observation when, with reference to its programmes, it states:

The importance of broadcasting in a developing country lies in the fact that it is the quickest means of communication with the largest number of people in the shortest time possible. Broadcasting serves to inform, educate and entertain.... People need to be informed about the social, cultural and economic practices in the different parts of the country. The FRCN has been playing a very big role ... along these lines....[47]

Just how adequate the FRCN has been providing these services in a developing Nigeria is best seen by an attitude of mistrust the general public maintains over it.[48] The FRCN has a traditional policy of summarising newspaper editorials from the major Nigerian dailies each day. But when a newspaper criticizes the government, the FRCN does not read such an editorial over its network.[49] The Nigerian public often questions this type of policy. A developing society is a rhetorical society where there are always pros and cons on issues. The level of conflicts on national development issues is so high that all sides of a case need to be presented for a rational public to make its choice. But the FRCN, through its programmes, hardly operates that way. It rarely, if ever, generates debates on controversial national issues. Rather, it only defends the views and policies of a government in power until that government is overthrown before it (the FRCN) begins to cast aspersions on that government it had loyally served. O'Kevbe Uyo makes the following criticism and specific references to such FRCN practices:

During the Gowon era...there were issues which the FRCN either suppressed, manipulated, or killed but which some newspapers reported. These include the affairs involving Tarka and Dabor, Gomwalk and Aku, and Ogbemudia and Iyare. With the revelations following General Muhammed's takeover of the leadership of this country, one could rightly say that FRCN had "fooled" the people with its "News in full." The practice is still continuing.

Six days a week...the FRCN broadcasts the *newstalk*. If the topic of the newstalk pertains to a government policy or action, never expect to hear that it was wrong or ill-advised....Not once was a daring finger pointed at the policies and actions of Gowon and his team. But the venom with which the FRCN newstalk attacked the policies, actions, even the personality of Gowon and his team after their downfall is non-parallelled; a classic case of ex-post facto or retroactive Journalism.[50]

The FRCN lacks a comprehensive national policy in its programming of important controversial issues. This has led to a lack of public confidence and trust.

The demise of public trust and confidence in the NBC actually began in 1964 when a nation-wide labour strike in the major Federal Government establishments was staged against the Federal Government. When the strike gained momentum and had reached its peak, with thousands of workers taking to the streets or staying home in support of the strike, the NBC, in its news bulletin, broadcast that there had been a "massive return to work" by workers in all the affected ministries and departments.[51] Another instance where the NBC had tried to support the government in power was during the 1964 Western Region Election riggings. The election had been controversial and substantiated allegations of region-wide election riggings that took place had been proved. But the NBC still went ahead to broadcast the results of the discredited election. This angered some people in the Western Region and their "reaction to the NBC...was the cutting off of their rediffusion boxes which were relaying the NBC programmes in the former region."[52]

Also, during the May 1981 nationwide strike that was organised by the Nigerian Labour Congress, NLC, the FRCN and its NTA electronic counterpart lost their credibility when, through their network news and other programmes, intentionally broadcast lies in which they informed their viewers that practically all the affiliated labour unions had dissociated themselves from the impending strike action. When the strike began, the FRCN and NTA also denied that there was any strike action going on. Believing the FRCN and NTA, some businessmen who went to the various airports in the country to board planes for their day's business transactions found all the planes belonging to the national airline, Nigeria Airways, grounded. Also, government ministries had all heeded to the NLC's call for a strike action. When the strike was called off after two days, and after labour and government negotiators had reached an agreement, when the FRCN and NTA announced that it had been called off and that people should report to their various places of work, not a single worker heeded that media appeal. The government had to summon the national labour leader, Hassan Sunmonu; it

took him to the NTA studios and asked him to make a broadcast, to assure
the workers all over the federation that all the labour unions and the government had negotiated the main issues leading to the nationwide strike and that
agreements had been reached and that the strike action had been subsequently called off. It was after the workers had seen their labour leader on
the tubes that they believed the FRCN and NTA. The workers' argument for
not believing the FRCN and the NTA initially was how could the two
electronic media networks say that the strike was over when in the first instance they said that there was no strike action taking place in the country.
Empirical field studies have shown that in crisis situations, Nigerians prefer
listening to foreign radio stations such as the British Broadcasting Corporation (BBC) and Voice of America (VOA) to the national radio and television
network services for objective and factual information of the situation of critical events in their country.[53]

The 1978 Radio Decree

During the thirteen years of military interregnum in Nigeria, 1966 - 1979,
the military dictators did not only takeover the management and control of
the entire state government-owned broadcasting systems, but also centralised
radio broadcasting to ensure effective control. However, when the military
decided to retire to its barracks and hand over power to a democratically
elected National Assembly in accordance with the 1979 Constitution that
provided for a bicameral system of government, it promulgated the Federal
Radio Corporation of Nigeria (FRCN) Decree No. 8 of April, 1978. The
decree decentralised radio broadcasting and restructured the nation's broadcast industry.

The Nigerian Broadcasting Corporation (NBC), the doyen of broadcasting organisation in Nigeria, had its name changed to Federal Radio Corporation of Nigeria (FRCN). In pursuance of the provisions of the military
decree, the FRCN also handed over its state affiliate stations in each of the
nineteen states of the federation to the respective state governments as their
bona fide property. The following influential radio systems that possessed
powerful transmitters were re-organised and they consequently formed the
nucleus of the FRCN. They were the Nigerian Broadcasting Corporation
(NBC), the Broadcasting Company of Northern Nigeria (BCNN), the
Anambra Broadcasting Corporation (ABC), Imo Broadcasting Service (IBS)
and Broadcasting Corporation of Oyo State (BCOS).

The military decision for this new outfit for the broadcast industry was to
stop the installation of powerful transmitters in the country. Consequently,
the decree constituted FRCN into four restructured national broadcasting
linguistic zones, with their headquarters located in Lagos and the former
capitals of the former three giant regions of the North: Kaduna; the West:
Ibadan; and the East: Enugu. The Imo Broadcasting Service (IBS), Owerri,

was directed to exchange its powerful transmitter for Anambra Broadcasting Corporation's less powerful transmitter. Subsequent political developments overtook this directive, hence its non-implementation.

The four linguistic zones of the FRCN and their languages of broadcasting are:

KADUNA: Hausa, Fulfulde, Kanuri, Nupe and English
ENUGU: Igbo, Tiv, Izon, Efik and English
IBADAN: Yoruba, Edɔ, Igala, Urhobo and English
LAGOS: English.

Each of these zones is made up of a board of directors for policy decisions and implementation. A zone is headed by a director.

The Federal radio stations, handed over to the various state governments, as well as any subsequent ones to be established by the states, are restricted to transmit only on medium wave. It is only the four linguistic zones and the station at the new Federal Capital Territory, Abuja, that are allowed to transmit on the short wave. The decree that reorganises the industry also allows a maximum transmitter power of 10 kilowatts and a field strength of 1 millivolt per metre, as measured at the state boundary. These provisions were inserted in the decree to curtail the political influence of some ambitious, powerful state governments and their people, especially in periods of political crises.

This was how the military restructured Nigeria's broadcast industry due to the political sensitivity of the broadcast media organisation in the Nigerian political set-up. The aim was to ensure political stability, co-existence, national integration and, above all, national unity and understanding among the various ethnic groups in a nation of about 100 million.

Broadcasting Policy During the Second Republic

Immediately the civilians took over from the military in 1979, a bill to amend the 1978 FRCN decree was introduced by the executive arm of the government before the National Assembly. The amendment bill was aimed at breaking up the four FRCN zones and establishing a Federal Government-owned radio station in each of the states of the federation to compete with those of the various state governments. The Federal civilian government discovered that the structure the army had left for the nation incapacitated the federal might, especially in those states of the federation where the party at the centre was not in control. Also, the calculation was that if the party controlling the central government needed to be re-elected to power, it needed federal presence at the grassroot level of the society which the state governments monopolised, assisted by their monopoly ownership of the broadcast industry in the states they administered. The amendment bill was subsequently withdrawn as it was vehemently opposed by practically all the ten states of the North. They did not want Radio Kaduna to be dismantled, irrespective of the political expediency of the executive and his party cohorts.

The opposition to the amendment bill notwithstanding, the Federal Government did brazenly violate the FRCN decree by establishing high-powered transmitters for the radio stations in those states of the federation that the ruling party (NPN) at the centre was not in political and economic control. Between June and July, 1983, the Federal Minister of Information had commissioned seven such new stations at Owerri, Akure, Enugu, Jos, Abeokuta, Calabar and Ikeja.

It is worth noting that all these were located in states that were controlled by the various political parties opposed to the National Party of Nigeria (NPN) at the centre. The only exception was the one established in Calabar where the political fortune of the NPN was in doubt as the incumbent governor failed to get his party's (NPN) second ticket for re-election. The Unity Party of Nigeria (UPN) courted him and his followers. The Federal Government thus established the FRCN station in Calabar and started it with personnel whose loyalty was not to be doubted. Also, these "illegal" stations were commissioned at the heat of the 1983 national election campaigns to elect a President, governors, senators and representatives of the Federal and State Houses of Assembly.

On their part, the state governments did equally violate the spirit of the decree. Some of them went as far as establishing transmitters that could be picked up at a distance of 800 kilometers. The Radio Rivers Two FM Stereo is a clear example. This violated the limited 10 kilowatts stipulated in the 1978 decree for each state radio transmitter. Also, some of the state governments established multiple radio stations, especially FM stereo stations, in strategic locations to innundate their people with political propaganda. One of the reasons attributed to the Federal Government for the establishment of its own radio stations in various states was denial of access to present the Federal views by the state government-owned radio outlets. Federal Government activities were blacked out in some states. The result of such an unplanned and unnecessary competition was that there were no less than forty-eight radio and thirty-two television stations in Nigeria in the early eighties, that were sustained by a heavy dose of foreign disco music and entertainment programmes.

Military Re-entry and implications on Broadcasting

On December 31, 1983, in Nigeria's fourth successful military coup d'état and fifth since independence in 1960, the military ousted the Shagari administration, alleging maladministration, economic mismanagement, corruption in high quarters, insensitivity, indecision, and inefficiency. The coup abruptly ended a-four-year experiment on the borrowed American form of check and balance system of government. The interesting question then was what the succeeding military administration would do with those new radio and television stations that the Federal and most State Governments had established, some of which were economically and politically unviable?

Political considerations and fierce competition to win the support of the Nigerian mass media audience by the Federal and state governments, especially during the shortlived Second Republic, (1979-1983), led to the proliferation of ill-conceived radio stations that lacked articulated and conceptualised objectives relevant to the needs of a fastly developing society. The lack of a clear-cut objective and subsequent affiliation of radio broadcasting with politics consequently led to heavy reliance on music, mostly foreign, for the retention of the coveted audience; and partly for the sustenance of eighteen hours of broadcasting per day.

As soon as the military seized power in December 1983, all the state and Federal Government-owned radio and television stations started to hook-up to the headquarters of both the Federal Radio Corporation of Nigeria (FRCN) and Nigerian Television Authority (NTA) at Ikoyi and Victoria Island of Lagos, respectively, without being directed by the military administration to do so. From 1979-1983, the relationship between the Federal and most state broadcasting organisations was characterised by such a high degree of hostility that political thugs from an opposing political party were accused of setting ablaze the Anambra Broadcasting Corporation (ABC) studios in Enugu in December, 1982.

In subsequent years, Nigerian media watchers will continue to record new trends in policy formulation and decision-making that are politically-motivated. In October, 1984, the nation's former Chief of Staff, Supreme Headquarters, Tunde Idiagbon, while inaugurating a committee on the rationalisation of television services the Nigerian Television Authority (NTA) provides, with regard to the existence and coverage of the state television stations and the general duties of the authority as specified in the decree of 1977 that established the NTA, announced that all the "mushroom" radio stations the FRCN established in the states of the federation during the Second Republic were to be closed down.[54] He said that the zonal radio stations in Lagos, Ibadan, Kaduna, Enugu and the new Federal Capital Territory in Abuja "would be re-equipped to provide better services to the nation..."[55] In an apparent move to revert broadcasting to the structure the military had approved, as contained in the FRCN 1978 decree, before the politicians of the Second Republic used acts of the state assemblies to restructure the entire radio broadcasting system, Idiagbon indicted them for breaking the military covenant on broadcasting structure and condemned "the proliferation of radio and television stations in the last civilian administration, to engage in and disseminate open character assassination, all sorts of profanity, slander, falsehood and even pure incitement bordering on treason."[56] On further reflection on the politics of the broadcast industry during the second Republic, he was credited to have observed:

> ...in the prevailing madness, the basic patriotic objectives of setting up sta-
> tions to inform, entertain and educate were lost as the various political
> parties ensured that the government under their control engaged in the
> proliferation of television and radio stations throughout the country. The
> stations, without exception, became megaphones of political parties in
> power, suppressing or grossly distorting information to suit the whims and
> caprices of politicians and consequently fanning the embers of disunity,
> disaffection and disorder. They succeeded to such an extent that law and
> order broke down in many states of the federation... The present ad-
> ministration owed it a duty to provide a virile, functional and effective
> broadcasting system to the nation and could not sit idly and watch the sec-
> tor decay.[57]

Two months after Idiagbon's pronouncements, the FRCN state stations in Owerri, Ilorin, Calabar, Akure, Ibadan, etc., etc., were closed and about 2000 of their staff had their appointments terminated. To prevent rioting, the government posted armed anti-riot policemen to the affected stations; they were also to maintain law and order and guard against looting or probable sabotage of equipment and other facilities in the affected stations.

The broadcasting media have become so endemic in Nigerian political set-up that without them the political juggernauts are nobody. The result is that the affinity between broadcasting and politics is like the birth of Siamese twins, in which any surgical operation that is performed to separate them, that is not carefully carried out, might lead to the death of either, if not both.

It now seems customary that every military or civilian administration must leave a historical landmark in the sphere of radio and television broadcasting industry. The Babangida military administration that overthrew the Buhari/Idiagbon regime on August 27, 1985, has also effected a major restructuring of the FRCN zonal set-up. The Nigerian Television Authority (NTA) is also affected in the reorganisation of broadcast media structure of the Babangida administration. The decree that gives legal backing to whatever these changes are is yet to be promulgated. But the changes have been reported in authoritative government-owned newspapers. The latest reorganisation could well be to suit the administrative convenience of the Babangida regime.

FOOTNOTES

1. Ian Mackay, *Broadcasting in Nigeria*. Ibadan: Ibadan University Press. 1964, p. 2.
2. Edward C. Milton, *A Survey of the Technical Development of the Nigerian Broadcasting Corporation,* (Lagos: NBC) 1955, p. 13.
3. Penn Roger, *Broadcasting in Nigeria*. Master's thesis. American University, Washington, D.C. 1960, p. 8.
4. Milton, see citation in no. 2 above pp. 1-2.
5. *Headlines*. Lagos, May 1977, p.6.
6. *Ibid.*
7. Ian MaacKay, "Concepts of Broadcasting in Nigeria", *EBU 788*, p. 17.
8. House of Representatives Debates. Third Session. March 6-25, 1954. (Lagos, Federal Government Printer), pp. 595-6.
9. MacKay, *Broadcasting in Nigeria,* p. 46.
10. *Ibid.*
11. *Ibid.,* p. 52.
12. *Ibid.*
13. Nigerian Broadcasting Corporation Ordinance No. 39 of 1956.
14. *Ibid.,* p. 123.
15. *Headline,* p. 6.
16. MacKay, *Broadcasting in Nigeria,* p. 61.
17. *Ibid.,* p. 64.
18. *Ibid.*
19. *Ibid.,* p. 25.
20. *Ibid.*
21. *Ibid.,* p. 66.
22. *Ibid.,* p. 67.
23. *Ibid.,* pp. 67-68.
24. *Ibid.*
25. *Ibid.,* pp. 68-69.
26. *Ibid.,* p. 69.
27. *Ibid.,* p. 70.
28. *Growing up with the Nation: THE FIRST TWENTY YEARS 1957-1977.* (Lagos, NBC), 1977, P. 23.
29. Reports of the Constitution Drafting Committee. Vol. II p. 209. (Federal Ministry of Information, printing Division, Lagos), 1976.
30. *Ibid.,* p. 147.
31. The FRCN has now fully established its state stations in all of the nineteen states after the creation of the seven additional states that increased the total number of states in the country to nineteen.
32. Not all the Northern states have established their own broadcasting stations. They are still being served by Radio-Television, Kaduna. But it is expected that very soon each of them will start a station.
33. *The First Twenty Years,* p. 24.
34. *Ibid.*
35. Luke Uka Uche, "Credibility Factor in Opinion Leaders' Media Preference: A case Study of Foreign Broadcasts in Nigeria During Crisis Situations." A competitive paper presented to Mass Communication Division, International Communication Association (ICA) annual conference, San Francisco, U.S.A. May 24-28, 1984.
36. *First Twenty Years,* p. 15.
37. *Ibid.*
38. *Ibid.*
39. This map has been furnished by NBC's Public Relations department. It was designed by Econó-Media Ltd., Lagos. It is contained in the *First Twenty Years,* p. 28, 1977.
40. *NBC: Annual Report and Statement of Accounts*, 1975/76. Lagos, p. 19.
41. *Voice of Nigeria* (NBC, Lagos publication), 1977, p.2.
42. *First Twenty Years,* p. 19.
43. *Third National Development Plan 1975-80.* (The Central Planning Office, Federal Ministry of Economic Development , Lagos); 1977. Revised edition, p. 351. The 500 k/w has already been installed.

44.   *Ibid.*
45.   *Third National Development 1975-80 op.* cit. pp. 351-354.
46.   *Ibid.*, p. 18.
47.   *Ibid.*, p. 15.
48.   Luke Uka Uche, "Credibility Factor in Opinion Leaders' Media Preference: A case study of foreign broadcasts in Nigeria during crises at situations." Earlier citation.
49.   O'Kevbe Adidi Uyo, "Here is the NBC news in FULL...!" *UNILAG COMMUNICATION REVIEW.* Vol. 1, No. 1, January/March 1977, p. 12.
50.   *Ibid.*
51.   "Wake up Radio Nigeria" *Sunday Times,* May 1, 1977, p. 16.
52.   *Ibid.*
53.   Luke Uka Uche, earlier citation.
54.   "Mushroom Radio stations To Go" *Daily Times,* October 24. 1984, p.1.
55.   *Ibid.*
56.   *Ibid.*
57.   *Ibid.*

FOUR

TELEVISION BROADCASTING

Early History

The evolution of television in Nigeria followed the same pattern as that of radio. The irony here is that while it was the Federal Government that started the first radio broadcasting in the nation, it was the regional governments that first ventured into television broadcasting. It was on October 31, 1959, that the former Western Region sent out the first television signal in the whole of Nigeria and Africa.

The Western Nigerian television service was established by an Act of the region's House of Parliament. Although it soon became the richest commercial television broadcasting organisation in the entire federation, commercialisation was not the reason why it was established, per se. The reason was that of formal and informal education. The proponents of its establishment had argued in the Regional House of Assembly that the necessity of such a medium was its utility as an additional means of improving the regional school systems that were handicapped by the shortage of qualified teachers in certain subject areas.[1] They also argued that such a medium would act as a surrogate "teacher" in those understaffed schools in the region.[2] The potential ability of television to enhance educational objectives at both primary (grade) and secondary (high) school levels and adult education became the overriding factor for the establishment of the Western Nigeria Television (WNTV) and Western Nigeria Broadcasting Service (WNBS).

On October 1, 1960, the day Nigeria achieved independence from Great Britain, the former Eastern Region started its own television broadcasting system. The motive for its establishment was also the need for formal and informal education. But, it, too, soon abandoned this objective and joined the WNTV in commercial broadcasting. The same overseas company that built the WNBS radio and television systems also developed the Eastern Nigeria Broadcasting Corporation ENBC radio and television broadcasting facilities. The overseas company (Overseas Rediffusion) owned shares and assets in the broadcasting systems they had helped build in these two regions. They were influential in policy formulation and programme contents. This was because the two regions - East and West - lacked the technical know-how to manage their new television industries. This could account for the reasons why the early emphasis on programme contents was on foreign programmes. However, relations between the foreign firms and the two regions soon became strained and these overseas companies were eventually paid off by the regions.[3]

The Federal Government was somewhat embarrassed at the rapidity with which the East and West had established television broadcasting. When the Federal Government wanted to start a television project, some of its officials argued that it would be wise to save the resources by maximising the development of radio broadcasting.[4] They also argued that television was primarily a luxury of entertainment. But eventually, after much political rancour and filibuster, the bureaucratic huddles were surmounted when the Federal Economic Council of Ministers gave the order for the final approval of the establishment of a Federal Government-owned television studio to be located in Lagos.

There was a problem of not only technical logistics for the proposed Federal Government television, but there were also those of politics and economy. The WNTV, Ibadan, had scored a major political and economic victory when it became the first to exist. Its victory was based on the fact that it secured the allocation of two standard frequencies on Band One. The result was that the allocation of Band One meant that the WNTV could broadcast from both Ibadan and Lagos.[5] But the price the Federal Government paid for having started late was that, having assigned Band One frequency to the WNTV, it could only utilise one frequency for its own television channel. The economic and political price it paid for dragging its feet in starting television broadcasting in the country was that its transmission would have to be confined to Lagos only.

The American network-owned company of NBC-International was contracted to build the proposed Federal Government television in Lagos. The Federal Government television was christened Nigerian Television Service (NTS). In fact, when NTS went on the air in April 1962, from its location at Victoria Island, Lagos, it was jointly owned by both the Federal Government and NBC-International of America. The Federal Government signed a five-year agreement with the NBC-International which stipulated that at the expiration of the agreement, the foreign company would sell its shares to the Federal Government and it would become the sole property of the Nigerian government. Also, the agreement provided that Nigerian personnel, who would takeover the management from the foreign firm at the termination of the contract, would be trained by the NBC-International before the expiration of the contract on April 1, 1967.[6] Also, the NTS became integrated with the Nigerian Broadcasting Corporation (NBC) when the contractual agreement with NBC-International expired in April, 1967. The call letter of the television station then became NBC-TV.

Meanwhile, the Northern Region Government contracted with the overseas firms of Pye Ltd., and Granada TV Ltd., to build its own television service. It was on the air in 1962. It came to be known as Radio-Television, Kaduna (RTV-Kaduna).

The Failure of a Mission

It seems that television was introduced in Nigeria just for the novelty of the medium and prestige reasons. It hardly fulfilled those missions their proponents had made the general public to expect. This became evident from the nature of programmes the various television stations began to transmit from 1959 to 1975. If television is considered a big asset in transmission of national cultures and ideals, they were just big foreign cultural transmission houses in Nigeria from 1959 to 1975, especially.

When modern television broadcasting system came to Nigeria, they were specifically introduced to provide adequate services in education, social, and economic development. They were also to transmit both the Nigerian and African cultures, tradition, politics, literature, drama, and entertainment.[7] The devotion of Nigeria's televisions to education when they were newly introduced becomes quite apparent when we see that of the six and one-half hours that the WNTV was on the air each day (Monday through Friday), it transmitted educational programmes from 11.00 a.m. to 2.00 p.m. to about one hundred schools equipped with television receivers in the region; while the transmitting hours of the ENTV, Enugu, were just as devoted to educational broadcasting as those of the WNTV.[8]

When the Lagos NBC-TV came into operation in 1962, despite its American-oriented programmes (such as *Beverly Hillbillies, Gun Smoke, Alfred Hitchcock* etc.) it devoted 40% of its thirty-five weekly hours to Nigerian-oriented cultural and educational programmes.[9] In 1975, the NBC-TV was on the air for thirty-seven hours per week. Of these hours, light entertainment netted 33% of the total air time; different cultural groups in the nation, 17%; news and information, 12%; education, 11%; and commercial advertising, 10%.[10]

Until 1974, Nigeria heavily depended on foreign imported television programmes. Only 25% of the programmes were produced within the nation; the rest were shipped from abroad.[11] It also becomes very intriguing to see how, during its infancy, and with limited budget and manpower, television programmes relatively emphasised on culture and education. The stations spent a reasonable amount of time on the air, and about 40% of transmitted air-time programmes, in 1962, were produced in the nation. How does one reconcile this discrepancy with 25% in 1974? Where did the problem come from? Did it develop with the very nature of the system? Despite the slogans of "First in Africa" and "Second to None," television programmes woefully failed to live up to their declared objectives of transmitting programmes that would emphasise on education and national culture. There is hardly a Nigerian who would agree that the national psyche was adequately portrayed by television from the early 1960's to mid 1970's. How does a Nigerian relate to *Mod Squad, Dan August,* and *I Love Lucy*, to mention just a few prime time foreign television programmes that dominated the screens in all our national television networks in the 60's and 70's?

The Federal Government Intervention

Television broadcasting in Nigeria was increasingly becoming a vast wasteland when the Federal Government stepped in, in 1975. Before the Federal Government intervention, the industry had been bedevilled with so many problems. The greatest one was that of frequency allocation, besides lack of producing indigenous programmes. Many stations sprang up even before the Posts and Telegraphs (the department that allocates frequencies) had knowledge of their existence.[12] The reason for taking things for granted was that the state governments owned such stations and there was no way the P & T would deny allocation of frequencies due to the power of the states. Also, many state television stations had such powerful transmitters that enabled stations to be picked in neighbouring states. There was also a problem of bureaucracy among three government bodies: the Ministry of Communications, the division of the P & T which is under the Ministry of Communications, and the Ministry of Information. Each claimed superior jurisdiction on television broadcasting in the country. Eventually they formed a committee that was charged with seeing to the allocation of frequency, the measuring of standards in television broadcasting, their contents, coverage, and advertisement.[13] However, this committee hardly accomplished anything as bureaucratic rancours hampered its effectiveness. The state governments had greater power over television broadcasting in their areas of jurisdiction.

This was the situation when the Federal Government indicated its intention to takeover the management of all the television stations in the nation. The government said its action had been primarily necessitated "to prevent their proliferation at the expense of the tax payers," and as a way of enabling it "to effectively participate in the country's mass media to supplement its giant programmes on mass education."[14] The government press release on its decision to takeover all the stations in the country stated that it would like to see television "highlight the way of life of Nigerians particularly in the rural areas as against the present programmes of the television houses whereby foreign films which have no relevance to our way of life dominate their daily events."[15]

In response to Federal Government's sudden sweeping take-over of the major mass media organs in the country, the *Daily Times*, itself also a victim of this swift take-over, editorialised:

With all the radio and television stations in the country to be under Federal control ... the nation's mass media are now virtually under official control.

We appreciate the need to prevent the proliferation of our radio and television and the need to harness our limited resources of capital and manpower, but wonder if our existing radio and television networks have focused attention on different ethnic cultures in their areas of operation, thus promoting the on-going cultural renaissance in the country. The stations' heavy reliance on foreign films is a situation they cannot help in the first place, and which nobody can change overnight since it takes time to establish a film industry that will produce local films of quality.

It is therefore still to be seen that the Federal take-over will effect significant changes in the audio-visual industry, faster than what we have now. It may be too early to predict but we hope that we will not end up with another untouchable corporation enjoying undue monopoly just as one of our many inefficient corporations.

On a broader base, for the attainment of a healthy and balanced public opinion desirable for any democratic society, it is necessary that there should be other channels of communication apart from the government's.[16]

It is an irony to see how *Bonanza* and other Westerns and comedies, at the expense of the Nigerian culture and education, forced the Nigerian Federal Government to decide to assume direct control of television operations within the entire nation. The origin of the problem of malprogramming and tokenism in indigenous cultural programmes on Nigerian television is related to lack of preparation, and conceptualisation of objectives of television broadcasting when the regional and Federal Governments established them. They existed as national prestigious institutions. They failed to relate their programmes to the needs and problems of a developing society they were established to serve.

Structure and Management of the National Television Industry

Television broadcasting in Nigeria operates under the provisions of the Nigerian Television Authority (NTA). The only deviation came during the Second Republic (1979-1983) when some states, based on the provisions of the 1979 Constitution that made radio and television broadcasting a concurrent subject between the Federal and state governments, established their own stations that were independent of the NTA structure, control and management. Otherwise, the Authority is vested with a wide range of powers to supervise television industry in the country. On April 1, 1977, the Nigerian Federal Military Government formally promulgated a decree establishing a corporation to be known as the Nigerian Television Authority, (NTA). The NTA decree makes the Authority a policy-making body, made up of sixteen members - a chairman, the chairmen of the six zonal Boards, a director-general, a representative of women's organisations, and people with experiences from each of the following areas: the mass media, arts and culture, management, engineering, financial matters, and education. The tenure of office of the members of the Authority does not exceed three years at first instance; but members are eligible for reappointment. This excludes the director-general who is a public officer. The director-general is the chief executive of the Authority, and is responsible for the execution of the policy of the Authority. The decree also empowers the Authority to appoint a secretary to be in charge of keeping records and correspondence for the Authority.

The Functions of the NTA

The NTA was established to restore order out of chaos; to restore a sense of national destiny and propagate common cultural bonds, through television broadcasting, among all the ethnic groups in Nigeria. In order to accomplish these tasks, the decree places all Federal television stations in the country under the Authority's control. The decree specifically requires the Authority "to provide as a public service in the interest of Nigeria, independent and impartial television broadcasting...."[17] And, also, to "ensure that the services which it provides... reflect the unity of Nigeria as a Federation and at the same time give adequate expression to the culture, characteristics and affairs of each state, zone or other parts of the Federation."[19] The additional functions of the Authority, among others, include:

(a)   "to plan and coordinate the activities of the entire television network;
(b)   to ensure the establishment and maintenance of standards and promote the efficient operation of the entire system in accordance with national policy;
(c)   to establish and operate a formula for sharing funds among stations;
(d)   to act as liaison between the Federal Government and the Zonal operations;
(e)   to establish such number of production centres as it may consider necessary from time to time;
(f)   to specify the types of programmes which should be transmitted by the whole network and the quantity, type and contents of foreign materials;
(g)   to provide other persons with, and receive from them, matters to be broadcast;

(h)   to organise, provide, and subsidise, for the purpose of broadcasting educational activities and public entertainment;

(i)   to collect, in any part of the world... both news and information and to subscribe to news agencies...."[19]

The decree requires the Authority to see that programme contents are not "likely to offend against good taste or decency or likely to encourage or incite to crime or to disorder or to be offensive to public feeling, or to contain any offensive representation of, or reference to, a living person."[20] The decree further stipulates that:

(a)   Programmes maintain a proper balance in their content and be of a high standard;

(b)   news be presented with accuracy, impartiality and objectivity;

(c)   when matters of political, current public policy and industrial controversy arise, due impartiality be maintained;

(d)   programmes may not be designed to serve the interest of any political party;

(e)   equal time be granted to divergent views of political parties when they seek to explain their views and policies before the general public;

(f)   time allotment be given to ministerial speeches which seek to explain government actions and policy;

(g)   the Authority shall broadcast government announcements whenever such a request is made.[21]

One interesting area the decree delves into is in the field of television advertising. In the super industrialised Western world, especially in the United States, television advertising has become a controversial issue. The NTA decree empowers the Authority to accept commercial advertisements and allow its programmes to be sponsored. However, it imposes an important injunction:

(a)   "A special programme shall not be interrupted by an advertisement or sponsored announcement, but advertisements or sponsored announcements may immediately precede, or immediately follow, a special programme.

(b)   "Where a programme is specially broadcast for schools, the Commissioner may designate the types or classes of advertisements or sponsored announcements that may immediately precede or immediately follow that programme."[22]

The NTA Zonal Boards

The NTA decree divides Nigeria into six television zones. In each zone, the decree establishing the Authority provides for a Nigerian Television Zonal Board. These zones are established, according to the decree, for the purposes of variety and better reception of television programmes. Each zonal board is made up of a minimum of six members, or a maximum of eight members from divergent professions. Their term of office is also three years, and they are eligible for reappointment at the expiration of the three-year term. The decree also created a zonal chairman and a zonal managing director; they are all answerable to the NTA headquarters in Lagos.

The Functions of the Zonal Boards

The following are the specified functions of each zonal board. Each zonal board is therefore responsible for:

(a)   "The operation of its main station and production centres;

(b)   The control of the general policy of the zonal programmes in such a manner as to ensure that all zonal programmes are selected with due regard to the distinctive culture, interests and tastes of the people of the zone on the one hand and the fulfillment of national needs on the other, and conform to any standards laid down by the Authority;

(c)   The appointment of an advisory committee to advise the Board on any matter concerning television broadcasting in its Zone and any other business of the Board referred to it for advice;

(d)   The supervision and control of the acts of all employees of the Authority in its Zone in matters of executive administration in the whole field of television broadcasting and matters concerning the accounts and records of the Zone;

(e)   The disposition of all questions relating to the services of the employees of the Authority in its Zone and their pay, privileges and allowances subject to the approval of the Authority;

(f)   The performance of such other functions as the Authority may from time to time delegate to it,"[23]

This decree also established a news department for the Authority and gives it all the duties of any news organisation. It created the post of a news director and puts him/her in-charge of the news department. He/She is also answerable to the director-general.

The NTA Zones

Besides its national headquarters at Victoria Island, Lagos, where the National Television Production Centre (NTPC) and NTA Two channel 5 are also located, the following are the zones that make up the zonal structure of the NTA, together with the stations in each zone:

Zone A: Ibadan, Ikeja and Abeokuta
Zone B: Benin, Aba, Akure and Port Harcourt
Zone C: Enugu, Markurdi and Calabar

Zone D: Kaduna, Kano and Jos
Zone E: Maiduguri, Yola and Bauchi
Zone F: Sokoto, Minna and Ilorin

The stations are grouped in their respective zones on the basis of similarities in linguistics and cultural affinity, and the factor of geographical contiguity; though the later does not quite apply in all the zones, as currently grouped. However, as we had observed in the previous chapter on radio broadcasting, the Babangida administration is about to alter the zonal structure of the NTA; if he has not already altered it. It could mean the elimination of the zones or some minor changes in NTA's administration. But chances are that when another new administration sets in, it could set aside whatever alterations the Babangida administration might have made; thus reverting it to its original structure; or it could totally abolish it; depending on administrative convenience and political expediency.

With the establishment of these zones, it is being expected that television will begin to play those basic roles for which they were established to perform. What is now most expected from the Nigerian Television Authority (NTA) is the encouragement of local talents and creativity in the production of national programmes as against importation of foreign ones. Local production of programmes must be encouraged; however, not just the production of *anything* that is local, but high quality local programmes, produced by professionals, that could compete with any local programmes that are produced anywhere in the world. At present, many of the local programmes are not only negative commentaries on our cultures but also too imitative of some foreign programmes and amateurish to get into the screens of any national television system that aims at informing, entertainment, public enlightenment, correlating and cultural transmission.

Administration of the Television Industry during the Second Republic

Soon after the NTA decree came into existence in 1977, a critic hastely observed that "the creation of a Nigerian Television Authority heralds the dawn of professional television broadcasting in the country provided it is allowed to function with all the impartiality a news and entertainment medium organisation requires in order to perform effectively. If it becomes free of any government interference, it will cure all the maladies and inadequacies that had in the past derailed effective orientation of Nigerian televisions to local cultures. It is also inconceivable to see how television had existed since 1959, and no authority was formed to be responsible for formulating policy in broadcasting organisation in a developing society."[24] The truth today is that the NTA decree that centralised broadcasting in the country has not brought about the desired changes the public was made to expect. While some state governments went about establishing their own television systems during the Second Republic, the NTA only existed to serve the interests and needs of the ruling party at the Federal level of government and in those states of the federation where the party that controlled the central government was also in power. The other states that were administered by the other political parties that were in opposition, were either blacked out or given unfavourable coverage by the NTA. Those who challenged this unorthodox form of democracy were rebuffed and told that bicameral system of government that the country was practising during the Second Republic meant "winner takes all".

The deposed president, Shehu Shagari, to ensure absolute control of the NTA and for it to be effectively utilised by his party for political spoils against the other political parties that were in opposition, redeployed the director-general of the NTA who had been in broadcasting industry since its inception in the country, to the Ministry of Communications to be an adviser on frequency allocation. He then appointed a political stalwart in his party (NPN), a former lecturer in the History Department at the University of Lagos, as the new director-general of the NTA. The President appointed his fellow political party man as the chief executive of the NTA to make sure that the other political parties were not given fair deal in the election campaigns and coverage. He wanted the NTA to portray only himself, NPN party members, supporters, their programmes and accomplishments. This was in utter violation of the entire provisions of the NTA decree. When the military deposed the Shagari administration, the former director-general was recalled from his "French leave" of frequency allocation in the Ministry of Communications to come and assume his former assignment as the director-general of the NTA. In a contemptuous manner characteristic of the Nigerian military, neither did it formally communicate to the Shagari political appointee that he had been relieved of his duties as the NTA director-general nor redeployed to any other government parastatal or ministry. The former president's political jogglings in the administration of the NTA demonstrate the extent to which the television system in Nigeria was politically abused, especially during the Second Republic. Its consequence was that a hitherto national media outlet that owed no allegiance to any political party, at least as the enabling decree that established it makes us believe, became politicised. This inevitably led to loss of public confidence and trust in the NTA and the eventual demise of the Authority's credibility. Its election theme of "VERDICT '83" for nationwide coverage of the futile 1983 general elections was instantly nicknamed then by the erudite Nigerian public as "VOID'83". Perhaps, the following newspaper account of how an anchorman at the Nigerian Television Authority (NTA), Enugu, instead of reading the news the way it had been written for him, with what he alleged to be "false information", wildly protested before his viewers, demonstrates the gravity of the situation during the Second Republic:

An NTA newscaster caused a major "air wave shock" on Thursday evening when he announced his resignation shortly after he had been cued on screen to read the 7.00 p.m. news bulletin.

Mr. Chuma Edozie, who had been primed to read the bulletin, scanned the scripts and discovered that one of the stories contained "false information".

He immediately threw down the bulletin and let loose in full glare of viewers: "I am fed up with this false information. I hereby tender my resignation. I can't continue with this stuff; no, no, no, I am fed up," he screamed, and walked out on camera in apparent disgust.

Completely taken unawares by Mr. Edozie's reaction to the bulletin, the studio hands were all said to have been thrown into a state of confusion.

As a result, viewers had to stare at blank television screens as the station went off the air for about 10 minutes.

A senior broadcaster, Mr. Chike Ubaka, was hurriedly called in to read the news bulletin abandoned by Mr. Edozie.[25]

The Seeming implication of this episode is that news lost its values and credibility as it became an instrument of insult and falsehood to be used against one's political opponents. That was the sad story of television broadcasting in the country during the Second Republic.

Until 1979, television broadcasting in the country was the exclusive monopoly of the Federal Government, after the military administration had, in 1975, taken over the management and control of all the television stations from their former owners (the state governments). This warranted the enactment into law for the establishment of a body, the Nigerian Television Authority, to be the sole administrator of the industry in the country. It is also important to note that Nigeria's 1979 Constitution stipulated that wireless broadcasting (radio and television) shall be owned and controlled by only the Federal and state governments. Private organisations and individuals are forbidden to own, manage or control any television or radio station.[26] On the basis of such a constitutional provision, during the Second Republic, some states of the federation that could financially and materially (in terms of personnel), afford it (especially Imo, Anambra, Oyo, Ogun, Lagos, Bendel, Ondo, Plateau, Maiduguri and Kano) established their own television broadcasting systems that came to challenge the Federal Government monopoly and manipulation of the industry. This led to the proliferation of 32 television transmitting stations in a country that does not even assemble television sets, not to talk of manufacturing them. At least a television station exists in each state capital. The confusion and contradictions in the administration of television broadcasting in the country is the fault of the Murtala/Obasanjo military administration of 1975-1979 that promulgated the NTA decree which made the Federal Government the sole administrator of television broadcasting at the exclusion of the state governments. It was also the same military administration that supervised the drafting and adoption of the 1979 Federal Constitution that made television and radio broadcasting concurrent subjects between the Federal and state governments, oblivious of the fact that it had, by the NTA decree of 1977, centralised television broadcasting in the country. The setting up of a committee in 1984 by the Buhari regime's second in-command, Tunde Idiagbon, to rationalise television broadcasting in the country and make recommendations to the Federal Government, was as a result of the number of television stations in the country and the millions of dollars that were being spent in the payment of staff salaries and emoluments at the various stations, most of whom were unproductive. The committee subsequently recommended the dismissal of a good number of the stations' staff and the retention of the NTA state stations. What is not known is whether those stations the state governments established on their own during the Second Republic will be allowed to stay or not. But as at now, they are still operating. The implication of the politics of the electronic media industry (radio and television) in the country is that decrees, acts of either Parliament or National Assembly exist only for the administrative conveniences of the respective regimes.

Television Programmes and Management

By 1979, all the television stations in the country had begun colour trans-mission. The first colour television transmission in the country was started by the NTA-Jos, Plateau State. The NTA-Lagos is on the air for 61 hours a week. Its programmes of broadcast include news and current affairs, religious items, educational drama, sports, etc., etc.,. There also used to be a-thirty-minute national network news at 9.00 p.m. until during the second quarter of 1986 when it was hiked to 45 minutes. The network news always originates from the Lagos national studios of the NTA. During this period, all the NTA stations in the country, together with those owned by the state governments, switch over to Lagos for the network news. Formerly, throughout the entire news slot, and in compliance with the decree that established it, paid adver-tisements were not aired; advertisements could only precede or follow news slots and other network programmes. But in recent times, without any amendment to the decree establishing it, the NTA has been interrupting its news and other network programmes to advertise commercial products or to air paid announcements. The forty-five minute news slot has been divided into four parts so that advertisements could come in-between at the end of each of the four segments of the news. The point being made here is that government institutions should respect the laws under which they are set up. The NTA has every right to advertise, and as a matter of fact, should be al-lowed to get into competitive and aggressive advertisement in order to rely less on tax Payers money for its subvention, but as at now it must operate within the limits of the law that established it, until the necessary amend-ments are effected into law. Because of people's penchant and flair for publicity, the NTA introduced a package that surcharges $5,000.00 for personality and business news items. This charge is for those news items that seek to promote personal egos and business products.

Besides the NTA news programmes that get network coverage, there are certain other programmes that are simultaneously transmitted nationwide by all the NTA stations in the country. These programmes could originate from any NTA station in the country, if approved by the zonal committee responsible for national programme selection. Programmes of this nature are also referred to as network programmes.

The 1975-1980 third national development plan appropriated about $203.6 million for the development of television projects in the country. It was during that plan period that the white and black monochrome service in Lagos was converted into a nationwide colour television system. All television stations in the country transmit in colour. All the NTA stations in the country are linked by a domestic rebroadcast satellite system. This involves the installation of both earth and television stations. Originally, the aerostat transmitter system, involving airborne of transmitters, that was to have been installed in 1978, which was thought would have made it possible for a receiver to pick up each programme from each television zone on six channels, three on VHF and the other three on UHF, became a white elephant. It failed. The aerostat project became cumbersome and soon obsolete before its take-off. The NTA spent millions of dollars preparing grounds for its installation and eventual take-off. It became a wasted and costly venture, and was subsequently abandoned as the power brokers at the NTA reluctantly agreed at last to let it go when they became convinced that the aerostat technology had already been abandoned in the industrialised Western country that was handling its contract in Nigeria because of its numerous faults. Moreover, latest technological advancements had already rendered it obsolete.

The Buhari regime was so angered by the millions of dollars that had been invested into the aerostat project which yielded nothing that it instituted an investigative panel of inquiry to ascertain why so much was invested when it was obvious that aerostat had become obsolete and unsuitable for Nigeria's terrain. Unlike India and some other fastly developing Third World nations where broadcasting and communication through satellite have become highly successful and effective, it is yet to make any significant impact in Nigeria. For the first time the NTA had to broadcast its network news and other programmes from the new Federal Capital Territory, Abuja, in June 1986, during the summit conference of the heads of state of the Economic Community of West African States (ECOWAS), the reception to Lagos and other parts of the country was of the poorest quality. It then dawned on Federal authorities who hardly travel outside Lagos that the Abuja experience via satellite was the experience NTA network news and other network programmes subject the rest of the country to. It is most likely that in the foreseable future, policy-makers will realise that the time has come to invest in reliable and effective communication satellite systems for the entire country.

FOOTNOTES

1. A reference to the Western Region House Debates between May 1958 through May 1959 will give additional information on this. Also, Wilbur Schramm notes this point in his book *The New Educational Media.*
2. *Ibid.*
3. Ian Mackay makes reference to these strained relations in his book which has been extensively foot-noted here.
4. See *Radio-TV Times,* April, 1977, p. viiii.
5. *Ibid.*, April and May issues, 1977.
6. *Ibid.*
7. UNESCO, *Television Traffic - a one-way street?* Reports and Papers on Mass Communication. No. 70, Paris: UNESCO 1974, p. 12.
8. UNESCO, *World Communication: Press, Radio, Television, Film.* Paris: UNESCO, 1964.
9. Roger Bower, "In Nigeria talent is easiest problem" *Broadcasting.* May 25, 1964, p. 107.
10. UNESCO, *Television Traffic - a one-way street?*
11. *Ibid.*
12. Interview with Mr. George Bako, then deputy director-general, NBC technical services, on May 19, 1977, at Lagos. He eventually retired as the Director-General of the FRCN.
13. *Ibid.*
14. *Daily times.* November 10, 1975.
15. *Ibid.*
16. *Ibid.*, November 13, 1975.
17. Decree No. 24 - Nigerian Television Authority Decree 1977 p. A 124.
18. *Ibid.*
19. *Ibid.*, A 125.
20. *Ibid.*, A 126.
21. *Ibid.*
22. *Ibid.*, A 127.
23. *Ibid.*, A 128.
24. Luke Uka Uche, "Mass Media Systems in Nigeria; A Study in Structure, Management and Functional Roles in Crisis Situations". Unpublished Ph. D. Thesis. The Ohio State University, Columbus. 1977.
25. "Network movie turn real live drama on Enugu NTA". *Sunday Concord.* July 31, 1983, p. 12.
26. 1979 Constitution of Federal Republic of Nigeria. Section 36.

FIVE

BROADCASTING, CULTURAL IDENTITY AND DEPENDENCY

Nigeria, like most Third World nations, hired Western communication experts to establish and assign roles to the mass media institutions to accelerate the rate of national development. The result was the patterning of her media institutions, especially radio and television, similar in structure, management and contents to those of the industrialised Western societies. This pattern of development also contributed to what critics refer to as *media imperialism*; another critical school of thought prefers to call it cultural *synchronisation*. In this chapter, the term media *imperialism* refers to the overwhelming universal influence the mass media products of the industrialised countries exert over the media programme preference of media administrators in Nigeria and other Third World countries, that have contributed to the imbalance in international flow of media products and contents, whereby local cultural autonomy and awareness are threatened and relegated by external cultural values. The consequence is that there is a risk of an assumed cultural imposition on the people of Nigeria and their counterparts in the Third World from the media source countries. The media contents of the industrialised nations are in most part cultural transmission. Their contents constitute cultural frame of reference to most viewers in Nigeria and other Third World countries. On the other hand, the term cultural *synchronisation* refers to exogenous influence on receiving cultural systems which may be imposed or may be actively invited.[1] According to Cees Hamelink, the originator of the term, it also "implies that a particular type of cultural development in the metropolitan country is persuasively communicated to the receiving countries," with the result that the whole process of local social inventiveness and cultural creativity is thrown into confusion or is destroyed."[2]

As this chapter is a critical evaluation of the local vis-a-vis foreign cultural content in electronic media broadcasts in Nigeria, and the degree to which foreign programmes compete with the locally produced ones, at the expense of the promotion of national culture through broadcasting, the subsequent pages that follow will therefore demonstrate that *media imperialism* or *cultural synchronisation* (whichever school of thought you prefer) is attributable to the following:

1. adoption of the Western professional media tradition in the development of print and electronic media in Nigeria and other areas in the Third World;
2. the media of the formerly colonised territories depended on those of the metropolitan Europe and the U.S.A. for programmes, standards and formats;
3. unpatriotic acts that sabotage national economic and developmental goals that manifest in the award of international media contracts and kick-backs in foreign exchange transfer of funds when placing orders for foreign media programmes and hardwares by the local media administrators;
4. exploitation of the Third World media markets to ensure maximum profit by selling action-packed sensational movies that impede the development of cultures and artistic creativities in local media programmes.

Nigeria's electronic media and cultural dependency

The construction and early management of broadcasting systems in Nigeria came under the auspices of some foreign companies. These foreign companies jointly owned the media with the Federal (central) and regional governments. Their ownership was only phased out as the nation assumed a more militant role. However, the consequence of foreign ownership and construction of the broadcasting systems was that these foreign owners defined the concept of broadcasting and media management in Nigeria. This was primarily based upon the operative norms in their home countries, which became their cultural referents in their programme preferences and priorities. A former British Broadcasting Corporation (BBC) employee, who later was sent to Nigeria by the BBC to become the director-general of the former Nigerian Broadcasting Service, which was later changed to the Nigerian Broadcasting Corporation, and in 1978 it was also renamed the Federal Radio Corporation of Nigeria (FRCN), patterned Radio Nigeria's programmes and technical facilities in the image of the BBC. He defends the logic of his grafting of the BBC model as follows:

> ...we have unashamedly taken the best features of British broadcasting and adapted them to suit the very different conditions in a tropical and largely underdeveloped country of immense extent.[3]

Lately, scholars and critics in the field of mass communication have realised that the mass media systems of the developing countries have, in some instances, defeated the very reason for which they were established in some developing countries: those of economic, social, and political developments; and as instruments of marshalling support for modernisation of the society. The reason for the failure can be attributed to the structure and centres of the international communications, and their influence in world communications market. A leading UNESCO study of the 1970's showed that Nigeria imported about two-thirds of her national television programmes from abroad; and her overseas suppliers were mostly the United States, United Kingdom, and East Germany.[4] As at today, the situation has not really significantly changed.

Some critics of media dependence suggest that the reason for the disparity between domestic production and foreign importation of programmes is due to lack of adequate funds within the developing nations; other critics attribute this phenomenon of high reliance on imported programmes as resulting from lack of technical equipment, trained personnel, programme material, and the cheapness of the imported programmes that the home governments have even gone to the extent of introducing legislations to be able to write off the costs for the companies as long as the companies' programmes for overseas markets promote the best cultural ideals of their societies.

The following account by Thomas Guback gives further clarification:

In 1948, the (USA) federal government established the informational Media Guaranty Programme to encourage export of printed matter and Theatrical films to soft currency areas from which companies had difficulty repatriating their revenues. The government agreed to buy with dollars certain foreign currencies earned by U.S. media companies, provided the materials exported reflected the best elements of American life.[5]

Guback goes further to reveal to us that:

American export of media materials... as well as the resulting cultural dominance and dependency relations that frequently exist, must be construed as an economic and political manifestation of a monopolistic, market-dominated media system. Because the United States is a powerful country, it exerts influence...over the cultural life of other nations. U.S. motion pictures account for only 6 or 7 percent of all feature films made annually in the world, but they occupy about half of world screen time and probably represent close to half of world box office receipts. U.S. television programs are shown in just about every country, and our news agencies dominate global news flow. Of the world's three largest music and phonograph record operations, two are American, and they probably control almost a fifth of the world market for recorded music.[6]

Besides the preceding factors that have promoted media dependency in the developing countries of the world, one of the reasons for this high dependence on foreign media programmes is primarily due to the origin of the media structure in Nigeria and other developing nations. A case in point was when two British-based firms, Granada Group Limited and EMI Limited, jointly established radio and television broadcasting systems in the former Northern Region of Nigeria, and their former British-born managing director gave an account of how members of the firms would fly back to London and would come back to Northern Nigeria with "considerable amount of different types of television film. Daily film shows were then shown to a representative cross section of the community. Questionnaires were filled in after each programme and a discussion was held on what had been seen. In this way the team got a fair idea of the type of programmes that would be popular."[7] In other words, the foreign firms exploited the audience excitement of the novelty of the new (television) medium for determining the popularity of foreign television films without attempting to promote those Nigerian cultural ideals for which radio and television were then being introduced to propagate.

Besides all these preceding factors, the greatest mundane factor that has made television entertainment programmes pawns of the Western media markets and/or establishments for continual dependence is the total lack of patriotism and nationalism, leading to fraudulent practices in foreign (currency) exchange transfers, that consequently result from the notorious 10% or more kickbacks when local television administrators place orders from their foreign suppliers. The amount of money for the order is usually inflated and shared in foreign currency. The following Nigerian experiences are evident. Following the December 31, 1983, coup d'état that ousted a civilian administration during Nigeria's Second Republic, the Nigerian Television Authority (NTA) began to notoriously make national newspaper headlines regarding illegal transfer of hard foreign currency for either television hardwares or programmes that were never supplied. During the 1983 general elections in the country, highly sophisticated made in God's own country (the U.S.A.) television equipment worth several millions of dollars were brought into the country. But, alas, they were never made use of, especially the jeep-mobile vans for live coverage of the elections.

At the time of writing this chapter, the Nigerian Television Authority (NTA) had taken a United Kingdom public relations firm in London to court just to recover the authority's money paid through the London-based public relations firm to help it procure the series, *Dallas*, a United States television film. The British public relations firm received the money but did not deliver the series. Today in Nigeria, it is generally believed that an interested Nigerian party could have suggested to the firm the sharing of the money, assuring the British public relations firm to discard the order on the *Dallas* series as nothing would happen to it (that is the firm). When this fraud was blown open, a newspaper headline, relating to the *Dallas* episode, proclaimed: "Adebanjo to help sort out N.8 million fraud at NTA." Part of the news story reads:

> Former Presidential Adviser on Information, Chief Olu Adebanjo, is to help the police over an alleged N.8 million (about U.S. $1,064,000.00) fraud at the Nigerian Television Authority (NTA). Informed police sources told the *National Concord* the NTA had sought the transfer of N.8 million in U.S. dollars to a United Kingdom company, Dynapulse, for a supply of serial films, *Dallas*, to the authority. But the money was alleged to have found its way into the purse of some NTA officials, while no film was supplied. This is the second case of alleged fraud that has been uncovered at the NTA within one week. Police sources had, last week, disclosed a deal involving an illegal transfer of N696,000.00 (about U.S. $850,000.00) into a London account of a Kano businessman.[8]

This is indicative of the many reasons why dependency on foreign films for our media programming, with the attendant cultural identity crisis of projecting a Nigerian personality and pride through the broadcast media, particularly the television, thrives.

From all indications, it seems that the quantity of foreign technical and non-technical aids that came to Nigeria had a latent dysfunctional effect of promoting the continual reliance on programmes that were produced from abroad, irrespective of their social and cultural relevance to the Nigerian audience in advancing the national psyche. The dependence on foreign media extended to the transferring of foreign media staff, and provision of equipment. It also seems that some of the donor countries and companies were locked up in a stiff "let us out-do our co-competitors" sort of rivalry. This further promoted the perpetuation of media dependence and parasitic relationship on the part of those responsible for developing mass media in the nation. At times one questions if there were enough genuine motives on the part of the donor countries and companies behind their aid-in programmes to Nigeria and other developing nations, in view of what Kushner says about the nature and motives of the USAID aid-in programmes to foreign nations, mostly located in Asia, Africa and Latin America:

> ...The USIAD tries to influence public attitudes in other nations in support of American foreign policy objectives. One of its methods is to make itself as useful as possible to the media in a host country. To the extent wanted by the host country, USAID provides it with goods and services, ranging from encyclopaedias to special VOA short-wave feeds in African languages.[9]

The activities of the USAID demonstrate how dependency is paternalistically perpetuated and how harmful and disadvantageous it could be to the developing nations in Africa and elsewhere in the Third World in their efforts to be as indigenous as possible in the media to meet the specific needs of their respective societies.

It was the United States' National Broadcasting Company-International (NBC-International) that was awarded the contract for the establishment of the Federal Nigerian Government television. This association, through contract, also resulted in high dependence on American-produced television programmes. This is discernable from the following admission of the NBC-International's former managing director to the Nigerian television service:

> We have the pick of top-rated films here and...every once in a while we get some adverse comments on our "many cowboy and Indian films" (*Rawhide, Gun Smoke, Rin-Tim-Tin*) and "murder and mayhen", *The Defenders, Alfred Hitchcock, Perry Mason, Naked City,* and *Beverly Hillbillies,* etc.[10]

However, foreign organisations cannot be solely blamed for this problem of dependence on foreign-produced television programmes, and the negligence of developing broadcasting programmes to the needs and cultural relevance of the country. In 1975, the Federal Military Government established a committee and charged it with the reorganisation of radio and television broadcasting systems in the country. The members of the committee quickly went to the United States Embassy in Lagos to request some data on how radio and television operate in the United States. The United States Embassy officials then dispatched the following telegram to the State Department:

> Nigerian Government has appointed a committee to recommend future organization and management of radio and television in Nigeria. Committee has asked USIS for material that might be useful as general background information. Following is suggested: (1) An FCC report of examination of radio and television broadcasting industries including recommendations for changes; (2) the legal instrument that established the FCC; (3) a copy of the broadcasting code that set forth advertising standards, morality and ethical standards; (4) a report on problems involved in establishing educational radio and television in a developing country...[11]

The mistake the members of the committee and the United States mission in Nigeria made in requesting this kind of assistance from Washington, D.C., was that of not coming to realities with the unique needs and problems of the Nigerian society. In the first instance, the Federal Communications Commission (FCC) of the United States was specifically established to bring order out of chaos and confusion that seemed imminent in the competition for the airwaves that are very scarce in face of thousands of privately-owned broadcasting radio and television stations in the United States. This led to the need for the creation of a regulatory agency for spectrum allocation. But, ironically in Nigeria, it is the government that controls the broadcasting media through the appointment of members of the board of governors, the director-general and other top executives of the radio and television systems. The monopoly ownership of the broadcasting media in Nigeria by the national government and its state (regional) counterparts is so extensive and total that the laissez-faire philosophy that operates in the American broadcasting industry is just the antithesis of what obtains in the Nigerian broadcasting organisation. Also, the FFC functions to see that radio and television stations in the United States, which are privately-owned, operate in such a manner as to meet public *interest, necessity,* and *needs* in the communities they serve. This is prompted by the fact that everybody does not have access to means of broadcasting.

The FCC, in order to make sure that the stations carry out their public commitments and obligations, licences all the radio and television stations in the United States. These licences are renewed every three years.[12] This gives members of the public the opportunity to challenge those practices of the stations they consider inimical to the public interest, necessity, and needs. There have been some instances where stations have had their licenses revoked, and stations sold to people whom the Commission considered better prepared and dedicated to meet the needs of the community they serve. In some occasions the Commission has had to renew licenses for only one year to give the affected stations, whose offences are not so intentional, chances to brush up.

The needs and cultures of a developing country that Nigeria is, are in no way compatible with those of the United States. If, as might have been expected, the then committee for radio and television industry in Nigeria had patterned its re-organisation programmes and structures after the FCC and the United States model of broadcasting, the probable consequence would have been a continued reliance on foreign-produced radio and television products that hardly relate to Nigeria's cultural values and media's utilisation in national development and for asserting and developing a high level of awareness of our cultural identity. It would have also negated the principle of the new world information and communication order that challenges the domination of international news and media products by the industrialised Western societies, consequently leading to imbalance in the media between the North and South. This committee that would have given Nigeria a photostat copy of broadcasting model of the United States was dissolved in 1975 when a new military government ousted the military regime that set it up.

**Cultural implication of the celebration of twenty-five years
of television broadcasting in Nigeria**

On October 28, 1984, the Nigerian Television Authority (NTA) began to celebrate a silver jubilee of television broadcasting in Nigeria. During the week-long celebration that ended on November 3rd, 1984, all the television stations in the country were directed to hook up with the NTA headquarters and simultaneously air the same network programmes for the national audience. The organising committee for the 25th birthday anniversary of television in Nigeria also forbade the airing of foreign television programmes in any of the television stations in the country throughout the period of the week-long anniversary of the silver jubilee of television in Nigeria. But just a few minutes after the chairman of the committee, appointed to see to the organisation of the silver jubilee, had announced the banning of foreign (non-Nigerian produced) television programmes during the anniversary week, the NTA began to advertise, over the same channel, for the supply of foreign television programmes by those who had them. Prospective suppliers were directed to contact the director-general of the NTA, at the Authority's headquarters in Victoria Island, Lagos, for the necessary guidelines on the foreign entertainment programmes to be supplied and the previewing of them, if they were already available in the country.

The advertisement for the supply of foreign entertainment programmes raised eyebrows among the vocal Nigerian elite class who questioned the probity, wisdom and propitiousness of the decision of the NTA management, particularly on the following grounds:

1. Nigeria had gone austere and bankrupt in her economy, and her external reserves had dwindled to such a poor level that citizens were allowed to travel out of the country with a paltry basic allowance of only US $70.00. The granting of import licenses and approval of letters of credit to businesses were virtually restricted to importation of essential commodities and raw materials to priority industries. The rationale of the NTA's decision to advertise for the supply of foreign entertainment programmes for television, a venture that would involve foreign (currency) exchange which would eventually reduce whatever was left in the country's external reserve, was critically questioned and challenged. When did foreign television programmes become priority raw materials for the essential manufacturing industries that were endlessly retrenching their workers? Also, when did foreign television programmes become classified as essential commodities (such as washing detergents, toilet soaps, sugar, milk, salt, vegetable oil, rice, beans, tooth pastes, etc., etc.,) that Nigerians swallowed their pride to queue for hours to get their rations?

2. In view of the shady deal surrounding the ordering of the *DALLAS* television series involving a British public relations firm, it was suspected that the NTA was up to something suspicious. The Authority's critics believed that some influential persons within the organisation could have made private arrangements with some overseas

television markets, and might have had the foreign programmes in their possessions prior to the military takeover of government on December 31, 1983. The Authority, being such a powerful and easily manipulated political entity, it was probably thought that the military authorities could have easily given in to NTA's request for the granting of import licenses to the Authority's prospective suppliers of foreign television programmes. This was to encourage it (NTA) to get any type of programme it needed, irrespective of where it was coming from, if it could just enable it (NTA) to retain the much needed followership and loyalty of its national audience through the attraction of foreign television programmes, to support the military administration and its iron-fisted programmes for the country. While the foreign programmes to be supplied to the NTA were already suspected to have been smuggled into the country, the selected "prospective suppliers" would then use the gimmick of the advertisement as a means of transferring the badly needed foreign currency for other private businesses abroad.

3. The advertisement for the supply of foreign programmes to be aired following the week of the silver jubilee anniversary invalidated the rationale for the ban on the airing of foreign television programmes in any of the nations's television stations. It also made the one-week ban on foreign programmes sound ludicrous, hypocritical, and look like window-dressing. What difference would it make if we did not see foreign television programmes for a week when we would still see *Charlie's Angels, The Return of the Saint, General Hospital, Different Strokes, Sanford and Son, The Jeffersons, The Best of Texas Wrestling, The Streets of San Francisco, Love Boat, Starsky and Husk, The Incredible Hawk*, etc., etc., for the other fifty-one weeks of the year?

The following is part of a newspaper report on the reaction of the former director-general of the Nigerian Television Authority (NTA) to public criticism of his establishment's *addiction* to the airing of foreign television programmes:

The director-general of the Nigerian Television Authority...has said that he has no apologies whatsoever to make on the purchase of foreign films.

He told the *Sunday Concord* that Nigerian television has the lowest percentage of foreign programme content in the world. He referred to a French research publication, UTNA, which listed Nigeria as having 30.68% of foreign programme content.

He said the NTA decided this year to go beyond its traditional programme suppliers in the United States to other areas of the world. "We want the widest varieties of programmes from the widest possible places," he said, emphasising that the recent advertisement NTA put out on the supply of foreign films did not mean that the Authority was planning to increase its foreign programme content.[13]

Besides educational radio and television broadcastings that come on the air during specific hours of the day when schools are in session, commercial television broadcasting in Nigeria is on the air from 4.00. p.m. to 12.00 a.m. (Monday through Friday), and from 8.00 a.m. to 7.00 a.m. (Saturday and Sunday) when both LTV-8, Lagos, and NTA-2, Channel 5 Lagos, introduced their marathon telecast. While the latter channel has abandoned its marathon week-end telecast because it was ill-conceived and politically motivated to challenge the political grassroot base of the Lagos State Government, with its capital at Ikeja, the former channel still continued with its 24-hour week-end round the clock marathon broadcasting until its studios and valuable equipment were burnt in a fire oubreak, origin of which was suspected to be arson by some members of its staff who were suspected to have embezzled the station's and corporation's funds.

But the real issue, with regard to the defence of the NTA's former director-general, is not the figure of 30.68%, a figure that does not really mean anything. It is meaningless because the second channel of the Authority in Lagos, NTA Two-Channel five, transmits more than 80% of its hours on the air on foreign films, to the most influential media audience, concentrated in Nigeria's most industrialised business, capital, educational and administrative hub-nob of the nation - Lagos; a city that is highly sophisticated and every Nigerian runs there in search of a job and better tomorrow. The NTA's second channel has become the most popularly viewed television channel in Lagos for children, teenagers and adults. Also, assuming that the 30.68% is anything to go by, the bone of contention is that the foreign programmes are shown at prime time. They depict grotesque violence and lovemaking scenes without warnings to the audience as to the types of programmes that it (audience) is about to watch. During the anniversary week of twenty-five years to television broadcasting in Nigeria, a member of the television audience in the country said that he had "completely lost faith in Nigerian television because of the preponderance of violence-oriented foreign programmes. Television in this country is one aspect that has continued to tie us to foreign values. The irrelevance of violence-dominated foreign programmes will have untold effects on children who constitute a high percentage of television viewers."[14] Another television critic accused the industry of only satisfying the desires of the Nigerian elites for foreign programmes, observing that "for such people the heavy slant in foreign programming is not only acceptable, but might also not be sufficient. Even local programmes like *Mirror in the Sun* and musicals like *Tea-Mac Show* are only local in form, but in terms of contents, ideology and values, innuendos are Western and foreign."[15]

It is not a fact, as the former NTA director-general would make us believe, that the NTA has the lowest foreign programme content in the world. Television stations in the United States only occasionally show non-U.S. produced television entertainment programmes. A few exceptions are only when major world events that affect America and the needs of her nationals occur; such as the Olympic Games, World (soccer) Cup, Miss Universe, etc. It is only then that one of the major three networks signs the contract for their airing. And yet studies have shown that 70% of feature films consumed world-wide originate from the United States media industries; whereas these United States-based media industries only produce between six to seven percent of total feature films produced in the entire world.[16] Recent researches have also revealed that of the five giant record industries that control the music industry in the world (CBS, WEA, RCA, Polygram, and EMI), the first three are owned by the United States corporations.[17]

It is appropriate to suggest, at this juncture, that foreign television programmes will continue to feature prominently for a long time to come until those Nigerians who are currently charged with the nation's broadcasting policy, who were brought up under the colonial tutelage, are excorcised of their colonial and neo-colonial mentality and personality complex. Such people would rather die of hunger than eat a major Nigerian dish of *eba* and *egusi* soup with their hands, instead of fork on the left hand and table knife on the right hand; the eating style the British taught them when we were colonised. It is not until a generation of culturally-minded radio and television managers emerges, shall we have a stupendous preference for such popular culturally acclaimed Nigerian television comedies as the *Masquerade, Jagua, Ojo Ladipo,* over such imported television programmes as *Doctor in the House, Mixed Blessings,* and *Mind Your Language.*

The dangers of cultural colonisation of the peoples of the Third World by foreign media programmes

There is an imminent danger that the values of those Third World countries that continue to court external cultural values, just to satisfy the tastes and curiosities of a few elites, educated in the Western societies, may be debased and forgotten forever. For the past two decades eminent scholars in the West have been crying out on the need to contain the invasion of Western cultural values, through the broadcast media, in the Third World. The concerned scholars do realise that a world of cultural diversity is far better than a world of monolithic culture. It is such a concern that prompted Herbert Schiller to detail out the bitter consequences of reliance on foreign programmes as follows:

(a)   The current tidal wave of international commercial broadcasting from the rich nations will continually lead to the exportation of social products with the least value receiving the widest circulation in the developing nations;

(b)   not only are these foreign programmes irrelevant to the needs of the developing nations, but also converting these nations into dumping grounds in order to make extra revenues from the foreign sales on these programmes will only discourage domestic programme production in all the developing nations;

(c)   these foreign programmes will lead to new cultural pattern to the detriment of the indigenous cultures because once cultural patterns are established, they endlessly persist, and as such the foreign programmes that are broadcast over the local networks of these nations may determine, in large measure, the cultural outlook and the social direction of the new nations for generations to come;

(d)   foreign programmes are produced without any iota of consideration for the requirements of the developing nations in view, and once they are shipped to these nations, they end up presenting "images and styles of life that are wildly out of keeping with the social necessities of most of the have-not states."[18]

Schiller is not the only critic of the potential danger of the impact of Western mass media programmes on the contents of mass media in the developing nations. Elihu Katz is just as unequivocal as Schiller in alerting the developing nations that continued dependence on Western media programmes for their broadcasting systems would be disastrous to their culture and development. Katz is essentially expressing the view that the adoption of borrowed goals and sets of professional norms from the Western mass media is inappropriate for meeting the needs of the small and developing nations.[19] First among these norms is the concept of continuous broadcasting which is the desire to broadcast as much as possible because Western and American broadcasting systems almost operate non-stop.[20]

Television broadcasters in the developing nations of the world, due to the nature of what Katz refers to as homogenised programmes they have acquired from abroad, forget the need for a variety of programmes for different audiences; members of the audience are taught to understand that all programmes are for everybody.[21] According to Katz, there is something functional in having an entire nation exposed to a shared cultural experience if the divergent ethnic groups in a developing nation are able to respond to the same messages which could result in the development of a shared set of symbols in terms of what they can communicate with one another. But Katz does not find anything functional to the audience of a developing country if the programme in question becomes *Bonanza* or *Hawaii Five-0.*[22] This leads him to question if programmes such as the last two are "shared cultural experiences that justify the huge national investment in television broadcasting?" or if these are "truly the programmes that audiences everywhere like the best?"[23]

We can now see how the mass media management and practice in Nigeria typify the problems Schiller and Katz have been able to identify. The nature of programmes the Nigerian Television Authority transmits to its national audience seems to be pertinent at this point. A former director-general of the Federal Radio Corporation of Nigeria (FRCN) once claimed that a relatively high percentage of programming on Nigeria's television stations was indigenous and produced locally, claiming that there was about a 50-50 division between local and foreign programmes. He said that most foreign programmes transmitted were the well-known drama series produced in the U.S. and Europe, such as *Mod Squad, Danger Man, Dan August, Bonanza* and *The FBI.*[24] The claim that there was a relatively high degree of indigenous and locally produced programmes in Nigerian television stations could not be substantiated by the available data at the time of the former director-general's claim. A UNESCO world-wide survey at the time showed that in Nigeria, for every 100% of television hours in each year, when the survey was conducted, only 27% of such transmitted hours aired locally produced programmes.[25] To the then management of the television broadcasting corporation, the statistics constituted a fifty-fifty balance; moreover, such imported programmes were "well known". Assuming they were "well known" programmes in the respective foreign cultures where they were produced, their relevance to the Nigerian culture still posed an unanswered question. Programmes ought to be evaluated and accepted based on the kind of educational dimension they contribute to the cultural enrichment and awareness of a society's values.

Another vocal critic of media dependence is Rita Cruise O'Brien who expresses the same concern of media audience maximisation in the developing nations that is brought about by a high preponderance of foreign television entertainment programmes that assume a mass audience and levelling of tastes. Her concern is that this results in flow patterns of information that assume a passive mass media audience which is only capable of receiving, but incapable of responding at the time to a (TV) medium that possesses the potentiality for effective exchange of information within a developing country.[26]

One is not far from the mark to suggest that electronic broadcasting systems in Nigeria are glaring examples of preference for foreign media products without ascertaining their suitability and relevance to the indigenous cultures of their audience by the managers of these electronic media. The second channel of the NTA-2, Lagos, as we have observed in previous sections of this chapter, transmits 80% of foreign-produced media products weekly to its viewers. On the other hand, Radio Nigeria Two, AM-FM, devotes an unusually high percentage of its hours of transmission to foreign popular music. Of the eighteen hours of transmission it is on the air per day, 15.5 of the hours are devoted to music. On the selected week-end day it was monitored to obtain data for the nature of its broadcasts for the International

Communication on Youth Culture (ICYC) consortium project on Youth and culture industry, out of a total of 154 records air-played, 70% were foreign sounds, 26% were Nigerian records, while the remaining 4% were sounds from other African countries, other than Nigeria.[27] The intensity with which Nigeria's broadcasting systems promote foreign cultural values at the expense of national culture prompted the researcher to conclude his investigation of the culture industry in Nigeria for the International Communication and Youth Culture (ICYC) consortium, first phase report by observing that his data have indicated that there is:

> ...a total rejection of music of the Nigerian musicians and an overwhelming preference for foreign music by the Nigerian youth. It thus seems that the music format of the Radio Nigeria Two, RN-2, influences the music preference of the youth. This is significant because about 60% of the audience of Radio Nigeria Two (AM-FM Stereo) consist of those whose ages range from 15 to 25. The implication then is that when we talk of cultural imperialism and the endangering of the local culture, we should as well be equally concerned with and be talking about the structure, programme priorities, and orientation of the local electronic media establishments, in addition to cultural policies of the developing nations in particular.[28]

From the above observation, it is appropriate to suggest that a Third World country that relies on external cultural values for the greater part of its hours of broadcasting is only debasing *la raison d'etre* of its indigenous culture as well as its existence as a nation.

The relevance of a national cultural policy

Lagos, as our previous section has noted, commands the largest market share of radio and television audience in the country. Its media audiences are the most influential in policy and decision-making apparatus in the nation. In apparent recognition of the need for the preservation of her cultural identity among her people, Nigeria, within the past few years, has been drafting a new national cultural policy. What are the implications of some of the suggestions being embodied in the draft cultural policy for the mass media, especially radio and television?

The draft national cultural policy, if accepted and implemented, recommends that:

1. the media should be used for the dissemination of cultural and artistic products for the purposes of preserving Nigeria's cultural heritage;
2. the media should enhance Nigeria's cultural development by broadening the citizens' horizon, awakening their imagination and stimulating their aesthetic awareness and creativity.[29]

In order to achieve the foregoing objectives, the draft cultural policy recommends that the philosophy to govern the mass media should be to relentlessly inculcate and propagate Nigeria's culture throughout the country through the medium of radio, thus:

I.   the radio is at present the most accessible means of reaching the largest number of Nigerian people;
II. primacy should be given to Nigerian culture in the production and transmission of radio programmes;
III. the state should exercise some measure of control to ensure selectivity in the number and quality of both Nigerian and non-Nigerian broadcast materials available to Nigerians;
IV. as it is very important that this medium of communication should be democratised, a national policy is needed that would make radio easily available to the Nigerian masses.[30]

The proposed national cultural policy also recognises the television medium, thus:

I.   it is now universally known that television is the most effective and most graphic means of reaching the largest number of people in any community;
II. in Nigeria, primacy should be given to Nigerian culture in the production and transmission of television programmes;
III. television is a great consumer of materials. The capacity of Nigerians to produce authentic Nigerian television programmes of high quality is as yet limited. Nevertheless, it is desirable that at least 80% of the total number of television programmes represent authentic Nigerian materials;
IV. effort should be directed therefore towards strengthening the production capacity of television establishments in Nigeria to the end that they can produce high quality Nigerian materials amounting to not less than 80% of their total programmes;
V.   the state should exercise some measure of control to ensure selectivity in the quantity and quality of both Nigerian and non-Nigerian broadcast materials available to Nigerians;
VI. television sets should be made easily accessible to Nigerians.[31]

The proposed national cultural policy may not achieve anything meaningful as its recommendations sound very abstract rather than concrete. It recommends that 80% of total television programmes represent indigenous Nigerian materials without specifying the modality of achieving the 80% content in indigenous programme. If the draft cultural policy for the nation is ratified in its present form, there will be no guarantee that dependence on foreign media programmes for the local electronic media will not persist.

Conclusion

This chapter has not only critically evaluated the cultural consequences of the patterning of the Nigerian radio and television systems after the Western media model and the subsequent dependence on foreign media programmes, but it has also challenged the cultural relevance and suitability of such imported media programmes to Nigeria. For the mass media systems of Nigeria and other developing nations to be effective in promoting the national cultures and aspirations of their people, the mass media managers need to evolve media programmes that reflect and promote the ways of life and accomplishments of their people as well as the cultural values of their societies.

This chapter has attempted to show that Nigeria is tied to the apron strings of the Western media because of her adoption of the Western media model. The international influence of imported Western media products, according to Jeremy Tunstall, "lies in the styles and patterns which most other countries in the world have adopted and copied. This influence includes the very definition of what newspaper or a feature film, or a television set is".[32] The centralisation of television broadcasting in Nigeria in 1975 did not solve the problem of media programme dependency as the Federal Government policy statement made observers and watchers of Nigeria's media system to believe. Dependency syndrome on foreign programmes even escalated during the Second Republic when foreign television programmes and equipment became major sources of foreign exchange earner for the politicians and other charlatans in the media houses and board memberships through kick-backs. In 1980, the NTA successfully knocked out a Lagos State Government-originated television that started broadcasting in channel five wave band, through jamming. Having forced the State television to a VHF band eight, it (NTA) took over the controversial channel five band and converted it into a Nigerian Hollywood television studio, as more than 80% of its transmitted programmes are devoted to mostly United States Hollywood-produced programmes as well as some British. The practice still persists. Having survived the onslaught of the jamming and forcible takeover of its original wave band that led to a futile court case, the State television began to refer itself as "LTV-8 alive".

On the other hand, the Federal Radio Corporation of Nigeria (FRCN), we must admit, is a powerful political establishment in the country. It has played one of the leading roles in unifying the various cultures of Nigeria through its broadcasts. It gave the nation a degree of legitimacy when ethnic rivalry and schism threatened the political, economic, and cultural coexistence of its people. The Federal Radio Corporation of Nigeria, as our earlier observation indicates, is perhaps the only institution in the country that, through a variety of ingeniously conceived local programmes, presents and perpetuates a certain degree of feeling of common national identity and belonging. It has an array of diversified cultural programmes that can appeal to all groups of persons.[33]

The 1978 radio decree a former military administration in the country promulgated has achieved more latent cultural functions than the manifest political functions for which it was promulgated. The division of the country into four linguistic zones has led to coverage of the country in twelve major Nigerian languages. Such a structural set-up is gradually diminishing the colonially-imposed English language as the nation's only official language. In this regard, Ekundayo Simpson has noted that "Radio Nigeria has striven to be a pace-setter.... In the absence of a well-formulated national language policy for the country, the corporation has gone ahead to reflect the mood and political reality of the country in its prime role as agent of national integration."[34]

Finally, Nigeria and some other Third World countries are undoubtedly faced with cultural conquest, via the electronic media, by the industrialised Western societies that once colonised them. However, culture cannot be forcibly imposed on any group of people who are unwilling to be acculturated by foreign values.[35] It therefore means that a sound national cultural policy that will be effectively implemented and policed; which broadcast media managers are very conversant with; that encourages artistic development of broadcast programmes that reflect on the best ideals and cultures of their societies; is the only alternative to resisting the cultures of the erstwhile colonial lords whose colonial tutelage created the current crisis of cultural identity in the wake of decolonisation.

FOOTNOTES

1. Cees J. Hamelink, *Cultural Autonomy in Global Communications.* New York: Longman. 1983. pp. 5 & 6.
2. *Ibid.*
3. Tom Chalmers. "Introduction." In *Survey of the Technical Development of the Nigerian Broadcasting Service.* (Lagos, Nigerian Broadcasting Service, 1955), p. ii. This has been quoted from Penn Roger, *Broadcasting in Nigeria.* Master's thesis. American University, Washington, D.C., 1960. p. 17.
4. UNESCO. *Television Traffic --- a one-way street?* Reports and papers on Mass Communication. No. 70. Paris: UNESCO. 1974. p. 12.
5. Thomas Guback. "International Circulation of U.S. Theatrical Films and Television Programming." In *WORLD Communications: A Handbook.* Gerbner, George and Siefert, Marsha (editors). New York & London: Longman. 1984. p. 157.
6. *Ibid.* p. 155.
7. Leslie A.W. Diamond. "Bringing Radio and Television to Northern Nigeria." *European Broadcasting Union (EBU) Review.* 938. September 1965.p. 27.
8. "Adebanjo to help sort out N.8 million fraud at NTA". *National Concord.* February 1984. p. 16.
9. James M. Kushner. "United States Information Agency." In *Broadcasting in Africa: A Continental Survey of Radio and Television.* Head, Sydney (editor). Philadelphia: Temple University Press. 1974. p. 223.
10. Roger Bower. "In Nigeria talent is easiest problem." *Broadcasting.* May 25, 1964. p. 107.
11. This was the text of a telegram the United States Embassy in Lagos, Nigeria, dispatched to Washington, D.C., as quoted by Kushner in his own chapter in Sydney

Head's *Broadcasting in Africa.* Earlier citation. p. 234.

12.   In some instances the Federal Communications Commission has revoked the licenses of some stations whose violations of the Commission's rules and regulations were very vagrant. Also, the broadcasting industry has been lobbying the U.S. Congress for quite some time now to extend the renewal period of licenses to five years. A House Bill to that effect has been introduced. But it faces serious opposition from citizens' interest groups. See full details in *BROADCAST LICENSE RENEWAL.* Part I. Serial No. 93-35. U.S. Government Printing Office, Washington, D.C., 1973.

13.   "Foreign films on NTA defended." *Sunday Concord.* October 28, 1984. p. 16.

14.   *The Democrat Weekly.* October 28, 1984. p. 12.

15.   *Ibid.*

16.   This revelation on the quantity of feature films produced in the United States in comparison with those produced in the rest of the world is also contained in the same chapter contributed by Thomas Guback in *WORLD Communications: A Handbook,* edited by George Gerbner and Marsha Siefert. Earlier citation. 1984. p. 155.

17.   Deanna Campbell Robinson. "Youth and Popular Music: A Theoretical Rationale For an International Study." *Gazette* (37). 1986.

18.   Herbert I. Schiller. "National Development Requires Some Social Distance.\" *The Antioch Review.* Vol. XXVII No. 1 (Spring 1967). pp. 64-68.

19.   Elihu Katz."Television as a Horseless Carriage." In *Communications Technology and Social Policy: Understanding the New "Cultural Revolution".* Gerbner, George et al. (editors). New York: John Wiley & Sons, Inc. 1973. p. 387.

20.   *Ibid.*

21.   *Ibid.* p. 338.

22.   *Ibid.*

23.   *Ibid.*

24.   Christopher Kolade. "Anglophone West Africa; Nigeria." In *Broadcasting in Africa.* Sydney W. Head. 1974. Earlier citation. pp. 85-86.

25.   UNESCO. See earlier citation footnote no. 4. p. 15.

26.   Rita cruise O'Brien. "Domination and dependence in Mass communication: Implications for the Use of Broadcasting in Developing Countries." *Institute of Development Studies Bulletin.* Vol. 6. No. 4. March 1975. p. 89.

27.   Luke Uka Uche. "Youth and Music Culture: A Nigerian Case Study". *Gazette* (37). 1986.

28.   *Ibid.*

29.   *Draft Cultural Policy for Nigeria.* Federal Department of Culture, Lagos, Nigeria. 1982.

30.   *Ibid.*

31.   *Ibid.*

32.   Jeremy Tunstall. "Media Imperialism." In *Reader in Public Opinion and Mass Communication.* Third edition. Janowitz, Morris and Hirsch, Paul (editors). New York: The Free Press. 1981 p. 185.

33.   Luke Uka Uche. *The Mass Media Systems in Nigeria; A Study in Structure, Management and Functional Roles in Crisis Situations.* Unpublished Ph.D. thesis. The Ohio State University. Columbus, Ohio. 1977. p. 193.

34.   Ekundayo Simpson. "Translating in the Nigerian Mass Media: a sociolinguistic study." In *Mass Communication, Culture and Society in West Africa.*Ugboajah, Frank Okwu (editor). New York: Hans Zell Publishers. 1985. p.136.

35.   Luke Uka Uche. "Imperialism Revisited.." Media Education Journal No. 6/1987. pp. 30-33. *Media Education Journal* (5) 1986.

SIX

THE PRESS: GROWTH AND ROLES IN NATIONAL POLITICS

Early History

The first newspaper ever to exist in any part of Nigeria was the *Iwe Irohin*, a Yoruba language newspaper. It was started by an English missionary, Rev. Henry Townsend, in Abeokuta in December, 1859.[1] In a dispatch to the Church Missionary Society in England, out of excitement over this unique accomplishment in a predominantly illiterate society, he noted: "I have set on foot a Yoruba newspaper.... My objective is to get the people to read... to beget the habit of seeking information by reading."[2] With these words, Rev. Townsend became the first person to introduce modern means in the process of mass communication which gradually led the way in replacing our talking drums and village troubadours as means of communication. The important thing is that it was an individual, rather than an organisation or government, who first conceived of the idea of the essence of a mass system of communication that would reach heterogenous members of the audience.

After *Iwe Irohin, the Lagos Times* was started in 1880[3] by a group of Nigerians. *The Times* became defunct in 1883 just after three years of what some had thought would lead to an establishment of a permanent fortnightly in Nigeria. *The Times* was ingeniously organised; it had depots outside Nigeria, in places as far away as London, Freetown, Cape Coast, Accra and Little Popo.[4] But *the Lagos Times* did reappear on the streets of Lagos in 1890.[5] *The Times,* no doubt, opened the way for a militant and nationalistic press in Nigeria. It started the first pitched press war between the Nigerian nationalists fighting for independence and the British colonial administrators when it editorialised:

We are not clamouring for immediate independence ...but it should always be borne in mind that the present order of things will not last forever. A time will come when the colonies on the West Coast will be left to regulate their own internal and external affairs.[6]

And that time did come in 1957 and 1960 when Ghana, Nigeria and most of the West African countries attained independence, respectively, from the European colonisers.

A flurry of newspapers emerged in the early 1900's but very few of them did survive long enough. But one of the most successful and influential early newspapers included *the Lagos Weekly Record,* which had a forty-year existence, from 1891-1930.[7] Its editorials were incisive and pinpointed on the colonial administration. *The Lagos Daily News* was another important newspaper the founding father of Nigerian nationalism, Herbert Macaulay, established in 1925. It became the first newspaper ever to exist along the West Coast of Africa as a daily.[8]

In 1926, some European interest groups in the Lagos Chamber of Commerce launched the Nigerian *Daily Times.*[9] The *Daily Mirror* group of newspapers did eventually acquire the majority shares of the assets and liabilities of the *Daily Times.* But in 1932, an intellectually oriented and edited weekly newspaper, *the Comet,* was started by Duse Mohammed Ali, an Egyptian. He took up residence in Lagos after graduating from London University. Ali is credited with introducing something unusual to Nigerian journalism of the time: that was nonpartisanship and objective views in the politics of the country. "As a non-Nigerian," writes a Nigerian admirer of Mohammed Ali, "Mr. Ali was free from most of the local prejudices of family, creed or political party. He brought his Egyptian nationalist ideas and an unusual objectivity to bear on local and national issues."[10] *The Comet,* under Ali's editorship, was so national in outlook that its nationalist appeal led the founders of the powerful anti-colonial political movement, the Lagos Youth Movement, to change its name to Nigerian Youth Movement.[11] The unusual journalistic style Ali brought to Nigerian journalism is noticeable in the following observation of another Nigerian:

> ...It was *the Comet* that carried more influence and popularity. It possessed high literary quality and gave considerable coverage to news of foreign affairs.... Its editor said: "Our objective is to deal with larger issues affecting West Africa rather than the minor issues of Nigerian politics." But later the paper devoted much interest to fostering Nigerian nationalism and indeed helped to foster the growth and the cause of the Nigerian Youth Movement before the latter had its own organ.[12]

Azikiwe and his *"West African Pilot"*

Nigerian journalism took a new turn, for good, when Nnamdi Azikiwe arrived on the scene to begin his *West African Pilot* in 1937. Zik, as he was popularly known, soon became the doyen of modern Nigerian journalism and used his *West African Pilot* to wage war of independence against the British colonial rule. He studied in the United States where his contact with the

French "Declaration of Rights of Man" and America's 1791 "Bill of Rights" and the proclamation of independence from Great Britain by the American colonies encouraged him to fight for independence and rid Nigeria and Africa of all the vestiges of colonialism and racial inequality.

Cognisant of the power of the media in mobilising national consciousness, and realising that a nationally, as opposed to regionally based media would greatly aid the independence movement in Nigeria, Zik quickly established the *West African Pilot* immediately he came back from Ghana where he had edited the *African Morning Post,* and had skirmishes with the British colonial government. He went about establishing a nation-wide newspaper conglomerate in the important cities where political discourse was the issue of the day. The aim was to arouse empathy and political awareness in the demand for independence from Great Britain. *The West African Pilot* became a newspaper chain with different names in many cities. In Port Harcourt city, Zik's Press Limited launched the *Eastern Nigerian Guardian* in 1940; this was followed in 1943 by *the Nigerian Spokesman* in Onitsha and *Southern Defender* in Warri.[13] Zik's group of newspapers quickly bought over Mohammed Ali's *Comet* in 1945, and four years later, converted it into a daily newspaper.[14] It was later transferred to Kano city, in 1949. It thus became the first daily newspaper in the North.[15] Also, in 1949, the Zik group of press established the *Northern Advocate* in Jos.[16]

With the *Pilot* based in Lagos, as headquarters, and with branches under different names in strategic areas of the country, Zik thus became the father of modern Nigerian journalism. He was very imaginative in his plan of awakening political consciousness through the print media. His was a new journalism that replaced an archaic and improvised journalism that had previously existed. The first edition of the *West African Pilot* appeared on the streets of Lagos and other places within the nation on November 22, 1937.[17] The impact of the *Pilot* on the Nigerian mass audience could only be imagined by the following observations two of Zik's arch political rivals, Anthony Enahoro and Obafemi Awolowo made:

...The *West African Pilot* blossomed into every corner of the country as the champion of the common man...the teacher, the trader, the clerk...it went right to the top.[18]

Enahoro indicted Nigerian journalism that had existed prior to Zik's arrival for having served the interest of the intelligentsia group, noting that "...those among the poor who were so privileged to read the newspapers looked upon them as the property and mouthpiece of the gods of their time. But here was a novel type of newspaper, catering to the taste of the people even in the remotest corners of Nigeria and, above all, edited by the colourful personality with those degrees! The people fell for him. The *Pilot* was made."[19]

And Awolowo had this to say about the *Pilot*:

The *Pilot*...whatever its literary defects, was a fire-eating and aggressive nationalist paper of the highest order....It was naturally very popular, the very thing the youth of the country had been waiting for. Newspapermen in the employ (sic) of the *West African Pilot* were better paid and they assumed a new status in the society. Civil servants, teachers and mercantile employees resigned good and pensionable posts to lend a hand in the new journalistic awakening. Some of these enthusiasts were eventually disappointed and disillusioned on other grounds, but the fact of a journalistic revival and revolution was widely recognised and acknowledged.[20]

The mass audience the *Pilot* took away from the other newspapers was so great that "the Nigerian *Daily Times* was very swiftly reorganised in order to meet the challenge of the *West African Pilot*. A substantial amount of foreign capital was injected into it, and the dead woods in the editorial section cut out to yield place to younger and imaginative elements...."[21]

Despite the successes it had, the *Pilot* had far greater problems that threatened its existence. One was a problem of location and the other was that of financial security bond to be posted. Perhaps, Jones-Quartey's recollections of how Zik encountered accommodation problem for his booming printing business vividly illustrate the point:

His first business and printing premises were in one of the most congested corners of commercial Lagos, Market Street. Later he moved into slightly more suitable and spacious quarters in Broad Street, part of the property of Sir Adetokunbo. Barrister Ademola...complained that the operation of Zik's printing presses and other machines was a source of nuisance to him on account of the constant noise and vibration. Secondly...the vibration was in turn a source of danger to his building, because he felt that the foundation as well as the walls were being undermined. Zik replied that he had put all his money and hopes into the present establishment and had no prospects whatsoever of acquiring suitable alternative accommodation at short notice. He thought Mr. Ademola's fears about the building were out of proportion, but undertook to do his best to abate the nuisance of the noise by a readjustment in the hours of operation. Mr. Ademola did not think this was satisfactory; Zik thought Mr.Ademola's attitude was unsympathetic and unreasonable. Eventually the case went to court. Zik lost. He was ordered to move from the lawyer's premises...to his immense distress."[22]

It was after this incident that a permanent site was found for the *Pilot* at 34 Commercial Avenue, Yaba, Lagos. However, it is most probable that the colonial rulers, who were being tormented by the *West African Pilot*, in a typical British gun-boat diplomacy, could have covertly created Adetokunbo

Ademola's fears.

Zik's other problem was that of people to stand as his sureties. In those days, Nigeria's colonial press laws required two people to sign as security sureties for a publisher. The two men who had earlier agreed to back him up as sureties withdrew their names without notifying him.[23] This crisis was so enormous that it threatened the survival of the *Pilot*. Zik was rescued by two well-meaning Nigerians, Kofo Abayomi and Akinola Maja.[24] Jones-Quartey adds that "...it is quite clear that the greatest support of the financial sector of Zik's enterprise was the Yoruba elite of Lagos."[25]

In the final analysis, the argument can be advanced that without privately-owned press by Nigerians, such as the *West African Pilot, Lagos Weekly Records, Comet, Lagos Times, Lagos Daily News,* etc., the Nigerian independence could have taken a longer period to arrive. The early newspapers in Nigeria led to mass participation in politics. They became the agenda-setting media by fanning the air of nationalism. They heralded the dawn of political articulation, rallying the general public and teaching it what it meant to be sovereign in one's own country. The more these early nationalists were sent to jail by the British colonial officials, the more their popularity and charisma were acclaimed and their followers became more committed and determined.

The colonial government controlled the broadcasting medium (radio) which it used to refute the charges the nationalists and their press were levelling against it. But the *Daily Times* and the *Daily Express* remained quite aloof and unconcerned in the nationalist struggle for an independent Nigeria. These two daily newspapers were controlled by private British business enterprises and were basically interested in exploiting a hitherto untapped and potentially rich market with a very active media audience. The *Daily Times* reluctantly admits that it did not get involved in putting across political views during pre- and post-independence periods in Nigeria because "since the original company was absorbed by overseas interests... it has maintained a neutral role in party politics, while at the same time attempting to promote economic and social interests of Nigeria as a whole."[26] This is contrary to too much, unmerited adulations being showered on overseas pioneer media in Nigeria and the rest of Africa. These media were hardly interested in the politics and cultural education of the African in preparation for an eventual self-determination and independence. Instead, their prime motive was exploitation and profit-making by selling sensational news that lacked enlightenment. Evidence of this is that in certain black African countries today, other than radio, there hardly exists any acceptable form of mass media. The former French West African colonies are just good examples. The paradox of it all is that mass media did flourish in these countries prior to independence. The foreign proprietors apparently became apprehensive and feared that the exit of their home government, the so-called metropolitan government, would not guarantee their continued operation. Their thinking must have been that independent black Africa would not tolerate the laissez-faire market that ensured profit-making for media products at the exploitation of the emerging nations.

Political imperatives of government ownership

It is rather ironical to see how the preceding pages have shown how some privately-owned newspapers emerged and accelerated the momentum of the Nigerian independence. But in post-independence Nigeria, the press is virtually owned and operated by the Federal and state governments of the federation. It was the three former regions... the North, the East, and the West... that started the practice of government ownership of the press in the geographical areas of their jurisdictions. The North was the first to start a government-owned weekly newspaper in 1939 when it launched the *Gaskiya Ta Fi Kwabo* ("Truth is worth more than penny.")[27] The same Northern Literature Agency that started *Gaskiya* also started the English daily newspaper, *Nigerian Citizen*, which was owned and operated by the Northern Region Government. The *Nigerian citizen* eventually gave way to the influential *New Nigerian* that emerged on January I, 1966. It was also founded and owned by the Northern Region (and later Northern states) government. Why was a government newspaper necessary in the North? A former editor of the *New Nigerian* said:

> The orientation of the North was rather different from that of the South. The North believed in controlled modernisation and emphasised the need for the changing society to adopt modern methods without destroying its own qualities. The South believed in an unthinking gallop towards everything European and Western, without considering its relevance or its dangers to the community. In this caution... of Western methods, notably education, lay a source of danger to the Northern region, because the North became educationally backward, and thus was likely to suffer in the distribution of national jobs. The then Northern Government was subjected to pressure by the Northern elite not to let the North suffer. The North therefore had to have a voice to put across. It was a society with an old history and revered administrative and legal traditions, which the South (and the colonialists) neither understood nor liked. But in the new Nigeria, where paper qualifications were the primary criteria in the distribution of jobs, the North was at a great disadvantage. So a government paper, *the New Nigerian,* was necessary to (i) get across the views of the Northern elite and mobilise them in order to achieve its goals; (ii) fight the Northern case in all disputes at the centre.[28]

Although the former editor of the *New Nigerian* colours the mission of the *New Nigerian* newspaper with historical and cultural differences existing among the various Nigerian ethnic groupings and states, he is obviously addressing the same reasons why the other regions' or states' mass media sprang up. And among such reasons is the major one of orienting the mass media of a region or state for the interest articulation of its people to the central government.

The former Eastern Region Government launched the *Eastern Outlook* in 1949. It later changed its name to *Nigerian Outlook* in 1955.[29] The Federal Government started its own newspaper, *the Morning Post*, in 1961. In 1964, the former Western Region started its own daily newspaper, *the Sketch.*

When Nigeria attained independence in 1960, the mass media orientation shifted towards reinforcing tribal and sectional loyalties in preference to the goal of national unity, identity and integration. The press and other media became parochial in their content. They dedicated themselves to the articulation of particular ethnic interests. The Federal Government's own press, *the Morning Post,* became defunct in early 1973. Its circulation had terribly fallen and the Federal Government was running it at a greater deficit; the Nigerian audience of the *Morning Post* had eventually revolted against reading Federal Government bulletins and press releases that overtly contained only pro-government news that became characteristic of the contents of the *Morning Post*. The *Post* "died" because it took its audience for a ride. It failed to recognise that it had a nationally-based audience, hence an element of objectivity in news content was essential in presenting all sides of controversial issues that were quite sensitive when the nation was faced with a series of crises of identity and legitimacy.

The one reason why state government-owned newspapers, especially those of the North, East and West, have survived and increased in their circulation is due to their policy to even bite the fingers that feed them; at times their anti-government stance on certain issues even embarrasses the governments. Frank Ugboajah had observed that "...of Nigerian newspapers one of the most critical is *New Nigerian*. Its anti-government opinion on some volatile issues of development in the Nigerian society is noticeable."[30] But the defunct Nigerian *Morning Post* always praised the government even when such praises were inappropriate.

When the Nigerian devastating crises of the late 1960's occurred, all the national press instantly took sides with their regional governments. Of course, such a course seems to be a natural tendency anywhere in the world. Failure to support one's national or ethnic line of action, particularly during crisis situations may expose one to being labelled a saboteur and an unpatriotic element. The following discussions a former Nigerian military head of state, Yakubu Gowon, and the former Igbo (Biafran) leader, Chukwuemeka Ojukwu, and some other Nigerian military leaders had at Aburi, Ghana, during an obortive conference to find a solution to the then impending civil war, illustrate the implications of the regionalisation of the media and terrible performance of the press during those crisis periods:

Lt.-Col. Gowon: On the Government Information Media I think all the Government Information Media in the country have done terribly badsic. Emeka would say the *New Nigerian* has been very unkind to the East.

Lt.-Col. Ojukwu: And the *Post* which I pay for.

Lt.-Col. Gowon: Sometimes I feel my problem is not with anyone but the *Outlook.*

Lt.-Col. Ojukwu: All the other information media have done a lot. When the Information Media in a country completely closed their eyes to what was happening, I think it is a dangerous thing.
Major Johnson: Let us agree it is the situation.

Lt.-Col. Ejoor: All of them have committed one crime or the other.

Lt.-Col. Hassan: The *Outlook* is the worst of them.

Lt.-Col. Ojukwu: The *Outlook* is not the worst, the *Post* which we all in fact pay for is the worst followed closely by the *New Nigerian.*

Mr.T. Omo-Bare: Let us make a general statement on all of them, no distinction.

Lt.-Col. Gowon: I think we agreed that all Government Information Media should desist from making inflamatory publications that would worsen the situation in the country.[31]

It is ironical that the press that brought colonial rule to an end in Nigeria became parochial and lost the nationalistic orientation it had earned. The above bitter but frank exchanges among the Nigerian military rulers of the 1960's explicitly show the degree of the involvement of the press and its partisan stance in Nigeria's fragile political process.

Each of the states of Nigeria is launching its own press. Those of them that have not started running their own newspapers have since completed plans to do so. In Nigeria, a state that does not have its own press is seen by the public not to have yet met the important requirement of maturation into statehood. The press has become the traditional organs of the governments, a legacy the former three giant regions bequeathed them. But one important observation must be made here: since the termination of the Nigerian Civil War, the press has virtually stopped the practice of perpetuating parochial interests, loyalties and ethnicity; excepting isolated cases that occurred during the Second Republic. There is a new change towards developing national awareness through all the mass media, irrespective of where they are located. So, for the time being at least, ethnic fractionalisation of the press is no longer a perceived danger to national integration. What seems to be the perceived danger is the current trend towards a monolithic mass media system, owned and controlled by the Federal and state governments. There are, as at 1986, twenty influential daily newspapers in the nation. Out of this number, only six are privately owned; the others are mostly owned and operated by the Federal and state governments. Even the six private newspapers have limited areas of circulation, excepting the *National Concord* and the *Guardian*. Their eventual existence was rocked to the foundation when the Federal Government, in 1984, favoured only the government-owned newspapers in import license allocation for the importation of newsprints. The problem and politics of newsprint have now abated since the commissioning of a local newsprint manufacturing industry at Oku-Iboku, in Nigeria's Akwa Ibom State.

In 1975, the Federal Government announced that it had acquired a majority of the equity of 60% shares of the leading independent newspaper and the most successful of all the newspapers in the country...*the Daily Times*. The government said the reason for its decision to participate in the ownership of the *Daily Times* was "to provide a channel of communication with the public without...having to set up an additional newspaper in competition with the established press."[32] However, it is interesting to note that the Federal Government has not had any newspaper of its own, quite unlike the state governments, since the demise of its *Morning Post*. Also, although the *Times* was originally a foreign financed newspaper, by 1974, Nigerians had bought up all its shares and the London *Daily Mirror* was paid off. The *Times*, over the years, had grown to be the largest circulating newspaper in Nigeria due to its neutrality and non-allegiance to any political party until during the Second Republic when the Shagari administration converted it into a party propaganda organ. The then Obasanjo/Murtala Military administration also took over the control of the *New Nigerian* newspaper from its former owners, the ten Northern states, and converted it into a Federal enterprise. It said that it would like to see the *New Nigerian* expand its activities to cover more effectively all parts of the country.[33]

PRESS AND POLITICAL INFLUENCE DURING THE SECOND REPUBLIC

When on October 1, 1979, Nigerians enthusiastically embraced the American bicameral system of government as a better alternative to thirteen years of military dictatorship, little did they know that their imitation of the American-styled check and balance system would be shortlived. After only four years and three months of experiment, Presidential democracy crumbled when the military sacked the Shehu Shagari administration. Prior to the military interruption of the Second Republic,[34] the Western media had

portrayed Nigeria as the World's third largest democracy.[35] Whereas most
Nigerians had anticipated military intervention, when it did occur it was quite
a rude shock to the West. The purpose of this section is to analyse the growth
of the newspaper industry and level of political awareness it generated in
Nigeria during the Second Republic. The *National Concord* has been used as
a case study to demonstrate the extent to which a newspaper had a tremendous political influence during the period of the Second Republic. Also, the
passage into law of the section 120 of the 1982 Electoral Act that established
a National Advisory Council (NAC) to supervise the contents of
government-owned mass media three months before and one month after
elections presupposed that the media were so powerful in Nigeria that their
contents at election time could influence the electorate's voting behaviour to
the way and manner the originator of such media messages desired. The
most important question that emerged during the era of the Second Republic
was whether the press (as represented by the *National Concord*), the media
gag laws, and the 1982 Electoral Act's section 120 that established the National Advisory Council (NAC) on government-owned mass media, contributed to the fall of the Second Republic.

If the quantity of newspapers and the fearlessness of their editorial
opinions and reportage are taken as measurements of level of political awareness and consciousness prevailing in a country at any given period, then the
growth of the newspaper industry in Nigeria, between 1979 and 1983, the
period of the duration of the Second Republic, could aptly be said to represent a high level of political participation and interest articulation in a
democracy. Every political pressure group established its own newspaper as a
medium of putting its message across the political spectrum and seeking
entry and recognition into the political decision-making process. With the exception of the well edited broadsheet *Weekly Democrat* that made its debut in
January, 1984, and suddenly disappeared as soon as it had come, the following newspapers developed to represent one form of political interest group or
the other: *National Concord, Satellite, Guardian, Nigerian Call, Eagle, Okigwe
Voice, Trumpet, Daily Nation, Echo, Daily News, Record, Stamp, Advocate,
Premier, Hope, Graphic, Sun* and *People's News*. Ralph Waldo Emerson's observation that in the United States of his time they had the newspapers that
did their best to make every square acre of land and sea give an account of
themselves at one's breakfast table[36] is just an appropriate political epigram
to describe the proliferation of the newspaper industry during Nigeria's
Second Republic. The only three newspapers out of the above eighteen that
survived after the fall of the Second Republic are the *National Concord,
Guardian* and *Satellite*. The eventual survival of the *Satellite* is uncertain as
its publisher/owner, who was the former Governor of Anambra state, Jim
Nwobodo, has been found guilty of corruption while in office and subsequently sentenced to more than forty years imprisonment by a special
military tribunal.

The *National Concord* is the only privately-owned post-independence Nigerian newspaper that has had a very influential impact on Nigeria's political development. The *National Concord* wielded a very wide political influence during the Second Republic. Founded on March 1, 1980, by a Nigerian multi-millionaire and chairman of the powerful American ITT for the Middle-East and African zone, the *National Concord* came to exist in order to protect the economic, religious and most especially, the political interests of the then ruling National Party of Nigeria (NPN) as well as to disseminate the ideals of the party, NPN, in a most convincing manner. Its founding followed the controversy, antagonism and bitterness the 1979 general elections had generated. The emergence of the *National Concord* added greater confusion to Nigeria's political intrigues. Its publisher professed that he believed in a free flow of information on issues of the day for the survival of any democratic system, claiming that dissemination of information had been one-sided in Nigeria. According to him, the *National Concord* was established to "give hearing to the other side of ideas; to challenge old myths and taboos whilst according full respect to those institutions that aid our growth as a virile nation."[37]

The Political Setting

The full political influence of the Nigerian press (especially the *National Concord*) on Nigeria's politics during the Second Republic cannot be fully understood without a brief recapitulation of Nigeria's political setting and its attendant intrigues. Since the attainment of independence in 1960, Nigeria's political administration, as previously stated in chapter two, has been fiercely contested and dominated by three prominent ethnic groups: the Hausa-Fulani of the Muslim North; the Yoruba of the Muslim cum Christian West; and the Igbo of the Christian East. Political parties have always evolved along ethnic lines in which their solidarity depended on ethnic loyalty. Consequently, it has not been possible for any of the three dominant ethnic groups, because of their tribal orientation and affiliation, to command national consensus and mandate at any of the general elections. The result has always been uneasy political alliances that lead to coalition governments, culminating into political instability each time the alliances break up. Nigeria's political scene was dominated by three giant political personalities, representing each of the three dominant ethnic groups. And they were: Nnamdi Azikiwe (Igbo of the East), Obafemi Awolowo (Yoruba of the West), and Late Ahmadu Bello (Hausa-Fulani of the North). Ahmadu Bello was assassinated in 1966 during the January 15, coup d'état. When the Nigerian Civil War broke out in 1967, the Yorubas, who initially sympathised with and supported the Igbos, teamed up with the North and other minority tribes, to wage war against the Igbos until the latter's defeat in 1970.

From 1967 to 1979, the Northern military and political leaders and their Yoruba counterparts, who together shared the economic, political and military war booties after the defeat of the Igbos, ruled Nigeria interchangeably. Before the military handed over political powers to the politicians in 1979, Nigeria was politically restructured into nineteen states in which equality of the states was emphasised in the 1979 Constitution that followed. The Yorubas of the West, with an ethnic population of about twenty million, had four states created for them. The Igbos of the East, with a comparable population of about twenty million, had only two states created for them. The Hausa-Fulanis of the North, totalling about twenty-seven million, had five states created for them. The military, prior to handing over power to the civilians in 1979, had approved and registered five political parties, all formed and dominated by the members of the three dominant ethnic groups. Three of the five registered and recognised political parties were headed by politicians of Northern origin. These parties were the National Party of Nigeria (NPN), Great Nigerian People's Party (GNPP), and People's Redemption Party (PRP). A Yoruba politician headed the only Political party in the West, Unity Party of Nigeria (UPN). Also in the East, an Igbo politician led the only registered political party, Nigeria People's Party (NPP) that represented the Igbo ethnic interest.

When national elections were held in 1979, three presidential candidates emerged from the North and one came from the East and West, respectively. The National Party of Nigeria won the majority of total votes cast during the presidential elections. But it did not win the constitutionally required two-thirds of the nineteen states.

When the Federal Electoral Commission declared the presidential candidate of the NPN, Shehu Shagari, winner of the presidency, the UPN presidential candidate, Obafemi Awolowo, together with the leader of the GNPP, Ibrahim Waziri, went to the Supreme Court of Nigeria where its justices surprisingly upheld the submission of the NPN's leading counsel who argued that mathematically, two-thirds of nineteen was twelve and two-thirds (12 2/3). Despite its victory that was upheld by the Supreme Court, the NPN could still not form its Federal cabinet because it did not have enough Senators and members in the House of Representatives in the National Assembly to pass any of the President's bills and other legislative requests. It therefore had to enter into a political alliance with the NPP, led by Nnamdi Azikiwe. But the alliance did not last as both the contracting parties accused each other of a series of violations of the accord and bad faith.

National Concord and Politics of the Second Republic

The National Party of Nigeria, in order to give its members, especially those of them from the East and West, a national sense of belonging, worked out a zoning policy plan whereby national offices were to be shared among the zones. The office of the President of the nation was to rotate among the North, East and West. It was therefore in realisation of his personal ambition to become the President of Nigeria at the expiration of Shagari's first term of office in 1983, that multi-millionaire Moshood Abiola launched his *National Concord*. Realising that he hails from the same Yoruba state of Ogun with the leader of the Unity Party of Nigeria (UPN), Awolowo, a charismatic Yoruba leader, who commanded a towering political image, and was regarded among the Yorubas as only next to Jesus Christ and Prophet Mohammed, Abiola had to destroy that myth and also the person of Awolowo in order for him (Abiola) to emerge as the only serious Yoruba presidential candidate who would not be overshadowed by Awolowo's political image and popularity. In a series of investigative journalism reports, the *National Concord* revealed how Awolowo, the leader of the UPN, had "immorally" acquired 360 plots of land in reservation areas of Maroko Village of Lagos at a paltry purchase price of $1.5 million. This revelation of Awolowo's capitalistic tendency constituted a political embarrassment to his image and credibility as a presidential aspirant who fancied and advocated socialism and its unquestionable acceptance in Nigeria. The Nigerian public, influenced by the *National Concord's* exposé on Awolowo, began to doubt his sincerity and commitment to the masses if he had such an insatiable capitalistic urge. The public confidence in Awolowo's integrity for the highest public office in the land further eroded when his political party's director of research and publicity said that Awolowo "had a right to own property.... The fact that the UPN leader was preaching socialism did not mean that he should be a poor man."[38] Meanwhile, the National Party of Nigeria, the archrival of the UPN, in a reaction to the Maroko land scandal, observed that Awolowo was "wearing a toga of deceit, wanting the nation to see him as a socialist while he was busy perpetuating capitalist ideas."[39] When confronted by journalists to defend himself on the land scandal, Awolowo said that the issue was strictly personal and that the *National Concord's* exposé had not had any effect on his political career. But at a later press conference, Awolowo told reporters that the deeds of conveyance of the land showed that he had ceased to own the lands (360 plots) since February, 1976, when he transferred the land to his family company, Dideolu Estate Limited, which, he said, was a private limited liability company "in which the only shareholders are myself, my wife and our children."[40]

The *National Concord,* bent on smearing Awolowo's political image, career and ambition and to prevent him from winning the presidency, questioned his probity in a series of editorials relating to the land scandal. These are some excerpts from two of such numerous editorials:

By multiple acts which can hardly pass moral, legal or ethical tests, Chief Awolowo or Dideolu Estate Limited has held 360 plots of prime land, and we do not think this is good enough for someone who claims to be the most qualified person to be the President of Nigeria.[41]

The picture one gets from the Chief's defence is not one of a socialist but a greedy, egocentric leader who however engaged in acts of philanthropy whenever his conscience pricks him.[42]

The credibility of the *National Concord* as an authoritative, respectable and non-tribal newspaper began to erode when it made a surprising U-turn to support the presidential candidature of Awolowo whom it had set out to discredit and destroy politically, as evidenced from the preceding pages. When the National Party of Nigeria, at a hurried party convention on June 12, 1982, renominated Alhaji Shehu Shagari, the incumbent President of Nigeria then as its flag-bearer for the 1983 general and presidential elections, the *National Concord* believed that its publisher, Abiola, had been jilted by an ungrateful party machinery. It thought that it was the turn of a Yoruba to be the party's flag-bearer for the 1983 general elections in accordance with the party's zoning policy. Its publisher, Abiola, ought to have been the choice. It was in preparation for Abiola's presidential race, among other reasons, that the newspaper was established. And to accomplish that objective of becoming a serious presidential candidate capable of defeating UPN's Chief Awolowo, the *National Concord* had to expose what it believed to be Awolowo's political scandals to tarnish his political image. Also, Awolowo hailed from the same Ogun state with Abiola, his fellow tribesman. Frustrated by denial of party nomination as a presidential candidate for the NPN, Abiola, at a press conference, announced his withdrawal from active and partisan politics. He also renounced his membership of the NPN and said that he did not plan to join any other party. He accused the Hausa-Fulani (Northern) politicians in the NPN of treating the rest of the country as second class citizens. He vowed to reject the leadership of anybody whom he did not consider to be as "competent" as himself and "who cannot show that he has contributed more as an individual to Nigeria."[43] The leader of the UPN, Awolowo, sent him a telegram, congratulating him for having left darkness (NPN) and that the light he had just seen would make him free.

Its publisher, having left the NPN, the *National Concord,* in an editorial that tacitly endorsed the presidential candidature of Awolowo of the UPN, whom its previous editorials and exposé on the Maroko land episode had ridiculed, humiliated and scandalised, wrote in part:

Chief Awolowo, veteran Nigerian politician and UPN leader, turned 74 on March 6, 1983. The elder statesman of Nigerian politics has cause to rejoice in the manner he has done in the last few days.... When in 1981 the chief stridently rang the alarm bell to warn the nation of the clouds gathering around her economy, he was accused of playing politics with the economy. Subsequent events proved him right. That has led to the perception of him in certain quarters as a far-sighted leader who could bail out our economy from the downturn in which it is now. It is a new Awo who is conciliatory to his opponents and is prepared to recognise the

religious, ethnic and geographical complexities of Nigeria. He certainly
has come a long way since 1979. New vistas seem to be opening up for the
UPN. The party hitherto perceived as a tribal outfit has made impressive
gains in Cross River, Rivers, Kwara, Sokoto and Gongola states. The vistas opening for the chief and his UPN have already led to talks of the Mitterand principle operating in his favour this year. French President Mitterand got elected after so many tries. If Awo should be that lucky, it
would certainly be a fitting crowning of the efforts of a dogged and principled fighter who refused to permit the accident of his birth to keep him
down.... Awo's grandfather, in the world beyond, would be proud of him.
So is Nigeria. We rejoice with Awo on his 74th birthday."[44]

The contradictions of the *National Concord* and its adaptation to the
intrigues of the Nigerian politics are aptly summarised by a critic, thus:

The image of the UPN leader which the *Concord* sold to the reading
public is best summarised in the following attitudinal words and phrases
which the newspaper used to describe Awolowo in many of its editorials:
"aged and faded; truculent and irrascible; naked; anarchist; tribalist; dictatorial; holier-than-thou; inconsistent; power monger; illusionist; false
image; and mischievous." After its publisher had left the NPN, the image
of Awolowo in the *Concord* changed to the following: "far-sighted; dogged
and principled fighter; democratic; consistent."[45]

Within the same period, the *National Concord* carried the following
editorials that derided the person of the former President, Shagari, whose
administration and actions it had previously defended against mounting opposition from the other political parties, particularly the UPN and NPP. The
editorials, in part, read:

Since 1979 President Shagari has tried to put on the garb of an innocent,
pious, humble, honest gentleman of honour who was always being persecuted by opponents. Now it seems the real Shagari is breaking out of his
shell.[46]

President Shagari has in the last fortnight given the country a cause for
concern by his utterances which must not escape comment. Apart from
claiming to have built hundreds of unnamed schools in (American)
"Time" magazine, he also said he believed "there is a lot of corruption in
the private sector." As if that was not enough insult to the intelligence of
the generality of Nigerians, he also claimed there was nothing like food
scarcity in the country.... The President must not leave the impression that
he has little respect for facts. How could anyone in his position dare say
there is no food scarcity at a time food and other items cost 300 per cent
more than when he took office? How could he leave the impression that
corruption is limited to the private sector when public buildings and other

property running into scores of millions have gone up in flames in order
to cover shady financial deals, when his cabinet and party men are widely
being accused of having amassed wealth by virtue of their positions?[47]

The above editorial excerpts typify the chicanery of the *National Concord*
each time Nigeria's political fortunes did not favour the interests of its publisher. These editorials that appeared four months to the elections were undoubtedly aimed at influencing public opinion which would affect the outcome of the elections.

At a time when the public began to question what the *National Concord*
really stood for as it suddenly switched to support the presidential candidature of its publisher's fellow tribesman, some political thugs were suspected
to have set ablaze the newspaper's warehouse that housed its newsprints. The
newspaper lost substantial bundles of its newsprints in the blaze. This happened when the 1983 general elections were about to begin. The public sym-
pathy and support for the *National Concord* and its publisher were quite
tremendous and encouraging. It was widely believed that some politicians
who were being frustrated by *Concord's* editorials and news coverage,
decided to burn down the entire newsprints so that the newspaper would
have nothing to print on as the NPN central government would not grant it
import license to enable it place orders for newsprints.

The publisher of the *National Concord* was also involved in another political intrigue that had an international ramification, barely two months after
the fire incident. The *Nigerian Tribune* and *Daily Sketch,* two influential pro-
Awolowo and UPN newspapers, with Awolowo the owner of the former,
carried an alarming news story in their respective editions that appeared the
same day. Their identical news story had alleged that the U.S. Central Intelligence Agency (CIA) had concluded plans to "solve before the general elections the problems posed by the UPN leader, Awolowo, and Chief Abiola
through operations 'heartburn and headache' in which Abiola and Awolowo
would be killed."[48] The U.S. embassy promptly denied it. The Federal
Nigerian Government set up a-one-man investigative panel. The editors of
the two newspapers, *Tribune* and *Sketch,* sought and got court order not to
testify and disclose the source and authenticity of their report. Some people
blamed the Russian KGB for planting the news story in the two media establishments. But a more plausible explanation seemed to be that the UPN
leader, Awolowo, and his party hierarchy masterminded the whole episode in
order to draw Abiola and his *National Concord* closer to his side and the
UPN. Identification of a common enemy that threatened to eliminate both of
them physically, it was probably thought, would offer the gimmick and opportunity to win Abiola and his newspaper. But it did not work out that way.
Neither Abiola nor the *Concord* paid any serious attention to the entire story.

The OIC episode

It is interesting to note that the *Concord* group of newspapers, made up of the *National Concord, Sunday Concord, Community Concord* (located in Imo, Kano, Ondo, Bendel States and Plateau) and the vernacular editions of *Udoka* (Igbo), *Isokan* (Yoruba), *Amana* (Hausa) became the first newspapers in Nigeria to face a national audience revolt. In spite of the seeming contradictions, confusion and opportunistic tendencies of the *National Concord*, particularly during the Second Republic, it (i.e. the *National Concord*) became the largest circulating daily newspaper in Nigeria, within a short period of its establishment. This was confirmed by a 1983 market survey carried out by an advertising company for the Nigerian Television Authority. In 1985, the *Concord* group of newspapers took a nosedive when it took its Southern Nigeria readership base for a ride during the controversy Nigeria's formal membership of the Organisation of Islamic Conference (OIC) generated. Prior to the OIC controversy, the *National Concord* had recorded a circulation figure of 500,000. Despite its tribulations, it is still one of the most influential privately-owned newspapers in Africa South of the Sahara. Its distribution and networks are well co-ordinated in a country where transportation and communication facilities are problems that are not easily surmounted. It has had a chequered history in the development of Nigerian journalism, especially when christian clergymen instructed their congregations all over the country to stop reading the *National Concord, Sunday Concord* and all other publications of the *Concord* group. Most Nigerian christians, especially those belonging to the fundamentalist religious sects, responded and started to boycott the reading and patronising of the *Concord* newspapers in any form; this included advertising in them. Their action followed *Concord* group's unveiled support and campaign for Nigeria's membership of the OIC. When a christian religious group in Northern Nigeria paid for an advertisement in the *National Concord* to publicly air its views against Nigeria's membership, the advertisement was not carried by the newspaper. This also added to the boycott bandwagon effect. Eventually, *National Concord* began to carry those advertisements that reflected the opposition of Nigerian christians against their country's membership of the Organisation of Islamic Conference. But it was quite apparent that the boycott had taken its toll on the *Concord* group of newspapers' circulation. This, undoubtedly had its very adverse impact on production. At this juncture, it is instructive to inform the reader that Nigeria is a secular state whose population consists of moslems, christians, traditionalists and atheists.

The 1982 Electoral Act

Besides the political influence of the *National Concord*, the 1982 Electoral Act generated a great deal of political debate during the Second Republic. It also influenced the political orientation of the press during the Second Republic. The 1982 Electoral Act, among others, provided for the setting up of a National Advisory Council (NAC) to supervise and approve the contents of those Federal and State Government-owned mass media, three months before and one month after elections. The section 120 of the Act states:

> All the mass media controlled by the Federal and State Governments shall be brought under a National Advisory Council three months before and a month after an election. The National Advisory Council shall consist of one representative selected by each political party contesting an election during an election year.[49]

The nation's traumatic experience during the inglorious national parliamentary elections of 1964 was a learning experience for the inclusion of the National Advisory Council on mass media into the 1982 Electoral Act. During the 1964 general elections, the mass media (radio, television, newspapers) of the Federal and various regional governments announced false election result figures that favoured the political parties of the governments they represented. This led to a wide-spread rioting, thuggery and arson in the Western Region of Nigeria.

When this section of the 1982 Electoral Act was being debated upon, majority of the National Assembly members in the Senate and House of Representatives argued that the NAC was necessary so as to avoid a reoccurrence of the 1964 experience that made a mockery of voting and election results as an expression of democratic principles. They argued that the absence of such a legislation before the 1964 general elections encouraged fraud, through the mass media, in announcing false election results. But the section 120 of the 1982 Electoral Act that provided for NAC in mass media displeased the National Party of Nigeria, NPN, the party that controlled the central government. Also, the Federal Government, under Shagari's leadership, controlled the largest media outlets in the country. The opposition parties strongly suspected the NPN-controlled Federal Government of planning to rig the elections through the mass media. To most Nigerians, the Act, with its section 120, was a necessary evil if that would ensure free and fair elections and results that would command national respect and be acceptable to everyone.

The former President of the Federal Republic, Shagari, initially refused to sign the Act into law as it infringed on the freedom of the press. He eventually did sign it into law at a mini-conference of most of the presidential candidates from the various political parties and representatives of those who did not attend. The absentees had suspected a *coup de grace* on the part of the President and his party, NPN. A few days after the President had signed the 1982 Electoral Act into law, without expunging the vexatious section 120, as he had requested, a member of his party's legal advisory committee sued him (the President) and prayed a Lagos High Court to restrain him from approving the appointments of the representatives of any of the registered parties to serve in the National Advisory Council (NAC) on mass media because section 120 that established it was a regulatory instrument of the media. This, the plaintiff argued, was contrary to the provision of the 1979 Constitution of Nigeria that guaranteed press freedom. This suit had the President's tacit approval, hence it was brought about by a member of his party's legal advisory committee.[50] The Lagos High Court, however, struck out the suit as the plaintiff lacked locus standi. He was not a journalist and could not prove how the appointments of the members of the NAC by their political parties and the President's subsequent confirmation of their appointments would adversely affect him.

It was at this stage that the members of the NPN's legal advisory committee, the president's party, approached the governors of two of the states that the NPN controlled, Rivers and Kwara, to ask the editors of the *Nigerian Tide* and *Nigerian Herald* to go to their states' High Courts and seek court injunctions to restrain the President from inaugurating the NAC on mass media and accepting the representatives of all the parties. The above two newspapers are owned by the governments of the two states, Rivers and Kwara, respectively. The editors were political appointees of the governors. In fact they, likewise the editors of all the other Federal and state governments' newspapers in Nigeria during the Second Republic, were responsible to the President and governors, respectively. Also, the High Court judges in the two states were considered to be very friendly and sympathetic to the president's party, NPN.[51]

This was the irony of the separation of powers, especially the much publicised independence of the judiciary in Nigeria during the Second Republic! The judge of the Kwara High Court quickly gave the suit an accelerated hearing. A few days later, the editor of the *Nigerian Herald* had won his case! The Kwara state High Court Judge had granted an injunction that restrained the president from inaugurating and swearing in the members of the NAC on mass media as required by the section 120 of the 1982 Electoral Act. Any contrary act on the part of the president would have tantamounted to contempt of the court. So, he did not contravene the court order. It was just exactly what he and his party had sought for, all along. He was later to tell the other parties that his hands were tied down by a court injunction.

The 1983 elections were not only rigged but false and bogus election figures were also released over the Federal Government-owned media and those of the states the NPN controlled. The opposition parties in control of the other states also released their own election result figures that conflicted with those of the NPN, through the media they also controlled. As a matter of fact, the then governor of Imo State, Samuel Mbakwe, without waiting for the Federal Electoral Commission to officially announce and release the gubernatorial election result for Imo State, went and seized both the radio and television studios his government owned and controlled, to make a live broadcast declaring himself winner. The Imo Television had just been built few months prior to the 1983 general elections. The following day, the Imo State Government-owned newspaper, the *Nigerian Statesman,* unstatesmanly carried the election results as declared by the then governor Mbakwe. Governor Mbakwe took the Federal Electoral Commission, FEDECO, and the Federal media unawares. He outfoxed them. He had suspected a foul play. His fears were not unfounded as numerous court cases and the judgments that followed the elections nullified some election results and reverted them to what the courts thought to be the real result. Some appeal courts over-ruled the judgments of the lower courts. The Federal Supreme Court, the highest court in the land, also did over-rule and uphold some of the rulings of the Appeal Courts. In Ondo State, an angry mob burned down the Nigerian Television Authority station, Akure, for allegedly declaring falsified results that made the incumbent governor the loser. Eventually, the incumbent governor of Ondo State emerged the winner after numerous court verdicts and counter-verdicts.

The fury and attendant consequences the 1982 Electoral Act generated notwithstanding, the enactment into law of the NAC on mass media by the Executive arm and the two Houses of the National Assembly during the Second Republic, tended to give the impression that the mass media were so powerful that monopoly control of exposure of their messages to the public by one political party was sufficient to sway the political attitudes, behaviours and orientations of the electorate. This assumption is tantamount to a belief in the hypodermic persuasion needle model of mass media effect that once postulated that the effects of the mass media messages on a mass audience were direct, immediate and powerful.[52] This model has since been largely abandoned because Seminal works since that of Joseph Klapper have debunked the assumptions of the 'hypodermic' model of media effects to change the attitudes and behaviours of the significant portions of the media audience on vital political issues.[53] This belief in the direct effect of the media at election period partly contributed to the fall of the Second Republic.

THE NEWS AGENCY OF NIGERIA (NAN)

Nigeria was a laggard in her decision to establish a national news agency. While such African countries as Ghana, Zaire, Algeria, Egypt, etc., etc., had established effective and functional news agencies immediately they attained independence, it took Nigeria, the giant of Africa, 16 years of indecision after being a sovereign nation, to promulgate a decree establishing a news agency. It also took her two years of bureaucratic processing and interpretation of the decree before the news agency finally took off. Had it not been for the un-favourable international coverage foreign media gave her during the Civil War (1967-1970); the negative coverage Africa generally receives from the Western media; her emergence as an African power; her financial, political, diplomatic and moral commitment to dismantling the apartheid system in

South Africa by countering Pretoria's well-entrenched international propaganda machinery that aids in prolonging her apartheid system; the emergence of a sub-regional economic community of the Anglophone and Francophone West African states (Economic Community of West African States: ECOWAS); and UNESCO's doctrine of new world information and communication order that challenges the uni-directional flow of information from the Western democracies to the Third World countries; perhaps, Nigeria would have still not considered it appropriate to start a national news agency.

Unlike the United Press International (UPI), the Associated Press (AP), Reuters and their types in the West, the News Agency of Nigeria (NAN) is a Federal Government parastatal under the supervision of the Federal Ministry of Information. It was established on May 10, 1976, by a military decree number 19. The decree that established it details its main objectives to be the following:

(a)   to seek, obtain and otherwise receive through subscription, payment, exchange or other means, international, regional, local and other news and features;

(b)   distribute such news, news material and news features to subscribers against payment either in the form of fees or news exchange or on such other terms as may be agreed;

(c)   present complete, objective and impartial information, news material or features on any matter of public or national interest within and outside the federation; and

(d)   report truthfully, and fairly without prejudice to public and national interest, the views of all sections of the population of the federation.[54]

The decree also mandates the News Agency of Nigeria (NAN) to have the monopoly of gathering news in Nigeria for sale to foreign news agencies.[55] It also created a board of directors for policy and decision-making. The general manager of the agency is an ex-officio member of the agency's board. He is charged with the day to day affairs of the agency and for the implementation of the decisions of the board.

Before the agency went into operations in 1978, the supervising ministry (Information) had, in March 1977, set up an implementation task force to develop the modalities of its operations. The task force also recommended that the functions of the news agency must revolve around the following guidelines, besides the provisions of the decree that established it:

(a)   "The primary duty of the News Agency of Nigeria is to uphold the integrity of the Federal Republic of Nigeria and promote harmonious relationships among the different groups in Nigeria.

(b)   News and comment emanating from the Agency must be truthful, honest and fair, but must not jeopardise peace and harmony in the country.

(c)   The Agency must bring enlightened opinion to bear in discussing national and international issues. It must positively influence public opinion and contribute to the evolution and formation of correct national policies.

(d)   The Agency is enjoined to promote understanding among the peoples of the ECOWAS sub-region, the OAU and the world in general. It is also enjoined to respect the integrity of member countries of the ECOWAS and OAU.

(e)   In its role as the national purveyor of news and opinion, and espousing the public good, the News Agency of Nigeria must not act as an institutional opponent to any government or interests; but where it is in the public interest to report criticisms of public policy, it must do so in a restrained and objective manner.

(f)   In matters that affect the sovereignty or unity of Nigeria, neutrality is not expected of the Agency. It must come out firmly on the side of Nigeria without prejudice to its adherence to the truth which must all times be its guiding light and governing principle."[56]

Undoubtedly, all these injunctions place NAN's reporters in a nerving and ambivalent situation. One such occasion occurred in early 1984 when most media establishments in the country carried a NAN despatch that the military governor of Ondo state under the Buhari regime had ordered 35 members of staff of Radio Nigeria, Akure, to be flogged for coming late to work. Some days later, the governor denied it and NAN accordingly despatched the denial to media houses, but without really apologising that its earlier report was inaccurate and unfounded. The general manager of NAN at the time had to summon a meeting of all his zonal editors and top management staff. At the meeting, he reminded them that NAN was not only a government-owned news agency but also that it existed to assist the government through dissemination of information in the execution of its programmes and policy. The Akure (Ondo) bureau editor was queried. But the fact remains that 35 workers of the FRCN in Akure were flogged, based on the accounts given by those of them who were flogged, and other eyewitness accounts. But the NAN headquarters' concern was that if Radio Nigeria, Akure, whose own workers were flogged did not have the courage to report the incident, why should NAN? Was it NAN that had its own personnel flogged? Was the NAN editor or any of his state correspondents there to witness the flogging? It was along these lines that NAN management rebuked and queried its Akure zonal editor. This incident demonstrates the orientation of the NAN management in the agency's news gathering approach. It instils the fear of not reporting the truth.

NAN's Structure

The NAN, like its electronic media counterparts, experimented with the zonal structure system for national coverage before abandoning it due to bureaucratic hurdles the news had to pass through before reaching its national headquarters in Lagos. The zonal system considerably slowed down news. In some zones, before the news could reach Lagos, it had already become stale. The five zones that once made up the agency's national coverage, besides its national headquarters in Lagos, were:

Bauchi: Bauchi, Borno, Gongola and Plateau states
Benin: Bendel, Imo and Ondo states
Enugu: Anambra, Benue, Cross River and Rivers states
Ibadan: Kwara, Ogun and Oyo states
Kaduna: Kaduna, Kano, Niger and Sokoto states.

The agency's news reports from the states used to pass through its zonal headquarters where they were processed and transmitted to Lagos.[57] Each of the zones was headed by a zonal editor whose functions included the coordination of the agency's services in the zone. The following account of how its zonal news items got to its national headquarters in Lagos at the time the zonal system was still functioning illustrates the degree to which lack of or inadequate existence of basic communication infrastructure (telephone, teleprinter, telex, radiophones, etc., etc.,) rendered NAN's operations ineffective:

The journey of the news from the state offices to Lagos has also not always followed the original plan. Initially, because of communication difficulties, NAN correspondents in the states had to resort to a variety of means to get their reports to the Lagos newsroom. Those of them who had access to Nigeria Airways sent their reports to the Airlines Public Relations office in Lagos from where a despatch rider collected them every day.

Reports from Owerri reached Lagos through the Chidi Ebere Bus Service! The correspondent in Minna sent his stories via the train once a week, while those in Akure resorted to express mail which in most cases took over a week to reach the Lagos office! For a long while, NAN was unable to establish contact with its correspondents in Yola and Maiduguri.... Yola, however, continues to present a serious problem. Most reports from the Gongola state capital still reach Lagos as telegrams, sometimes three weeks after they were despatched.

In Lagos, the news gathering problems have been mainly those associated with the traditional traffic bottle-neck. NAN has tried to ease this problem through the purchase of vans equipped with mobile radio-teleprinters which are used to transmit reports from Ikeja and Lagos Island to the newsroom in Iganmu.[58]

After the dissolution of the five zonal bureaux that grouped all the states of the federation into various zones, there are now twenty NAN bureaux, besides its Lagos national headquarters, each located at the state capital of each of the states in the country and the new Federal Capital Territory at Abuja. As at 1984, each state bureau was staffed with five correspondents for statewide coverage. By this very structural arrangement, NAN is ineffective in its coverage of the country, as it is currently urban-based. It hardly pays any attention to what is happening in rural areas of the country where the majority of Nigerians live. One would have also expected NAN to have located correspondents in each of the local government areas in all the states of the federation for effective national coverage of both the urban and rural dwellers.

Some years ago only four of its zonal headquarters in Kaduna, Enugu, Ibadan and Bauchi were linked to the Lagos national headquarters by high frequency transceivers that provided only one-way (receive-only teleprinter) that served for both news gathering and distribution to all the states. Today each of NAN's bureaux is currently located in the capital of each of the states and Abuja is linked with all of them and its Lagos headquarters by a two-way high frequency teletype communication network.[59] Outside Nigeria, the agency has divided Africa into four regional pools whose function is primarily to assemble news from the respective national news agencies and send such news items down to Lagos. The NAN bureaux outside Nigeria are:

Abidjan: covering West African and ECOWAS countries
Nairobi: covering East and central Africa
Harare: covering Southern Africa
Cairo: covering North Africa and Middle East. [60]

The news agency has also established the following bureaux outside Africa, to cover the other areas of the world: New Delhi, for the Asian continent; New York, for the United Nations, Canada and the West Indies; Washington, D.C., for the continental U.S.A., Central and South America; London, for Western Europe; Belgrade for Central Europe; and Moscow for the U.S.S.R. and Eastern Europe.[61] But the economic depression Nigeria started experiencing in the middle of the 1980's has threatened the operations of the agency's foreign bureaux. The introduction of the second-tier foreign exchange market (SFEM) has financially crippled the agency's overseas bureaux due to lack of hard foreign currencies to sustain them.

In compliance with the provisions of the decree that established and empowered it to be the sole collecting agency of news in Nigeria for sale to other international news agencies, NAN has subsequently entered into a co-operative agreement with the Associated Press (AP), Deutsche Presse Agentur (DPA), Agence France Press (AFP), and TASS for the supply of news and in exchange for news about Nigeria that NAN gathers. As a result of this co-operation, NAN now receives in its Lagos newsroom, newscasts from DAP, TASS, and AFP by radio teleprinters.[62]

Funding

The agency is funded by the Federal Government. By 1987, the Federal Ministry of Information that supervises its operations expects it to generate about 50% of its revenue and to pull out of the unified salary structure of government ministries and parastatals because of its potentials to be self-sustaining.[63] Will the agency be able to sustain 50% of its income by 1987? A look at the following table that provides the figures of the annual subvention from the Federal Government and the revenue the agency generates from its services to its clients does not only provide the answers to the types of services NAN provides but also says a lot as to its ability to generate about 50% of its revenue.

In 1982, the news agency was allocated a budget of N4,500,000.00 (about US $6.8 million as at then) by the Federal Government. But the then Special Adviser for Information to the President, Olu Adebanjo, whom the Ministry of Information he was in charge of its affairs supervised and still supervises NAN, by his own fiat, ordered the diversion of about three million naira (US $4.7 million) of that year's budget allocation to NAN to the Nigerian Television Authority (NTA) where he had proclaimed himself the sole administrator and awarded various categories of contracts, having sent its director-general and chief executive, Vincent Maduka, on compulsory and indefinite leave. Despite protests from, and resistance by NAN's board of directors, the Special Adviser to the President on Information had his way without any qualms. The diversion of its fund demoralised the agency's personnel and derailed most of its projected capital development programmes. As the nation's purse got thinner over the years, the Special Adviser's approach to the development of a virile, aggressive and financially sound news agency (NAN) undoubtedly contributed to the agency's shortcomings.

There is a shortfall in the agency's self-generated revenue because most government establishments that receive its services do not regularly pay for the services they get. It takes the agency a series of pleadings, via memos, to extract some portions of debt these government-owned establishments owe it. However, the agency's cyclostyled duplicating sheets of foolscap papers with which it provides services to its clients are unattractive and unbefitting of a news agency. Its management does admit that it had originally planned to provide wire service at its inception, but that the post and telegraphy department of the Ministry of Communication did not provide it with the lines needed to go wire. However, as at January 1985, seven years after it came

NAN'S BUDGET SINCE ITS INCEPTION

FISCAL YEAR	RECURRENT	CAPITAL	NAN'S OWN-GENERATED REVENUE
1977/78	1,407,490,00	1,000,00	-
1978/79	1,407,490.00	-	-
1979/80	2,000,000	240,000	149,215.00
1980	4,275,000	6,343,000	203,752
1981	5,700,000	1,260,000	481,545
1982	4,500,000 but received only 1,500,⁽ᵛ	1,500,000	596,244
1983	3,604,500	4,989,000	544,123
1984	3,063,830	585,680	690,931
1985	3,063,830	-	-

into operation, only eight of its subscribers in Lagos receive its services by wire. The eight are: FRCN, NTA (Ikeja) *Punch, National Concord, New Nigeria,* State House, NTA (Victoria Island) and Commodity Board. As at early 1985, the news agency had run out of stock in teleprinters, else the services in wire would have been extended to those customers that could afford to pay for the installation and the subscription charges that would follow. In spite of so many odds it has had to face, it has more than 180 local subscribers. Its clients include newspapers and magazines, electronic media, academic institutions, government ministries and parastatals, diplomatic missions, Nigerian missions abroad, commercial, financial and industrial establishments. The agency plans to set up radio receiver system attached to the teleprinters. It started providing photo services from January, 1985. This is not facsimile service, however.

The News Agency of Nigeria (NAN), like those other news organisations the Federal and state governments own, does have enough room for innovative approaches to news gathering and reporting. The Federal Government hardly interferes as to what is to be reported or not. Like its counterparts in the country, its management, particularly during its first seven years, has imposed self-censorship in news gathering and dissemination, fearful of what government reaction would be if a particular news that may be potentially controversial is disseminated. Because of NAN's management caution, grovelling sychophancy and self-imposed censorship in an agency the Federal Government has, in no mistakable terms, stated its goals and modus operandi in the decree that established it, the News Agency of Nigeria, may continue to convey the wrong impression of government control.

FOOTNOTES

1. Increase Coker, *Landmarks of the Nigerian Press,* Lagos, 1968, p.1.
2. *Ibid.,* p.7.
3. *Ibid.,* p.9.
4. *Ibid.*
5. *Ibid.*
6. *Ibid.,* p. 32.
7. *Ibid.,* p. 117.
8. *Ibid.,* p.16.
9. *Ibid.,* p.19.
10. *Ibid.*
11. *Ibid.*
12. Kalu Ezera, *Constitutional Developments in Nigeria.* Cambridge: Cambridge University Press, 1964, p. 52.
13. Increase Coker, *Landmarks of Nigerian Press.* p. 21.
14. *Ibid.*
15. *Ibid.*
16. *Ibid.*
17. Jones-Quartey. *A Life of Azikiwe.* Baltimore, MD: Penguin Books. 1965, p. 147.
18. *Ibid.,* p. 148.
19. *Ibid.*
20. *Ibid.*
21. *Ibid.,* p. 149.
22. *Ibid.,* p. 146.
23. *Ibid.,* p. 149.
24. *Ibid.*
25. *Ibid.*
26. *Nigerian Year Book.* 1975. p. 179.
27. Increase Coker, p. 60.
28. Mamman Daura. "Editing a Government Newspaper in Nigeria." In *Reporting Africa,* Ed. by Olav Stokke. New York: African Publishing Corporation. 1971, pp. 39-40.
29. Increase Coker, p. 60.
30. Frank Okwu Ugboajah. "Nigerian Media Behaviour On Development Issues of Conflict." *Instant Research On Peace and Violence.* Vol. VI. No. 4, 1976.
31. John de St. Jorre. *The Nigerian Civil War.* London: Hodder and Stoughton Ltd. 1972, p. 345.
32. *West Africa.* September 8, 1975.
33. *Ibid.*
34. The first military coup d'état in Nigeria took place on January 15, 1966, when Nigeria's First Republic was overthrown after five years of parliamentary democracy.
35. "Nigeria's Test at the Polls." *Newsweek.* August 8, 1983. pp. 10-15.
36. Ralph Wado Emerson. "Newspaper". In *Using Good English.* Ed. by John E. Brown Summit, New Jersey: Laidlaw Brothers Publishers, 1962. p. 2.
37. *Sunday Concord.* March 1, 1980.
38. *Nigerian Tribune.* May 13, 1980.
39. *Nigerian Herald.* July 7, 1980.
40. *Nigerian Tribune.* April 28, 1980.
41. *National Concord.* July 14, 1980.
42. *Ibid.,* July 11, 1980.
43. *Ibid.,* January 19, 1983.
44. "Will Awo be another Mitterand?" *National Concord.* March 9,1983.
45. Olatunde Akande. "Influence of Publisher's Political Orientation on the Coverage of National Issues." Unpublished research project for the M.Sc. thesis. University of Lagos, 1984.
46. *National Concord.* March 22, 1983.
47. "Shagari's cheap shots." *National Concord.* April 27.
48. *Daily Sketch* and *Nigerian Tribune.* April 13, 1983.
49. The 1982 Electoral Act, section 120. Federal Government Printer, Apapa, Lagos. 1982.

50.   As a former personal adviser to the Special Assistant on Information to the President, I was adequately briefed of what the President wanted to achieve and the way of achieving it.

51.   The Secretary to the NPN legal advisory committee, a very good confidant, told me of the NPN's second option as soon as the Lagos High Court struck out his own suit against the President.

52.   Everett M. Rogers and F. Floyd Shoemaker. *Communication of Innovations*. New York: The Free Press. 1971, p. 203.

53.   Steven H. Chaffee, ed. *Political Communication: Issues and Strategies for Research*. Beverly Hills: Sage Publications, 1975. P. 24.

54.   *The Story of NAN*. Lagos.

55.   *Ibid.*

56.   *Ibid.*

57.   *Ibid.*

58.   *Ibid.*

59.   Interview with the editor-in-chief of NAN, Mr. Femi Adefala, on January 14,1985.

60.   *Ibid.*

61.   *Ibid.*

62.   *The Story of NAN*, earlier citation.

63.   "Presentation of the Department of Information to the Onosode Presidential Commission on Parastatals." Lagos, January 1982.

SEVEN

LAW, CENSORSHIP AND FREEDOM OF THE PRESS

The Nigerian press laws, as they relate to defamation, libel and slander, national security, contempt of court, copyright, sedition, reports of parliamentary and judicial proceedings, civil suits, obscenity, etc. etc. are patterned after the English laws. Every other institution in Nigeria has made a rapid change in the process of Nigerianisation since independence, but the Nigerian national press laws are still patterned after the British press laws. To meet the exigencies of the period, Nigeria only enacts some new laws and decrees to accommodate the interests of the ruling elite.

This chapter will, among other things, analyse certain press laws that are considered important due to their ramifications on the mass media industry and freedom of the press. This chapter will also make references to the origin of the press laws in Nigeria. The most important Acts of the former civilian administrations of the First and Second Republics, and military decrees in Nigeria, as they relate to the press, and the concept of press freedom, form the basis of analysis in this chapter.

The Nigerian press laws define a newspaper to mean:

...any paper containing public news, intelligences, or any remarks or observations therein printed anywhere in Nigeria for sale and published in Nigeria, or printed elsewhere and circulating in Nigeria periodically, or in parts, or in numbers at intervals not exceeding twenty-six days between the publication of any two such papers, parts or numbers, and includes any paper printed in order to be dispersed and made public weekly, or more often, or at intervals not exceeding twenty-six days, containing only or principally advertisements.[1]

The first newspaper law was enacted in Nigeria in 1903. It made provisions for the regulation of newspaper publications in Southern Nigeria;[2] the amalgamation with the North took effect in 1914. There was no such ordinance in the North because there were no newspapers being published over there by 1903. Among the provisions of the 1903 ordinance was that the newspaper proprietors were required to deposit a sworn affidavit with the registrar of the Supreme Court, giving details of the correct title or name of the newspaper, the address of the place of production, and the names and addresses of the printer, publisher, or proprietor. It also required a proprietor to post a bond in the amount of two hundred and fifty pounds sterling to be executed and registered with the Supreme Court Registrar by "one or more sureties as may be required and approved by the Attorney-General."[3] In 1917, Lord Lugard felt that the newspapers were extraordinarily irresponsible. He therefore introduced another newspaper ordinance as an amendment to that of 1903.[4] But there was hardly any substantial addition other than certain technical changes in terminologies and names; otherwise, it retained all the major provisions of the earlier ordinance of 1903.

In 1948 another amendment to the newspaper ordinance was introduced. Its main feature was that any person who wished to start a newspaper "pays an equivalent sum in cash to the government as a deposit to free him from the necessity of providing a bond."[5] The intention was to "ensure that in libel, the paper would be able to meet any claim arising therefrom and...in general it was meant to protect the members of the public from malicious attacks in newspapers."[6] But as soon as the 1948 amendment to the newspaper ordinance was introduced, Nnamdi Azikiwe, the proprietor of the *West African Pilot,* was reported to have put up a vigorous fight in the Legislative Council to pass a bill repealing the ordinance by eliminating the clause that required cash or any other deposits.[7] But Azikiwe lost his fight as the majority voted against the bill seeking to repeal the clause; and the ordinance was also passed.[8]

The Newspapers (Amendment) Act, 1964

It was just barely four years after independence from Britain that the Nigerian Federal House of Parliament passed a very controversial newspaper amendment act in 1964. The controversy this amendment act generated stemmed from the following provisions the newspaper industry found to be a thorn in its flesh:

(a) "Any person who authorises for publication, publishes, reproduces or circulates for sale in a newspaper any statement, rumour or report knowing or having reason to believe that such statement, rumour or report is false shall be guilty of an offence and liable on conviction to a fine of two hundred pounds or to imprisonment for a term of one year.

(b) It shall be no defence to a charge under this section that he did not know or did not have reason to believe that the statement, rumour or report was false unless he proves that prior to publication, he took reasonable measures to verify the accuracy of such statement, rumour or report."[9]

It is surprising to see that Nigerian leaders would engage in such a double standard when they became the law-makers of their country. If the colonial government had stringently imposed such sanctions, it would have been very doubtful that Nigerian nationalism would have seen light of day through the pages of newspapers. Ironically, we have just seen how Azikiwe, who later became the first Nigerian President, fought a 1948 newspaper ordinance that merely sought for the payment of cash as part of a security deposit prior to the publication of a newspaper. The free operation of the press hastened Nigeria's independence. The 1964 newspapers amendment act has only demonstrated that the political leaders of the First Republic did not want the press to *irresponsibly* challenge them as they *responsibly* challenged the colonial government. Another problem the 1964 act posed was its failure to give a definition of what constituted a rumour. Newspaper proprietors and editors feared that once they fell out with any politician, government official or the government, they could be charged with peddling a rumour through their newspapers. And that would be an effective way of gagging the press. The other provisions of the act included the following requirements:

(c) The proprietor and every publisher of a newspaper that is printed or published outside the Federal territory of Lagos shall establish a liaison office in the Federal territory for his newspaper if its circulation covers the Federal territory of Lagos. The proprietor is expected to notify the Minister of Information in writing when he implements this requirement.

(d) The penalty for not carrying out the above provision of the act would be a fine not less than ten pounds or not more than twenty-five pounds, or an imprisonment for a three-month term.

(e) The proprietor of a newspaper published in the Federal territory is required to appoint an editor whose job shall include the supervision and control of "all matters intended and suitable for publication in the newspaper." The appointed editor shall swear an affidavit that discloses his name and residential address, and register it in the office of the Minister of Information. The penalty for failing to comply with this requirement also carries the same penalty as (d) above.

(f) The editor shall sign and deliver a copy of every edition of the newspaper to the Minister of Information as well as any supplement of the newspaper under his supervision and control.[10]

In 1963, at an all-party conference aimed at changing the Nigerian Constitution to reflect Nigeria's status as a republic, the major ruling political parties in the country proposed to introduce into Nigeria a "Preventive Detention Act" by an act of Parliament. The entire Nigerian society denounced the idea. The rulers quickly heeded public antagonism and condemnation of the proposed bill of "Preventive Detention Act". The greatest denunciation of the idea came from the *West African Pilot,* which editorialised:

> Preventive Detention is like a snake which eats its own tail.... Nigerians must rise and fight with all their vigour against the move to rob them of rights guaranteed them in the constitution by the introduction of the primitive and wicked weapon of preventive detention.... While it may be necessary in time of war or in an emergency ...in time of peace it is no more than an instrument of intolerance and dictatorship. None of those who favour a Preventive Detention Act would have dreamt of such a bru-tal deterrent against critics, were they members of minority parties or in opposition. See how they whimpered and trembled under the gentle whip of the colonial sedition laws which we have retained. They all retreated into their shells like hermit crabs, afraid to say one word amiss.... These are the men who would want to hold people without trial. God help us.[11]

If the measure had been introduced and subsequently passed, people would have been indiscriminately jailed under the act for an indefinite period without trial. However, it is believed that the defeated "Preventive Detention Act" that did not become a legislation was aimed at silencing the critics of the government who were mostly journalists and political activists. It has also been widely speculated that the 1964 Newspapers Amendment Act was a way of getting the same idea across by its provision of punishment for reporting events the authorities considered to be rumours or false.

The Circulation of Newspapers Decree 1966

It was noted in chapter two of this book how the Western and Eastern regional local government areas and city councils banned the circulation of certain newspapers they disliked, especially if such newspapers were critical of their administrations. Local Government Councils in the East had, in 1965, imposed bans on the *Daily Times,* the *Morning Post,* the *Daily Sketch,* etc., for certain publications they thought to be inimical to them during the post-Western Nigeria election crisis. The Western region also retaliated by ban-ning the *Pilot, Outlook,* and *Nigerian Tribune.* The *Tribune* was even pub-lished in the Western Region, but was pro-opposition party. The Western Region government also forbade its entire regional population to listen to the Eastern Region's radio - Eastern Nigeria Broadcasting Corporation (ENBC, Enugu). The penalty was severe for anybody found violating these edicts that effected the bans on radio listenership and newspaper readership in the two former regions.

But when the military took over power in 1966, it promulgated a decree lifting these bans and making it free for a newspaper to circulate anywhere in Nigeria.[12] The decree stated that the provisions the local government councils, cities, or town councils and municipal authorities enacted that prohibited or restricted the distribution or general sale of any newspapers in any part of Nigeria had ceased to have effect, on the implementation of the new military decree lifting the bans. The decree also made the following provision:

> Any person who after the coming into force of this decree, whether alone or with any other person, and whether as a member of a municipal authority or otherwise, does anything calculated to prevent or restrict the distributing or general sale of any newspaper in any part of Nigeria shall be guilty of an offence and be liable on conviction to a fine not exceeding five hundred pounds or to imprisonment for a term not exceeding three years or both.[13]

One year later, the former Western Nigerian regional military government that was headed by Adeyinka Adebayo, violated this decree by imposing a ban on the circulation of the *Morning Post* and *Sunday Post* within the jurisdiction of the former region. The ban, was, however, lifted after two months.[14]

Newspapers (Prohibition of Circulation) Decree 1967

Another military administration, under Gowon, promulgated its own decree to prohibit the free circulation of newspapers in Nigeria. Although some have interpreted this decree to have been aimed at foreign newspapers that gave adverse coverage of Gowon's regime abroad during the Nigerian Civil War, it was only the Nigerian newspapers that suffered from this decree, whatever the intentions of the decree were. The decree made the following provisions:

> Whereas the Head of the Federal Military Government if satisfied that the unrestricted circulation in Nigeria of a newspaper is or may be detrimental to the interest of the Federation or of any state thereof, he may by order...prohibit the circulation in the Federation or in any state thereof as the case may require, of any newspaper; and unless any other period is prescribed in the order, the prohibition shall continue for a period of twelve months unless sooner revoked or extended, as the case may require.[15]

The penalty for non-compliance with the above Provisions of the decree includes the following:

(a) A fine of not less than fifty pounds or not more than one hundred pounds, or an imprisonment of not less than six months for an individual offender. If he commits the offence twice "the penalty shall be double that prescribed for a first offender."

(b) For any other person, there shall be a fine of not less than five
hundred pounds or not more than one thousand pounds.[16]

Public Officers (Protection Against False Accusation)
Decree 1976

One of the most controversial decrees ever passed by any political or
military administration in Nigeria was the 1976 *Public Officers Protection*
decree against the so-called false accusation. The decree made the following
provisions:

(A) "Any person who publishes or reproduces in any form whether written
or otherwise, any statement, rumour or report alleging or intended to
be understood as alleging that a public officer has in any manner been
engaged in corrupt practices or has in any manner corruptly enriched
himself or any other person, being a statement, rumour or report
which is false in any material particular, shall be guilty of an offence
under this Decree and liable on conviction to be sentenced to imprisonment for a term not exceeding two years, without the option of a
fine.

(B) In any prosecution for an offence under this Decree the burden of
proving that the statement, rumour or report which is the subject-
matter of the charge is true in every material particular shall, notwithstanding anything to the contrary in any enactment or rule of law,
lie on the person charged."[17]

The decree defined a public officer to include:

(a) any member of the Supreme Military Council, the National Council of
States or the Federal Council, the Military Governor of a State, any
Commissioner in the Government of the Federation or of a State;
(b) any member of the Nigerian Army, the Nigerian Navy, the Nigerian
Air Force or the Nigerian Police;
(c) any person who holds any office in (i) the public service of the Federation or of a State within the meaning of the Constitution of the
Federation or of a State; (ii) the service of a body whether corporate
or unincorporate established under a Federal or State law; or (iii) a
company in which any of the Governments in the Federation has controlling interest.[18]

One important observation here is that under this decree, corruption was
shielded. Very few newspapers, if any, took the risk of conducting investigative reporting. Also, this decree made it impossible to claim a privileged
reporting on the conduct of a public official as provided by the Nigerian press
law. However, as far as the military administration that promulgated it was
concerned, the decree was promulgated to curb irresponsible mass media

practices of emotional and sensational allegations at the expense of the accused person's civil liberties. But it seems to have gone too far to the point of
intimidating a newspaper from giving the public what is generally considered
to be investigative reporting.

**Public Officers (Protection Against False Accusation)
Decree No. 4, 1984**

When the *Guardian* newspaper decided to publish what it considered a
scoop on the list of ambassadors and high commissioners the Buhari administration had shortlisted for diplomatic appointments to Nigerian missions abroad, little did its management realise that the editorial decision to
make public the list before the military made a formal pronouncement would
be a fatal blow to freedom of the press in the country. The Federal Military
Government hurriedly promulgated a near-replica of the 1976 Public Officers
(Protection Against False Accusation) decree in 1984, as decree Number
Four. Specifically, the decree Number Four of 1984, made the following basic
provisions:

1. "Any person who publishes in any form whether written or otherwise,
    any message, rumour, report or statement, being a message, rumour,
    statement or report which is false in any material particular or which
    brings or is calculated to bring the Federal Military Government or
    the Government of a State or a public officer to ridicule or disrepute,
    shall be guilty of an offence under this Decree.

2. Any station for wireless telegraphy which conveys or transmits any
    sound or visual message, rumour, report or statement, being a mes-
    sage, rumour, report or statement which is false in any material par-
    ticular or which brings or is calculated to bring the Federal Military
    Government or the Government of a State or a public officer to
    ridicule or disrepute, shall be guilty of an offence under this Decree.

3. It shall be an offence under this Decree for a newspaper or wireless
    telegraphy station in Nigeria to publish or transmit any message,
    rumour, report or statement which is false in any material particular
    stating that any public officer has in any manner been engaged in cor-
    rupt practices or has in any manner corruptly enriched himself or any
    other person."[19]

The decree also empowered the Head of State to prohibit the circulation
in the entire country of any newspaper that may be detrimental to the interest
of the country. The prohibition order was for twelve months unless it was
revoked earlier or extended at the expiration of the twelve months.[20] It also
empowered him to either revoke the license granted to any wireless telegraphy station or order the closure or forfeiture to the Federal Government of

the wire telegraphy station concerned. The decree also established a tribunal whose membership shall consist of a serving or retired High Court Judge, as its chairman, and three members of the Armed Forces whose ranks were not below that of an army major or its equivalent in either the navy or air force.[21]

The decree provided stiff penalties for any contravention of its provisions. Any person who was tried and found guilty under it would be sentenced to a term not exceeding two years without any option of fine. In the case of a corporate body, a fine of not less than N 10,000.00 was to be imposed.

Besides, the tribunal was vested with the powers to order for all or any of the equipment of either the newspaper or wireless telegraphy station with which the offence was committed to be forfeited to the Federal Government.[22] The decision of the tribunal was final. Its decision was not to be appealed against in any court of law.

This decree led to the celebrated trial of two *Guardian* reporters: Nduka Irabor, assistant news editor, and Tunde Thompson, diplomatic correspondent. During the trial, the Attorney-General of the federation made the Federal Government presentations, while the *Guardian* and its reporters were defended by a prominent Lagos-based lawyer. The appearance of the Federal Attorney-General signified the determination of the Federal authorities to win a case they saw as a big apple. When judgment was pronounced after the case had lasted for weeks, the two journalists were found guilty and each sentenced to one year imprisonment. The *Guardian* newspaper was itself fined N 50,000.00.

The reaction of the Federal Government that culminated in the promulgation of the decree under which the two *Guardian* reporters and their newspaper were tried was surprising. In many circles, the government was condemned for an over-reaction and intimidating the rest of the country's journalists by using *Guardian* and its reporters as examples of what the military government had in stock for them. In defence of its action against negative public opinion, of its prosecution of the reporters, the Federal Government explained that its action was based on the so-called sensitive nature of the diplomatic list the newspaper had made a public consumption. It said the newspaper had no right at all to have made it public when it (i.e. the Federal Government) was yet to hear from the prospective foreign governments the ambassadors and high commissioners were being assigned to. Also, it was speculated that somebody who was looking forward to being appointed as an ambassador might have been disappointed when he did not see his name on the list. The speculators went further to suspect that the frustrated prospective ambassador could have influenced the prior publication of the list by the *Guardian* so as to force the Federal Government to withdraw it, as the alternate list likely had his name on it.

Some media critics also found it hard to agree with the *Guardian* that what it had published was anything but a scoop. The newspaper's news judgment was questioned. The question the critics asked was when did ambassadorial appointments become a national issue to warrant a prior publication of list of prospective appointees when the government was yet to make it public. Also, the rationale for the news judgment was further questioned at the time when a bag of 50 kilograms of rice was costing from $500 to $650 in open markets. While the Federal Government did not escape public indictment for reacting in such a harsh manner, irrespective of the "sensitivity" of the list, neither was the *Guardian* nor were its reporters found less guilty of promoting sensational journalism on trivial issues that serious-minded newspaper managers and editors would rebuke a reporter for wasting a whole day prying on government files that contained lists of prospective ambassadors and high commissioners.

However, the fact remains that the *Guardian* carried a report other national newspapers in the country had similarly carried at one time or the other in the political history of the country. Also, until politicians and retired military officers stop influencing the press, and until the newspaper public in Nigeria opts for more serious news items than what it currently pays for and gets, the Federal and State Governments in the country might as well begin to ignore some of the frivolities the newspapers carry as news. Perhaps, sensationalism may be the current mood of the nation's newspaper audience. If this be the case, the government, in order to restore its good image in the annals of Nigerian journalism, acclaimed in all parts of the world as the freest in Africa, may have to financially compensate *Guardian's* Nduka Irabor and Tunde Thompson for their period of confinement as a result of irresponsible journalism and poor news judgment emanating from their unnecessarily excessive excitement over a news story that would hardly be considered news at all, not to talk of it as a "sensitive" government document, as claimed by the Federal Government and its officials.

When the Buhari administration was ousted, the Babangida administration that unseated it repealed the notorious Decree Four and restored the freedom of the press, if the administration's doctrine of human rights was to make sense. Furthermore, the Attorney-General of the Federation and Minister of Justice under the Babangida administration, issued Nduka Irabor and Tunde Thompson certificates of pardon by the Federal Government.

THE CONCEPT OF FREEDOM OF MASS MEDIA IN NIGERIA

Nigeria is a country of over 100 million with different cultural patterns, temperaments, political cultures and languages before the British amalgamated the more than 52 "nationalities" into one single political entity as we have noted in chapters one and two. It is such a unique background that has made freedom and other fundamental human rights to be cherished ideals of the Nigerian people as well as controversial issues in the Nigerian polity. Some Nigerians hold the view that the press of their country is the freest in the entire African continent. Others contend that besides being the freest, the press has gone wild and irresponsible, implying that freedom means responsibility and decorum. Others still believe that the freedom the press enjoys is moderate; while to some others, there is no press freedom in Nigeria when compared with what obtains in the Western democracies, with particular reference to the United States whose presidential form of government Nigeria practised from October 1, 1979 to December 31, 1983.

It therefore becomes imperative for us to define our concept of press freedom as it relates to Nigeria. Within the context of this book, the concept of freedom means the right of the mass media (radio, television, newspapers, magazines, films, books, etc) to communicate ideas, opinions, information; the right to criticise the political, economic and social institutions of the country; the right to help in the enlightenment of every Nigerian by providing him/her with the day's intelligence in an open market place of ideas, without any overt or covert systematic means of applying censorship, pressures or any form of inhibition on the part of both the Federal and state governments, institutions, organisations, and individuals within the country; within the laws of libel, defamation and obscenity.

The military suspension of some portions of the 1979 Constitution notwithstanding, fundamental human rights and freedom are still enshrined in the 1979 Constitution that forms the bedrock of Nigeria's democracy. Besides sections 21 and 41 of the Constitution that assigned non-defined, abstract and ineffective supervisory role to the press over those that govern the country, the section 36 of the Constitution unequivocally provides that:

> every person shall be entitled to freedom of expression, including freedom to hold opinions and to receive and impart ideas and information without interference ...every person shall be entitled to own, establish and operate any medium for the dissemination of information, ideas and opinions provided that no person, other than the Government of the Federation or of a State or any other person or body authorised by the President, shal own, establish or operate a television or wireless broadcasting station for any purpose whatsoever.[23]

Part of the main objective of this section of the chapter is to identify and describe those factors that have influenced press freedom in Nigeria. This is an important subject because of its controversial nature, especially in a country where both the Federal and-state governments are the principal owners and financiers of the major newspapers and all the radio and television stations. It therefore becomes interesting to describe how freedom thrives under such ownership and control pattern.

Factors determining Press Freedom

In one of a series of research reports [24] that resulted from an elaborate field study of communication in crisis situations, which the present author conducted in Nigeria some years ago, the following factors were identified as influencing the degree to which press freedom exists in Nigeria:

Type of Mass Media Ownership

Nigeria has the reputation of enjoying the freest media in the entire continent of Africa. Even under the various military administrations, a former chairman and managing director of the leading Nigerian newspaper, the *Daily Times,* made the following remark:

In Nigeria, the tradition of a vigorous and virile press dates back beyond the period of British colonial administration. Although the arrival of the soldiers had not advanced the cause of unfettered freedom, I am glad to say that comparatively today, throughout the length and breadth of Africa...no press enjoys the kind of freedom being currently enjoyed in Nigeria under a military regime. Even the elected government of the First Republic was not as tolerant of the press as the present benevolent military government is....It is to the eternal credit of the military in the country that there has been no press censorship - even throughout the thirty-months' civil war.[25]

The above assessment has not accurately portrayed the picture of the degree of press freedom in Nigeria. It is contradicted by the following, much perceptive and objective analysis of the situation in the country, at least during the Civil War period which the preceding assessment did make a reference to in crediting the government with permitting freedom of the press. A critically well informed foreign journalist, who covered the Nigerian Civil War, makes the following observation:

The press on both sides of the line came out of the war of words badly, succumbing with hardly a token resistance to the pressures exerted on it by military governments...the press lost its nerve and censored itself into a state of grovelling sycophancy. This reached such a pass that it eventually upset the army commanders themselves by embarrassingly claiming military victories long before they were a fact. One of the worst but not untypical "whitewash" examples...was by the formerly highly reputable *Daily Times*... when it reported the International Observer Team's report on the killing of four European relief workers by Federal troops in Okigwe. The deep banner headline on the front page read: "TROOPS CLEARED ON THE OKIGWE DEATHS." Lower down, the sixth paragraph had this to say. "The report, however, claimed that soldiers deliberately and without provocation by the persons concerned shot and killed two Red Cross Officials and two World Council of Churches representatives." An outstanding contradiction by any standard.... The famed freedom of the Nigerian press, the liveliest and most independent in black Africa, died with the civilian rule and there is still little sign of its ressurection.[26]

The above remark has shown how benevolent and tolerant the military governments in Nigeria were (and still are) to the press and its freedom.

The type of mass media ownership in Nigeria is obviously related to the degree of press freedom that prevails in the country. In a country where there are about twenty national daily newspapers, only six are privately-owned. And all the laws of the mass media are aimed at regulating the few existing independent dailies. Government-owned media do not engage in certain exposition of malpractices in high government establishments if a government paid civil servant or public office holder is involved.[27] Also, during a confrontation (relating to the "Zombie" record that satirised the Nigerian Army) between Nigeria's famous and controversial Afro-beat musician, Fela Anikulapo-Kuti, and some Nigerian soldiers, during which the former's Kalakuta "republic" residence was burnt down by the soldiers,[28] no government-owned newspaper reported the incident. It was only the privately-owned *Punch* that reported it to the general Nigerian public. When the government-owned media eventually did decide to join the *Punch* in reporting the incident, they distorted the true story.

Type of media ownership becomes an important factor because the existing literature has indicated that Nigeria enjoyed the greatest free media in Africa when there were multiplicities of independently-owned newspapers that existed during the pre- and post-independence era under the colonial and civilian administrations, respectively. There was an incident during one military regime when two editorial writers of the *Daily Times,* the paper the Federal Government controls 60% of its equity, were suspended because they refused to let the government-appointed censor control their editorial thought.[29] They refused to show the censor the editorial they had written prior to its appearance on the paper. Moreover, the censor was considered incompetent as he had no media expertise. It was the duty of the censor to scrutinise and approve all the contents of the paper before its publication.

The freedom of the press can be impeded if the press is under the dominant monopoly of a single ownership. Frank Ugboajah made an insightful observation when he noted that "the establishment of one media-voice through overall government ownership of the media is a killing of variety. Thus the concept of development support communication seems to lend absurdity to accepted journalistic principles of the free flow of information."[30] In Nigeria, the few cases of exposé on corrupt government officials who had at one time or the other embezzled public funds and/or committed certain unethical acts in which their morality was questioned, were all spearheaded by the private media,[31] their minority in number notwithstanding. There has never been an occasion when a government-owned newspaper has seized the intiative to expose, through investigative reporting and researching, a public figure or official for either corruption or maladministration. It also means that now the governments of the federation virtually control all the influential media in the country, and the frequency with which military administrations enact press censorship laws, as exemplified by the implementation of the public officers protection decree of 1976, with its 1984 edition, investigative journalism will always be an endangered aspect of our development communication.

Type of Political System

The nature of a political type of regime prevailing in Nigeria at any given period constitutes an influential factor in determining the degree of freedom of the press. Already, the case has been made that greater press freedom prevailed in Nigeria during the periods of First and Second Republics than during the military regimes. In fact the picture of the press under the *type of ownership* variable that has earlier been discussed, shows self-imposed censorship by the press during a military government. Also, during the civilian administrations in Nigeria, the political system was pluralistic as opposed to one-party political system of government. The result was that each political party, besides the Federal and state governments, had its own party press and this led to greater freedom of the press; what the press of one party or state tried to suppress, the press of the opposing party or state exposed it.

In Nigeria and practically all of the African continent under black and white leadership, there is a great interlink between the media and political system. In racist and apartheid South Africa, there is a high degree of freedom of the press in as much as the press upholds the doctrine of the apartheid and the false image of the superiority of the white race in that country. Any press functioning otherwise, is charged with numerous offences that could close it down. In Zimbabwe, the white minority, racist government press during Ian Smith's brief rebellion was free also in so far as it defended the supremacist policy of the rebel regime of Ian Smith. In most black African countries, the press is free only when it does not criticise the government in power and does not promote the interest of the opposition party. The impact of the political system as an influential variable in determining the degree of freedom of the press makes Colin Legum's claim that the mass media are as much an institution as any of the other political institutions existing in African Political systems a valid one. His observation is that "to talk... of 'press freedom' in idealistic terms is useful only as a guide to action, but it becomes meaningless...if we simply go on to assert the principles by which a free press should be judged, without...relating the conditions for the existence of a free press to the circumstances of the society and its times."[32]

One rarely comes across any literature on Africa's mass media without reference to late Kwame Nkurumah's prescription of what the African mass media must be doing, and which, in fact, led to a systematic control of the mass media in Ghana during his regime. Nkrumah's address before the Pan-African Journalists Conference in Accra, Ghana, in 1963, typifies how the structure of the mass media in most African countries, especially those government-owned media, often determines the degree of freedom of the media and their functional role to the political system. Nkrumah said:

The true African journalist very often works for the organ of the political party to which he himself belongs and in whose purpose he believes. He works to serve a society moving in the direction of his own aspirations. How many journalists of the imperialist and neo-colonialist press have this satisfaction?[33]

Speaking on the functional role of the media, he said:

To the true African journalist, his newspaper is a collective instrument of mobilisation and a collective educator...a weapon, first and foremost, to overthrow colonialism and imperialism, and to assist total African independence and unity.... Our revolutionary African press must present and carry forward our revolutionary purpose. This is to establish a progressive political and economic system upon our continent that will free men from want and every form of social injustice and enable them to work out their social and cultural destinies in peace and at ease.[34]

The problem with this kind of defining the functional role of the media by a President of a nation is that criticism of his administration will inevitably be equated with treason. Tom Hopkinson had in mind this pattern of the impact of the political system on the structure of the African mass media and their control when he made the forecast that due to crisis of life and death, and non-tolerance of criticism of the media by the ruling elite, the African mass media could be exterminated before they were properly developed.[35] Another insight into the problem political system poses to free press is given by Frank Barton, a veteran journalist who has contributed significantly through the International Press Institutes, in Lagos and Nairobi, to the training of African journalists. He asserts that the defeat of African newsmen over the fight for the freedom of the media is now *fait accompli*. He claims that the freedom of the mass media does not exist in any recognisable form in Black Africa. He also notes the hypocrisy of the politicians as they "grind the media deeper into the dust, they at the same time proclaim how free their media is," (sic). From East to West Africa, his observation is:

The complete picture of the media in Africa varies only in its degrees: from Uganda, where editors are beaten or burned to death, to the slap-happy military junta of Africa's largest nation, Nigeria, whose engaging bags of tricks for the media ranges (sic) from horse-whipping to stripping and head-shaving. But at least in Nigeria there is one freedom left the journalist, and a very real one it is, too. He is allowed to sue the government when they (sic) beat him up.[36]

But Colin Legum thinks that "to talk of the 'decline of the free press in Africa' is to talk of something that never existed." With the pattern of the evolution of the mass media of Africa in mind, and the generic problem of structure that became embedded as they developed, Legum goes on to note that "it will readily be seen... that the circumstances or opportunities for a free press or for other forms of mass media were hardly propitious."[37] But Peter "Pan" Enahoro, a one-time self-exiled Nigerian journalist, subjectively explores this problem when he remarks:

The African's reluctance to invest in the press is not all economic. The African entrepreneur wishing to go into the newspaper industry finds that in addition to the security his bank will ask for, he must also be politically credit-worthy. It is one of the post-independence experience that African newspapers generally have less freedom to report and criticise today than they did under colonial administrations.[38]

There was not any occasion when, during any civilian administration, a Nigerian newspaper was forcibly closed down. But under the military regimes, such incidents became a common occurrence. A typical case occurred in November, 1969, when armed soldiers occupied the premises of the nation's leading newspaper, the *Daily Times,* for six days.[39] The reason for the occupation, during which period the paper did not publish, was never made known to the general public. During the six-day takeover of the paper, the police detained and interrogated the editor, the news editor, and the managing editor of the paper for three hours.[40]

Unlike the civilian administrations, the military does not hesitate to invade a newspaper room to stop an editorial or any major news story it has a prior knowledge of focusing on a controversial topic the government does not like. That was the experience of the *Daily Sketch* sometime during the reign of one deposed military regime:

Police have raided the offices of the Government-owned *Daily Sketch* in Ibadan and removed an editorial intended for the next day's issue....The newspaper appeared with no editorial comment and the opinion column instead had the slogan, "Long live one Nigeria." A front-page statement said, "Readers, please pardon our slight errors. We had unexpected visitors just before going to press...." The two-hour raid was carried out by 50 plain-clothes and uniformed policemen...who demanded to see the editorial and then removed it. Three people, including the night editor, were taken away but released after questioning.... Police told the staff during the raid that the activities of the newspaper within the last three months had been embarrassing to the Government.[41]

When some vocal press mounted a nationwide anti-corruption campaign, one of Nigeria's deposed military administrations threatened to, and did eventually, take unpleasant measures against the press. The then national police boss and commissioner of internal affairs stated:

The press has recently mounted a campaign against the Federal Government putting pressure on it to institute an enquiry into the conduct of certain government functionaries and levelling accusations against individuals. Publishing inciting articles, books, and pamphlets capable of whipping up sectional sentiments and disrupting law and order has become the order of the day. This is nothing short of blackmail. The government will not allow itself to be blackmailed by the press or stampeded into taking any action in any matter of public interest. The Federal Government will no longer tolerate press indiscipline and calculated attempts to undermine its authority. It may be forced to take drastic and unpleasant measures to curb the excess of the press.[42]

From 1966 to 1979 a decree proclaiming a state of emergency existed in Nigeria. The decree empowered the police and the military to arrest and detain anybody without a warrant.[43] The result was the arrest and detention of some editors and newspaper proprietors. The military, after overthrowing the Shagari regime in 1983, reinstated decree two that authorises detention without trial.

In a monolithic political system where political parties are proscribed and the tendency is to maximise public consensus in support of the activities of the regime in power, the coverage of certain exiled political leaders by the national press is even seen as a threat to the system maintenance of the regime in power. In May 1977, an incident occurred in Nigeria whereby the national security men impounded 50,000 copies of the *Newbreed* magazine at the Murtala Muhammed airport as the consignment was being discharged from an aircraft.[44] The particular issue of the *Newbreed* had carried the second portion of a two-part interview with Chukwuemeka Ojukwu, the former Igbo leader during the abortive Biafran secession. The editor-in-chief of the magazine and his other two officials were asked to be reporting to the police headquarters for interrogation.[45]

Certain outstanding specific cases have been used to demonstrate how a political system or political type can influence the degree of press freedom in Nigeria. Three claims can be made: (1) *The degree of press freedom in a country is related to the type of its political administration.* (2) *In a country where there is no democratically elected government, the freedom of the press will be at its lowest ebb.* (3) *Press freedom seems to thrive better in a pluralistic political system than in a one-party or monolithic (military) political system of government.*

Coopting

One of the most influential variables determining the degree of media freedom in Nigeria is *coopting*. The government uses certain preferential treatments to "buy" over the most influential journalists in the country. On numerous occasions, administrations in Nigeria had imprisoned journalists. The results were unexpected backlash on the government from the outraged general public, especially if the imprisoned journalist happened to be one of its most favourites. And governments in Nigeria eventually adopted the policy of appointing their influential critics in the media to top posts within the government.

When this tactic started working effectively for the government, many media professionals who used to be hypercritical of the government when its policies became questionable, softened their criticism so as to be appointed to top management post within the regime. The following instances will illustrate this point. In May 1975, a former managing director of the leading national daily, the *Daily Times,* told an international audience that "we have a benevolent military government.... There is no censorship, and no journalists, to the best of my knowledge, are at present in prison."[46] The fact was that to the best of this director's knowledge, many journalists were in prison at that time. One of the most celebrated cases that involved the Amnesty International even came to public attention in Nigeria through the pages of the *Daily Times* which he was the managing director. And the fact was that the same *Daily Times* published many statements the London-based Amnesty International sent to the Nigerian government asking for the release of the journalist. When eventually the Gowon regime was toppled in a coup d'état, the new administration released the journalist in August 1975, two months after the former managing director of the *Daily Times* had said that no journalist was in prison in Nigeria. The journalist used the columns of the *Sunday Times* (the Sunday edition of the *Daily Times*) to describe his prison ordeal, thus:

> In many ways, my detention was unique. It was unique because never before in the history of our country has a mere news gatherer been selected out for what amounted to systematic destruction. For upwards of twenty-three months, I was kept in the most nefarious solitary confinement.... So thorough was the police method of torture that I had thought the end was just near.... Any Nigerian with human sympathy will be shocked at the indignities which are inflicted on fellow Nigerians at the Maximum Security prison, Kirikiri. As a detainee I watched and occasionally wept how a Nigerian prison was systematically being converted into a Robben Island ....It was a very nasty experience...worth passing

through.[47]

The director who had no knowledge of journalists being in prison in the country was shortly appointed a state commissioner, and was later appointed to a higher Federal post in the area of mass media. This is one way coopting works. Just say something good about the government if you are a popularly known national journalist and a critic of the government, you are assurred of an important post when the government makes an offer to you. The point being made here should not be mistaken to mean that journalists who are qualified to help serve their national government, when they are called upon to do so, should refuse. Rather the problem is that of human greed for power whereby the human conscience is betrayed.

Another glaring instance of the effectiveness of the government coopting of journalists which invariably leads to less press criticsm was that of a Federal Government Commissioner of Information whose attitude embarrassed his former colleagues in the profession. He was a journalist and a former manager of a state broadcasting station. But once he was appointed the Federal Commissioner of Information for the entire country, he started unleashing such attacks on the journalists that the questions were being asked why he remained quiet and did not criticise his colleagues publicly when he was with them in the profession? In a televised national news interview, he condemned what he referred to as adversary journalism.[48] The Commissioner's utterances got so disturbing that the *Daily Times* editorialised, in part:

A Commissioner for Information is today required not merely to be an apologist for government. He is ... to preside over a momentous debate regarding the future health of the press in Nigeria. Mr. Ogunlade...seems to have opted voluntarily for the role of an interested advocate, and thrown all detachment to the wind. In numerous appearances, he has persistently voiced forceful opinions on every imaginative subject, on press freedom, on government control of the news media, on the quality of journalism in the Nigerian press, on the necessary distinction between Western and Third World journalism. And at all times his favourite mode of argument has been that of outraged defence counsel, ready to confound all opposition by the sheer weight of unctuous rhetoric.

In all the flurry of excitement...Mr. Ogunlade has caused in recent weeks, it is necessary to pause for a while to recall that he has been barely a month at his new post... four weeks are much too brief for anyone to have developed such definitive responses to so many questions.[49]

The above instances indicate that press freedom in Nigeria is precarious if those who are supposed to be its guardians are easily attracted to join the government in helping to suppress it. Coopting is then a systematic way of silencing the press as some national journalists vie for top government appointments by softening their criticism of bad policies of the government.

The Judiciary

The Nigerian judiciary is a very important influential variable in determining the degree of press freedom. Many important cases had gone before it and some of them had set the pace in landmark decisions. One of such landmark decisions came sometime in December, 1969, when one F.C.O. Coker instituted a libel suit against the *Daily Times* and the *Nigerian Tribune* for a series of malicious articles and editorial comments against him. During the trial, the *Daily Times* claimed to have been protected by privileged reporting, and that what it published on Mr. Coker amounted to fair comment on a public official. But in his final verdict, the judge, among other things, observed:

> In matters of freedom of speech, everybody is entitled to make statements as long as they are fair. But nobody is entitled to make statements which are untrue and which are likely to lower the reputation of others in the eyes of right thinking men. I take it that in law, for the defence of fair comments to succeed, there must be sufficient cause to warrant the comments. But no fair minded man could hold this to be so in this case. It behoves a writer to know what portions of his writing are facts and what are comments. Failure to exhibit this distinction carried (sic) its own risks and such a person cannot succeed by the defence of fair comments.[50]

The substance of *Daily Times* news reports and editorials on Coker was based on a report of an inquiry into the affairs of some establishments of the government of Lagos State. In short, the *Daily Times* called for the forced resignation of Mr. Coker due to his appointments into more than one government post.[51] It also noted that Mr. Coker and the former governor of Lagos State were cousins, and that Mr. Coker's appointments were tantamount to nepotism.[52] It said that no one man was indispensable, in response to an alleged answer from the office of the former military governor of Lagos State.[53] The judge found the comments and articles in the newspapers against Mr. Coker to be defamatory and malicious. Noting that they were libelous and that malice had been established, he awarded about $25,000 damages to the plaintiff on the suit against the *Daily Times*, and about $4,000 for the plaintiff in the second suit he brought against the *Nigerian Tribune*.[54]

Another landmark case came in 1975. A correspondent of the *Nigerian Observer* had reported about a dispute between the Rivers State union of teachers and that state's Ministry of Education. But for the fact that the article appeared on the 31st birthday of the Military governor of the Rivers State, Alfred Diete-Spiff, the reporter was arrested, flogged, and had his hair and beard shaved. The reporter was hospitalised. He instituted a court action. The verdict was astonishing. The reporter was awarded $1,600.00 for each stroke of the cane he received from those who tortured him; he was also awarded damages for the shaving of his hair and beard. His total damages came to about $35,000.00.[55] The Rivers State Government was asked by the court to pay the damages awarded against it.

In fairness to the Nigerian judiciary, it could be said that it has effectively acted as the "football umpire (referee)" between the press, the government, and the people of Nigeria. In some of its decisions, the excessiveness of irresponsible journalism has been checked. Also, it has protected the freedom of the newsmen to report without any threat to their lives. The two cases that have been used here, as examples out of many, illustrate these points. However, there had been some instances where some court rulings had been overturned by the military when such rulings did not favour the latter.[56] In some instances some military regimes had had to make sure that they appointed the judges/justices they were certain would rule in their favour when a controversial issue came before them.

Professional and Ethical Responsibility

The problem of developing a socially responsible press is one of the variables undermining the issue of freedom of the press in Nigeria. Some Nigerian journalists do not know that the power to disseminate and control the flow of information to a heterogeneous audience entails a high degree of responsibility and maturity. Some do not even know that the power of the media could spell the doom of someone's career. To some, to be a journalist is a license and privilege above all others. The argument is that the media are functioning as "watchdogs" against the excess of those in power, hence every topic is emotionally handled without ascertaining its accuracy.

Some of the most inimical laws inhibiting the freedom of the mass media in Nigeria were enacted to check the irresponsibility of the mass media practitioners in the country. The origin of the "Public Officers (Protection Against False Accusation) Decree 1976" and its version of Decree Number Four of 1984 were the aftermath of the Ohonbamu trial and *Guardian's* prior publication of a list of ambassadors. The accused, late Ohonbamu, a Senior Lecturer in Law at the University of Lagos, and also the publisher of a magazine - *African Spark* - had accused a former Head of State, prior to the latter's death, of corruption and acquisition of ill-gotten wealth. The following was part of his editorial in the *Spark* that came at a time when the late Head of State was carrying out the most courageous cleaning up of corruption in all levels of government in Nigeria:

But for an effective cleaning operation, we of this paper appeal to Brigadier Murtala Muhammed to let charity begin from home. If he should take the initiative by declaring his own assets and passing the ones he can't account for to the state, then the war against corruption is half won. The present nation-wide whispering campaign being waged against him about his own alleged property in Kano and his fleet of vehicles must have been crushed before any damage is done to his image and regime. After him all his associates must follow suit, then none of us can hide under the slogan "physician heal thyself".[57]

Ohonbamu was consequently charged with sedition against the state of Nigeria for publishing what was "likely to cause fear and alarm to the public knowing or having reason to believe that such a statement is false."[58]

Towards the end of the trial, Ohonbamu pleaded guilty. He was verbally reprimanded and set free. But the Federal Government, a few days later, promulgated the "Public Officers Protection Decree Against False Accusation."

The point here is that some Nigerian journalists and publishers still believe that one can attack anyone and the government under the cloak of journalism and freedom of the press without bothering to ascertain the facts of their allegations. In any democratic society, the publisher of the above editorial would not go unpenalised if a libel suit was brought against him for malicious assault on a citizen on the pages of a publication. The fact is that he has to prove that the person he has alleged of possessing a fleet of vehicles, does indeed possess them and that they have also been possessed by illegal means, or through kickbacks. Failure to prove this could lead to substantial damages being awarded in favour of the plaintiff. Rather than being professionally responsible, some Nigerian journalists and publishers do let their emotion and dislikeness for someone control their professional competence.

Even the most leading national daily, the *Daily Times,* has on numerous occasions failed to set the pace for responsibility in the profession of journalism. It has on several occasions attacked people and officials without first bothering to properly investigate into the issue at stake. Immediately the Gowon administration was overthrown in 1975, the new military rulers ordered city councils in all the major cities and towns in the federation to change the names of streets named after those members of the toppled regime. When the Lagos City Council carried out this order, the *Daily Times,* not caring to find out why the Lagos City Council did what it had done, editorialised, in part:

...the announcement at the weekend by the Lagos City Council to change the name of Yakubu Gowon Street in Lagos to its old one of Broad Street is too petty a decision and totally unnecessary...it is the height of meanness on the part of the Lagos City Council authorities to want to wipe out his (Gowon's) name in the history of this nation. Rather than engage in the fruitless exercise of street-name changing, the council should concern itself with its many problems. Evidence of its failure is the deplorable state of the city of Lagos and its environ. The ordinary man... is more concerned with the quality of life that the government can provide than to bother himself over what street is named after whom. The overriding interest of the LCC should be how to make life worth living in its areas of jurisdiction. It should first of all clear the bankruptcy beam from its eyes before looking for diversionary issues like the street-name changing. We appeal to the supreme authorities in this country to call the meanness and pettiness of the LCC to order.[59]

The Town Clerk to the Lagos City Council came up, two days later, with the following rebuttal:

I wish to register my protest about the content of the editorial in yesterday's issue of your paper. This editorial, which concerns the change of the names of certain streets on Lagos Island, is not only unfair to the Lagos City Council, but it is also insulting and uninformed. It is insulting in that the language used by the editor against a statutory body like the city council is very unbecoming of a national paper. It is also uninformed because if the editor had taken the trouble to find out, he would have come across the facts about change of street names as contained in the Federal Government statement of August 18, 1975. In that statement, the government had made it clear that Nigerians living and dead, who had contributed outstandingly to the progress of this country, will be appropriately honoured at the right time.... It is therefore most unfair for the *Daily Times* to use abusive language in condemning the action of the Lagos City Council which was in accordance with a deliberate policy of the Federal Government as passed down to the council.... It is in the interest of this country that editors should check their facts before going to the press and that they should also use refined language in their comments on public issues.[60]

There are countless instances when the Nigerian press has either consciously or unconsciously engaged in careless reportage that lacked professional discipline. Needless to say that the consequence has been promulgation and enactment of laws that have reduced the newspapers to mere public relations bulletins and official government news releases. This has, of course, adversely affected the freedom of the press. Unethical conducts and lack of professional responsibility form a variable that threatens press freedom.

Media Expertise

The problem of professional responsibility is related to the degree of media expertise. No one can become a medical doctor or a lawyer without the formal education which, among other things, teaches ethics, responsibility and expert knowledge in the profession. But one can become a publisher and journalist without going to the university or any other institution of higher learning for a formal education to acquire expert knowledge of the profession. It is this deficiency in formal education in the profession of journalism in Nigeria that has led to semi-professional media with the result that the cause of freedom of the mass media is retarded.

There is the urgent need for a formal education in the profession. Without formally educating the personnel of the media, the media's management will always be under the control of excited rascals. This will lead to a great disarray and confusion.

It is essential for news reporters, talents (anchormen), top personnel management and other important staff to acquire the professional knowledge in their field through formal education. Non-acquisition of higher knowledge at the university level has already created a formidable social demarcation between an average media reporter and a government official whom he goes to interview. In such a situation, there is a cultural awareness on the part of the reporter that he is interviewing his superior in every respect. In certain situations, a senior official delegates a member of his junior staff to give an interview on the inquiry the reporter seeks when he becomes too conscious of his superiority in social ranking. Formal professional education seems to be the only way to surmounting such obstacles that are on the way of free media.

However, some institutions of formal education in mass media have been established in Nigeria. They have started making a great impact on media profession. There are the Departments of Mass Communication at the University of Nigeria, Nsukka; University of Lagos, Lagos; Bayero University, Kano; University of Maiduguri, Maiduguri; and University of Cross River State, Uyo. Nsukka and Lagos award both bachelor's and Master's degrees in Mass Communication. University of Lagos (UNILAG) started the Ph.D degree programme with the admission of four students during the 1986/87 academic year. Bayero, Maiduguri and Uyo award only bachelor's degree. Also, principal newspapers and broadcasting stations have their own on-the-job training programmes. About nine polytechnics and the Institute of Management and Technology (IMT), Enugu, admit students for a-two-year and a-four-year diploma programme leading to Ordinary National Diploma (OND), and Higher National Diploma (HND), in Mass Communication. It is therefore hoped that in all these academic institutions, the possession of higher knowledge and mastery of the profession will tremendously aid the cause of press freedom and build a great degree of respectability in the profession before the national audience.

Cultural Heterogeneity

It is the diversity of autonomous cultures within the Nigerian society that has promoted the relative degree of freedom of the mass media that exists in the nation. The heterogeneity of the culture is undoubtedly one of the leading factors that promote press freedom. There are high degrees of competition and diversity in value systems within the various cultures in the nation. Despite systematic government ownership of the media, the media are still reflecting the cultures and interests of their geographical locations. Frank Okwu Ugboajah had perceptively noted that "cultural plurality in the Nigerian society acts as a stop gap in attempts towards media control by the government. This also helps to bring sanity and compromise among Nigerian people in the resolution of conflicts."[61] It is not an exaggeration to state that the heterogeneity of the Nigerian society acts as an effective barometer in measuring the degree of freedom of the mass media.

However, cultural heterogeneity can also be seen as a double-edged sword. During the First Republic, as we have previously observed, local government council areas in the former Eastern Region banned the circulations of certain newspapers from Lagos and the Western Region in their areas of jurisdiction during the 1965 political crisis in the Western Region. In retaliation, the Western Region government also had to ban some newspapers from the East and Lagos, and forbade citizens within its jurisdiction to listen to radio ENBS, Enugu. Such actions do not, in any way, promote the freedom of the press in any democratic society, no matter how pluralistic such a society is in its cultures.

Despite this shortcoming, however, the orientation of both the Nigerian press and society makes it hard for a dictator to emerge. The mass media of various states act as a sort of "watchdog" over the developments of events in each of the states of the federation. The Amakiri incident (the *Nigerian Observer* correspondent in the Rivers State whose hair and beard were shaved, and who was flogged by the authorities in the Rivers State) proves this contention. Whereas the Rivers State newspaper, the *Nigerian Tide,* failed to report that there was a conflict between the state's union of teachers and the Ministry of Education, the newspaper of another state, Bendel State's *Observer*, saw the conflict between the two bodies in the Rivers State as a news worthy event to be reported to the Nigerian general public. This shows that if the government of one state muffles and gags its own media, Nigeria's cultural pluralism makes it possible for another state's media to disclose the hidden fact of another state.

Literacy

The concept of freedom of the mass media can only take root in Nigeria if the literacy rate increases. The high rate of illiteracy (about 80%) is such that only a minority of the population reads the newspapers. Some previous administrations have had to defend their clamp down on newspapers based on mass illiteracy. A former Federal Government Commissioner of Information during the Gowon Military Administration, went to the extent of saying that majority of Nigerians in the rural areas of the country were unaware of the existence of an emergency decree that was in force from 1966 to 1979.[62] Literacy therefore constitutes an important variable if mass media freedom is to take place in Nigeria. The belief is that if people are able to read and write, they will acquaint themselves with their rights and this would invariably promote the freedom of the press. But if only a minority can read, the freedom of the media becomes precarious.

The picture of literacy rate in Nigeria is very promising. With the introduction of a compulsory universal primary education scheme that lasted for a brief period, and many tertiary institutions being built at a great rate, illiteracy will be reduced to a very low level in the very near future. In fact the strength of the media depends on how many people can read and write. Literacy then becomes an important factor in determining the degree of freedom of the mass media in Nigeria.

The Audience Indifference and the Low Esteem of the Mass Media Profession

The profession of mass media suffers from a very low image credibility before the general audience in Nigeria. Members of the general public are indifferent and aloof in the struggle for a free press in the country. Tom Hopkinson has noted the inability of the African mass media to establish their influence before the masses, and to become respectable organs that are capable of shaping community opinion because the freedom of the press has become a highly unpopular cause, and the media are viewed with suspicion. The problem is compounded by the indifference of those residing in the villages where the bulk of the population lives. Because the whole concept of mass media and the philosophy of their freedom are Western in origin and context, it becomes impossible for the African media to rally enough public support. Hopkinson vividly describes this problem of the inability of the African mass media to muster national support, thus:

> To the man in the African village, the abolition of press freedom - where it exists - would mean little or nothing. Identifying himself with his new government, the first thing he asks of it is that it should be strong, should dominate. He expects the radio - which bears as a rule its country's name - to be the mouth-piece of the country's government, and though he accepts that the press is more independent than the radio, he often does not understand why it should be allowed to criticise, to "speak against", authority. Press freedom survives at all partly because, despite their quarrels with the press, many African leaders value the tradition of a free

press; having quite justifiably exploited press freedom on the way up, they have an honest hesitation about kicking the ladder away now they are on top. Partly also because an independent press in known to be highly valued in the Western World, and it is to the Western world that the newly independent states look for most of the financial help and technical know-how they so desperately need.[63]

There is a general apathy or indifference to the struggle for press freedom in Nigeria. The mass media are yet to garner people's support in their favour. The following two letters to editors of a prestigious newspaper, the *Daily Times,* and a prestigious weekly magazine, the *West Africa*, respectively, sum up the audience reluctance to support the media:

Although I am opposed to the arbitrary arrest of journalists in Nigeria, I believe that the journalist himself is not totally blameless. Why does the fault lie solely with the leadership or does the journalist have questions to answer as well? What is it about the Nigerian press system that makes it ineffective in society? The microphone, if properly used, can accomplish the following tasks in society: wipe out dictatorship; make civil war unnecessary; make military coups unnecessary; enforce social justice and assert equal rights; make democracy more successful in a communal society. The simple code to accomplishing these tasks is "give the mass media to the people". Do the mass of the Nigerian people have access to radio, TV, and newspapers to tell their own stories and lay their complaints before the country? How can journalism succeed when... 70,000,000 people... have no place in the country's mass media? Nigeria's problems remain until we realise that for a country to succeed nobody must be ignored.[64]

Two years after the above observation, another member of the media audience quipped:

I read with interest the article..."press and the government "... which stated that the present government is very fair to the press and that no Nigerian journalist lives in fear of detention or arrest which was the order of the day with past governments.... I wish to state here that this has been so because journalists today are not as daring as their counterparts of yesteryears and they dance too much to the tune of the government of the day. I cannot blame them because here in Nigeria the "sword is mightier than the pen." An average reporter in Nigeria knows his bounds as far as news gathering is concerned. He dabbles into predictable sources of news like news briefings, tribunals, parade and the like instead of 'engaging' in investigative reporting which is of more importance to ordinary citizens. In a situation where journalists know the extent to which they could operate, they would continue to enjoy a fair treatment from the government in power. The question of a fair treatment could only come in where journalists are free to publish and be damned and NOT where they operate in or out of fear.[65]

The reputation of the Nigerian press got worse when a former Army Chief of Staff, David Ejoor, publicly accused Nigerian journalists of being politically and financially corrupt.[66] A foreign correspondent in Nigeria at the time of this allegation against the Nigerian journalists, noted that "...one can find individual Nigerian newsmen who will take money or gifts for doing special favours. But ... Nigeria also has journalists who are not corrupt and whose skills and dedication compare favourably with those of newsmen elsewhere."[67] A famous Nigerian journalist, Peter Enahoro, ("Peter Pan") makes the following analysis which also gives credence to low image perception and non-recognition of the profession by the members of the general public in Nigeria:

> There is... this image that the profession of journalism is filled with underfed "boys" who are forever thirsty and who use their wits to corner free drinks and coerce donations towards the taxi fare back to the office. The reference to journalists as "press boys" with a stress on "boys" is standard among officials and symptomatic of the image in which the profession is held.... Even visiting foreign journalists are subject to the treatment which it is considered press "boys" merit.... African journalists are well informed on scandals, less on constructive information. Ministers consider them useful allies in waging personal feuds, but will not entrust them with important guidelines and background information. The sum total is that the African journalist is not as well informed as he should be. Consequestly he is accused of frivolity and professional incompetence.[68]

It is this negative and low credibility image of the journalist by the audience the press communicates information to that adversely contributes to the realisation of a fully guaranteed free media. The above analyses have shown that the journalists have little or no public support when they are in confrontation with the government. One of those interviewed during an empirical research project on people's perception of the functional roles of the media in crisis situations, made this comment:

> The Nigerian press shouldn't be free because we have not reached that stage of adversary journalism in our national development. After all, what is the percentage of the people who read the newspapers? Also, Nigeria isn't as developed as America, or any other Western community. The media in this country, I mean the press, concentrate on pointing out only the weakness of the government without pointing out the good side. The press is very negative in its attitude towards the government.[69]

The Nigerian press needs to re-orient its strategy. No mass media can enjoy freedom to disseminate information without the audience support. The audience indifference and low esteem of the press are two inseparable variables compounding the problem of achieving a free and virile press in Nigeria.

Other Related Factors

Among other factors that relate to the degree of freedom of the mass media in Nigeria are the following:

Social Structure: The society is highly stratified. Seniority in age and one's educational qualification are highly cherished values such that exposing the misbehaviour of one's senior is considered a social nuisance and disrespect. There is, therefore, the tendency of journalists trying to accept the social status quo and an attitude of "I am not the one going to change this country over-night". Most cultures in the society are authoritarian as opposed to egalitarian in nature.

Economic System: Nigeria practises both laissez-faire economy and state ownership of some basic means of production. However, the state is richer than any private sector. It is therefore not surprising to find the government-owned media thriving while privately-owned media are dying, resulting from economic hardship. When shortage of newsprints occurred some years ago, while the government-owned newspapers hardly felt it, some privately-owned newspapers reduced the number of pages they normally produced to the barest minimum so as to survive. Also, before the establishment of newsprint manufacturing in the country the private media owners used to pay heavy custom duties to import newsprints from abroad. In fact, if the government had decided then to close down the few private media in the country, it could have done so by quadrupling the custom duty paid on newsprints. In the past, low circulation of some private media had forced them to fold up. Economic survival thus becomes a determinant factor in the maintenance of the freedom of the media. The point is that if economic hardships lead to the folding up of private media, there will be a missing dimension in news reporting to a great extent.

Technical development of communication infrastructure: Lack of effective communication networks can lead to the derailment of larger communication systems. Such communication networks include efficient transportation systems - air, sea, land, etc.-; good and reliable telephones; as well as constant energy (electricity) supply source. These communication systems are still at the infant stage in the country. Without efficient delivery system and communication network, the freedom of the mass media will always sound strange to many members of the Nigerian public.

FOOTNOTES

1. Newspaper (Prohibition of Circulation)Decree 1967. Decree No. 17.
2. T.O. Elias, ed., *Nigerian Press Law*. Lagos: University of Lagos and Evans Brothers Ltd. 1969. p.1.
3. Increase Coker, *Landmarks of the Nigerian Press*, Lagos. 1968 p.51.
4. Kalu Ezera, *Constitutional Developments in Nigeria*, p. 50.
5. *Ibid.*
6. *Ibid.*
7. *Ibid.*
8. *Ibid.*
9. Newspapers (Amendment) Act 1964. (Lagos).
10. *Ibid.*
11. This has been quoted from Ezera's *Constitutional Developments in Nigeria*, p. 286. The editorial appeared in *West African Pilot*, Lagos, on July 24, 1963.
12. The circulation of Newspapers Decree 1966. Decree No. 2.
13. *Ibid.*
14. T.O. Elias, *Nigerian Press Law*, p. 133.
15. See Footnote no. 1 above.
16. *Ibid.*
17. Public Officers (Protection Against False Accusation) Decree 1976. Decree No. 11.
18. *Ibid.*
19. Public officers (Protection Against False Accusation) Decree 1984.
20. *Ibid.*
21. *Ibid.*
22. *Ibid.*
23. *Constitution of the Federal Republic of Nigeria*, 1979.
24. Luke Uka Uche: "Government-Media Relations in Nigeria: Factors Influencing the Degree of Press Freedom." Forthcoming in *Unilag Communication Review*. Accepted for publication on April 9, 1986.
25. "Press Freedom in Africa." Paper presented by Alhaji Babatunde Jose, former chairman and Managing Director of the *Daily Times* of Nigeria Limited, to the Royal African Society, London, April 10, 1975.
26. St. Jorre, *The Nigerian Civil War*, pp. 349-350.
27. In an interview on this problem of press freedom with a high ranking NBC management official on May 16, 1977, I was told, in response to my question of a particular "dash" to a custom officer at a road junction which I witnessed, that government-owned media are forbidden to engage in anything like exposé on government officials because such exposé would discredit the government before the general public.
28. The "Zombie" album Fela and his Afro Beat band had played was a satire on the Nigerian Army. The soldiers were said to have attacked Fela's "republic" as an act of vengeance on the satirical record because one of Fela's drivers had ignored an army order to stop his vehicle which he was driving on a day when vehicles with particular plate digits were forbidden to be on the road. Some soldiers were said to have pursued the driver when he refused to stop. It was then at Fela's residence that some thugs were said to have beaten up one of the soldiers into a state of unconsciousness. Reinforcement came from the Abati barracks that is close to Fela's residence, and a "war" began between the soldiers and Fela's group, whereby the soldiers set Fela's residence ablaze as well as that of his elder brother and others around the "combat" zone.
29. A Senior Lecturer in Education at the University of Lagos, told me of this incident which was later confirmed by many knowledgeable members of the public and some editors I talked to about the incident in *The Daily Times* office.
30. Frank Okwu Ugboaja, "Nigerian Mass Communication Trends in the African Context." *Gazette International Journal of Mass Communications Studies*. Vol. XXII. No. 3 1976 p. 161.
31. 'The *Daily Times*, before the government decision to acquire 60% of its equity, was the first to start the exposé on the Tarka and Daboh affair. This led to Tarka's resignation. The *Daily Times* also started the publication of the Gomwalk and Aku affair. Gomwalk was later exonerated by the Gowon regime. After the Gomwalk affair, the Gowon regime banned sworn affidavit as a ground for accusing a public official of corruption.

But another regime that toppled the Gowon administration found Gomwalk to be highly corrupt after a special commission of inquiry had probed his involvement in certain enterprises. Gomwalk was executed, and his wife imprisoned, for proven accomplice in the abortive coup of February 13, 1976.

32.   Colin Legum, "The Mass Media: Institutions of the African Political Systems." In *Reporting Africa*, pp. 27-38, (p.37).

33.   Kwame Nkrumah, *The African Journalist*. Dar es Salaam: The Tanzania Publishers. December, 1965, p. 10.

34.   *Ibid.*

35.   Tom Hopkinson, "The Press in Africa." In *Africa: A Handbook.* Edited by Colin Legum. Revised edition. New York: Praeger Publishers Co. 1966. pp. 437-226.

36.   Frank Baron, "Black Africa - no press freedom today". *IPI Report* Vol. 24 (June 1975) no. 6., pp. 1-2.

37.   Colin Legum, "The Mass Media: Institutions of the African Political Systems." In *Reporting Africa*, pp. 27-38. (p. 37).

38.   Peter Enahoro, "Africa's Besieged Press." *African Affairs*. No. 21. May, 1973.

39.   Alhaji Babatunde Jose: "Press Freedom in Africa." *African Affairs*. Vol. 74. No. 296. July 1975.

40.   *Ibid.*

41.   "Police Raid Sketch." *West Africa,* September 23, 1974, p. 1175.

42.   *IPI Report*, December 1974 No. 12, p. 8.

43.   *IPI Report.* No. 11, October, 1974.

44.   *Daily Times*, May 5, 1977, p. 1.

45.   *Ibid.*

46.   *IPI Report.* Vol. 24. June 1975, No. 6.

47.   *Sunday Times,* August 24, 1975, p.5.

48   NTA (Lagos) Interview with Ogunlade, the Federal Commissioner of Information on May 5, 1977. He was interviewed by a three-man panel.

49.   *Daily Times*, May 10, 1977, p. 3.

50.   *Ibid.* December 6, 1969.

51.   See the *Daily Times* issues of January 12, January 20, and February 3, all of 1969.

52.   *Ibid.*

53.   *Ibid.*

54.   *Daily Times,* December 6, 1969, pp. 1 & 3.

55.   *IPI Report,* June 1974.

56.   Incident of this type happened in 1969/70 when a Lagos High Court passed a judgment against the government of Lagos State which apparently angered the Federal Government. The latter, in a special decree, overruled the High Court.

57.   This quotation is culled from the *Daily Times*, November 8, 1975, p.1.

58.   *Ibid.*

59.   *Daily Times*, August 18, 1975.

60.   *Ibid.* August 20, 1975

61.   F. Okwu Ugboajah, earlier article cited on the journal *Instant Research on Peace and Violence.* p. 193.

62.   This was one of the major points of Edwin Clark's address before the International Press Institute (African) Assembly, held in Lagos, in May 1975.

63.   Colin Legum, editor, *Africa: A Handbook.* p. 437.

64.   *West Africa,* March 3, 1975, p 255.

65.   "Reporters are timid," *Daily Times,* May 4, 1977, p. 13.

66.   "Press and Regime clash in Nigeria", *New York Times.* April 21, 1975, p. 8.

67. · *Ibid.*

68.   *African Affairs.* No. 21, May 1973, p. 31.

69.   These views were expressed by an opinion leader, No. 2, during an interview on a media research project in Lagos, on May 7, 1977.

CONCLUSION

Some of the early theories in political communication, especially those propounded by Lucian W. Pye, Daniel Lerner, Wilbur Schramm, Samuel P. Huntington, etc., postulated on the relationship between the mass media and political development in the developing countries of the world. It is a truism that there is a natural affinity between the media and political structures in the developing nations. The Nigerian experience, as demonstrated in this book, gives credence to this assumption. Nigeria obviously possesses one of the world's most exciting press and electronic media systems. At best, her press and electronic media are most appropriately described as political institutions. The Nigerian mass media systems are microcosmic of Nigeria's crises of political development. Any critical appraisal of the performance of Nigeria's mass media systems has an obvious implication on her political culture. Part of the objectives of this book has been to critically appraise the structures and performance of radio, television, newspapers and the wire service in Nigeria and to relate them within the context of the nation's political, economic and cultural structures. A common theme that one easily discerns from this book is the trend towards a monolithic ownership of the media by the Federal and State Governments. This, of course, has been accentuated, since that fateful January 15, 1966, the first military coup d'état occurred. Since then, a series of successful, abortive and uncovered plans of military coup d'états has taken place. Some of these coup d'etats were selfishly motivated, encouraged by highly corrupt civilian administrators of the First and Second Republics that were indifferent to the welfare of the citizens that elected them to govern.

The net impact of the series of changes in political leadership has been a serious political strain on the nation which has also resulted into fluctuating economic fortunes due to punctuated instability in the nation's political administration. Consequently, a new dimension seems to be emerging in the Nigerian political development process. That new dimension is the constant military intervention in politics. Had it been that military administrations in Nigeria had instilled discipline and honesty in the management of the economy, nobody would have had the audacity to question why the military intervenes in political administration. But military administrations have had the impact of leaving Nigeria in worse political, economic and social conditions than what prevailed prior to the staging of the coup d'états that led to military rules. One hardly comes across military generals anywhere else in the world who retire at the youthful age Nigerian top military officers retire from active service, after accumulating obscene wealth while in government. Of course, the Nigerian military controls the legitimate instrument of violence: lethal arsenals. But their use has been to usurp political administration at the expense of liberal democracy. The military does not, of course, house the best of men with the intelligence quotient for the governing of a complex society that Nigeria is. In years to come, those politically ambitious military officers will have to make a hard decision as to whether to opt for a reputable gentlemanly career in the military in which the acquisition of filthy wealth through gunning one's way into the State House is seen as a vice and unmilitary; or to become outright military politicians and dictators through the barrel of the gun; or to shun military career and work towards becoming a civilian politician. Another option is to wait until one's retirement from active military service. Military coup d'états and subsequent military rules have had tremendous impacts in the structure, administration and contents of the Nigerian mass media. In most instances the military impacts on the mass media have been overwhelmingly negative. An outstanding case that readily comes to one's mind was the notorious Decree Four of the Buhari regime.

Also by implication and on the basis of the intentions and provisions of the 1982 Electoral Act on the National Advisory Council on government-owned media, there seemed to be a general belief on the part of both communication policy and law makers in Nigeria during the Second Republic that the mass media had the power to directly influence the outcome of elections or any other national issue. Presumably, they also believed that repetitive exposure to mass media messages could change the voting pattern of the electorates. This was apparently the thinking of the majority members of the defunct National Assembly when they passed the 1982 Electoral Act into law that, among other things, provided for the setting up of a National Advisory Council (NAC) to supervise those Federal and State Government-owned mass media (radio, television and newspapers) three months before and one month after elections.

The last chapter of this book, in part, highlighted on the specificity of some acts of the First Republic Parliament and Second Republic National Assembly, military decrees and the Constitution of the Federal Republic of Nigeria as they affected (and still do affect) the mass media institutions of the country. One easily realises that the uniqueness of all the laws as they affect the mass media industry, with the exception of the ill-fated Decree Four of 1984, is that they are mostly directed against the newspapers alone. There is hardly any particular legislation that its enactment is targeted to the electronic media. One can understand such a partiality in view of the fact that only the Federal and State Governments have the constitutional mandate to own radio and television broadcasting systems in the country. In the area where private citizens are allowed to operate their own media, especially in the area of the newspaper industry, laws are enacted to check them.

The degree of freedom the mass media will exercise in future will greatly depend on the extent to which journalists become aware of citizens' civil liberties. The freedom of the mass media should be of paramount impor- tance to any government that seeks to develop and enhance the knowledge of its people. It was Thomas Jefferson, one of the founding fathers of the United states, who has been credited with saying that if he were asked to choose between a government without a newspaper and a newspaper without a government, that he would not hesitate to prefer the latter. But govern- ments in Nigeria would not hesitate to prefer the former. The problem of freedom of the press in Nigeria entails an understanding among the press, the government, and the people of Nigeria. It is essential that there be a free press which the public uses to critically appraise the activities of those who govern them. A muffled press cannot hold a government accountable to the people; it must be free to function. Suffice it to say that in Nigeria, combina- tions of those factors identified in chapter seven determine the degree of her press freedom. It is hard to say that press freedom does or does not exist. The nation's press environment is influenced by various factors, some of which this book has analysed. Also the Federal and State Governments, as the main financiers and owners of the various media systems, influence the nation's press performance, in terms of freedom, due to their participation in media ownership.

The way modern mass communication systems evolved in Nigeria ham- pered their neutrality in mass politics and constructive criticism of the politi- cal system. This was largely due to parochial interests and tribal loyalties as the media championed the cause of their tribesmen. Also, the British colonial administrators and their policies were the main targets of opposition by the early Nigerian press. No wonder then that when the British left, after Nigeria's independence in 1960, the media had to look for someone or some- thing to oppose because the style had been geared towards insult, ludicrous and unsubstantiated accusations and sensationalism.

The evolution of the modern mass media systems leads to an inescapable conclusion that the media originated from the political structure of the country; hence their integration with the politics and interests of the various ethnic constituencies within the nation. The media were not neutral during the Nigerian Civil War. They actively supported the government of their geographical locations. They also acted as the leading organ of the regional and state governments in the articulation of the interests and needs of their constituencies in the federation. The following observation of Frank

Ugboajah's confirms this "...mass media behaviour appears moulded by the fact of geographical administrative location, independent of ownership.... Their attitude is usually a function of geographical location more than ownership, and certainly guided by the ethnic constituencies (they) serve."[1]

The trend in Nigeria's mass media philosophy and monolithic ownership of the press by the Federal and state governments is towards evolving a national consciousness. But the means of achieving it seems to be geared towards an imposition of consensus via the press. The latent dysfunction of this style is that constructive criticism on certain national issues could be misunderstood for, and equated with disloyalty. The imprisonment of two *Guardian* reporters in 1984 to twelve months, each, and a fine of N 50,000 ($60,000) against the *Guardian* for carrying the reporters' news stories that publicly disclosed the names of Nigeria's high commissioners and ambassadors before the military government made public the appointments, support this observation. Whatever be the case, be it military junta or civilian administration, the Nigerian mass media cannot be separated or divorced from the Nigerian politics. Whatever the Bible means to the Christian faith, and the Koran to the Muslim religion, is what the press means to Nigerian politics and politics of any social system that embodies democracy. The Nigerian press has effectively set the agenda and tempo of the Nigerian politics, from Nnamdi Azikiwe's nationalistic *West African Pilot* to Moshood Abiola's adventurous *National Concord.*

FOOTNOTE

1. Frank Okwu Ugboajah. "Nigerian Mass Media Behaviour On Development Issues of Conflict." *Instant Research On Peace and Violence.* Vol. VI. No. 4. 1976. p. 193.

BIBLIOGRAPHY

African Encyclopaedia. London: Oxford University Press. 1974.

Ainslie, Rosalynde. *The Press in Africa: Communications Past and Present.* New York: Walker and Co. 1967.

Akinjogbin, I.A. "Dahomey and Yoruba in the Nineteenth century." In *Africa in the Nineteenth and Twentieth Centuries.* Joseph C. Anene and Godfrey M. Brown. Eds. Ibadan: Ibadan University Press, 1966.

American Universities Field Staff. Reports Services on Countries: West African Series. V. 4-5, New York: American Universities Field Staff, Inc. 1961.

Anene, J.C. "The Peoples of Benin, the Niger Delta, Congo and Angola in the Nineteenth Century." In *AFRICA in the Nineteenth and Twentieth Centuries.* Joseph C. Anene and Godfrey N. Brown, eds. Ibadan: Ibadan University Press. 1966.

Baker, George W. et al. ed. *Man and Society in Disaster.* New York: Basic Books, Inc. 1962.

Barghausen, Alfred F. "Technical Problems of Spectrum Utilization." In *Broadcasting in Africa.* Edited by Sydney W. Head, Philadelphia: Temple University Press. 1974.

Barton, Frank. *African Assignment: The Story of IPI's Six-Year Training Programme in Tropical Africa.* Zurich: International Press Institute. 1969.

Bohannan, Paul and Curtin, Philip. *Africa and Africans* (Rev. edition). Garden City, New York: The Natural History Press. 1971.

Bower, John Waite and Ochs, Donovan J. *Rhetoric of Agitation* Reading, Mass: Addison-Wesley Publishing Co., Inc. 1971.

Bradfield, Robert M. et al. *The International Year Book and Statemen's Who's who* Surrey KTI, England: Kelly's Directories Ltd. 1976.

Broadcast License Renewal. Part 1. No. 93-35. U.S. Government Printing Office. Washington, D.C. 1973.

Browne, Donald R. "Africa: An Overview." In *National and International systems of Broadcasting.* By Walter B. Emery. East Lansing: Michigan State University. Press. 1969.

Coker, Increase. *Landmarks of the Nigerian Press.* Lagos. 1968.

Coleman, James S. *The Politics of the Developing Areas.* Princeton: Princeton University Press. 1966.

Collis, Robert. *Nigeria in Conflict.* London: Secker and Warburg Ltd. 1970.

Crowder, Michael. *The story of NIGERIA*. London: Faber and Faber, 1962, 1966.

Curran, James et al. (editors) *Mass Communication and Society*. Beverly Hills/London: Sage Publications. 1979.

Daura, Mamman. "Editing a Government Newspaper in Nigeria" In *Reporting Africa*. Edited by Olay Stokke. New York: African Publishing Corporation. 1971.

Davidson, Basil. *The Lost Cities of Africa*. Boston: Little, Brown and Co. 1959.

Doob, Leonard. *Communication in Africa: A search for Boundaries*. New Haven: Yale University Press. 1961.

Elias, T.O., editor. *Nigerian Press Law*. Lagos: University of Lagos and Evans Brothers Ltd. 1969.

Emery, W. *Broadcasting and Government Responsibilities and Regulations*. East Lansing: Michigan State University Press. 1971.

Ezera, Kalu. *Constitutional Developments in Nigeria*. Cambridge: Cambridge University Press. 1960, 1964.

Federal Department of Culture. *Draft Cultural Policy for Nigeria* Lagos, 1982.

Federal Ministry of Information. (Lagos). "News From Nigeria." No. 5, Section 10. January 18, 1961.

Federal NIGERIA. Vol. 1, No. 1.1976 and Vol. II, No. 1. 1977. Washington, D.C. The Embassy of Nigeria. Publications and Information Division.

Federal Republic of Nigeria. *Report of the Constitution Drafting Committee Containing the Draft Constitution*. Vol. I. Lagos: Federal Ministry of Information, Printing Division. 1976.

Federal Republic of Nigeria Reports of the Constitution Drafting Committee. Vol. II. Lagos: Federal Ministry of Information, Printing Division. 1976.

Federal Republic of Nigeria Third National Development Plan 1975-80. Revised Volume II. Lagos: The Central Planning Office Federal Ministry of Economic Development. 1976.

Feit, Edward. *The Armed Bureaucrats*. Boston: Houghton Mifflin Company. 1973.

Fisher Glen. *American Communication in a Global Society*. Norwood, New "Jersey: Ablex Publishing. Publishing Corporation. 1979.

Flint, John E. *Sir George Goldie and the Making of Nigeria*. London: Oxford University Press. 1960.

Forsyth, Frederick. *The Biafra Story*. Baltimore, Md.: Penguin Books Ltd. 1969.

Foster, George M. *Traditional Cultures: and the Impact of Technological Change*. New York and Evanston: Harper & Row, 1962.

Foster, Philip J. *Africa: South of the Sahara*. New York: The Macmillan Co. 1968.

Garnham, Nicholas. *Structures of Television*. London: British Film Institute. 1973.

Garbner, George et al. (editors). *Communications Technology and Social Policy: Understanding the New "Cultural Revolution"*. New York: John Wiley & Sons, Inc. 1973.

Gerbner, George and Siefert, Marsha (editors). *WORLD COMMUNICA-TIONS: A HANDBOOK* New York: Longman. 1984.

Hachten, William A. "Broadcasting and Political Crisis." In *Broadcasting in Africa: A Continental Survey of Radio and Television.* Sydney Head, ed. op. cit.

Hachten, William A. *Muffled Drums: The News Media in Africa.* Ames: Iowa State University Press, 1971.

Hale, Julian. *Radio Power: Propaganda and International Broadcasting.* London: Paul Elek Ltd. 1975.

Hall, Jr., William Edward. *An Analysis of Post-World War II Efforts to Expand Press Freedom Internationally.* Published Dissertation. State University of Iowa. 1954.

Hamelink, Cees J. *Cultural Autonomy in Global Communications.* New York: Longman. 1983.

Hanna, William John, ed. *Independent Black Africa: The Politics of Freedom.* Chicago: Rand McNally & Co. 1964.

Hartland, Robert. "Press and Radio in Post-Independence Africa." In *Africa and the United States: Images and Realities.* Washington, D.C.: U.S. National Commission for UNESCO. 1962.

Head, Sydney W., ed. *Broadcasting in Africa: A Continental Survey of Radio and Television.* Philadelphia: Temple University Press. 1974.

Hopkinson, Tom. "The Press in Africa." In *Africa: A Handbook.* Edited by Colin Legum. Revised Edition. New York: Praeger Publishers Co. 1966.

Huntington, Samuel O. *Political Order in Changing Societies.* New Haven: Yale University Press. 1968.

Huth, Arno G. *Communications Media in Tropical Africa.* Washington, D.C.: International Co-operation Administration. 1961.

Janowitz, Morris and Hirsch, Paul (editors). *Reader in Public Opinion and Mass Communication.* Third edition. New York: The Free Press. 1981.

Katz, Elihu. "Television as a Horseless Carriage". In *Communications Technology and Social Policy: "Understanding the New Cultural Revolution."* Edited by George Gerbner et al. New York: John Wiley and Sons, Inc. 1973.

Katz, Elihu and Lazarsfeld, Paul F. *Personal Influence.* Glencoe, Illinois: Free Press. 1950.

Kirk-Greene, A.H.M. *Crisis and Conflict in Nigeria.* Vol. I January 1966 - July 1967. London: Oxford University Press. 1971.

Krasnow, Erwin G. and Longley, Lawrence D. *The Politics of Broadcast Regulation.* New York: St. Martin's Press. 1973.

Kushner, James M. "United States Information Agency." In *Broadcasting in Africa.* Edited by Sydney W. Head. Philadelphia: Temple University Press. 1974.

Lasswell, Harold D. "The Structure and Function of Communications in Society." In Lyman Bryson, ed. *The Communication of Ideas.* New York: Harper. 1948.

Lee Chin-Chuan. *Media Imperialism Reconsidered: The Homogenizing of Television Culture.* Beverly Hills/London: Sage Publications. 1980.

Legum, Colin, ed. *AFRICA: A HANDBOOK*. New York: Praeger Publishers. 1966

Legum, Colin "The Mass Media: Institution of the African Political Systems." In *Reporting Africa*. Edited by Olave Stokke. New York: African Publishing Corporation. 1971.

Lerner, Daniel and Schramm, Wilbur, eds. *Communication and Change in the Developing Countries*. Honolulu: East-West Centre Press. 1967.

Mackay, Ian. *Broadcasting in Nigeria*. Ibadan: Ibadan University Press. 1964.

Melody, Williams H. et al. (editors). *Culture, Communication and Dependency*. Norwood, New Jersey: Ablex Publishing Corporation. 1981.

Milton, Edward C. *A Survey of the Technical Development of the Nigerian Broadcasting Corporation*. (Lagos: NBC).

New York Times Index 1975: A Book of Records. Vol. II. New York: The New York Times Co. 1976.

Nigerian Broadcasting Corporation. Annual Report and Statement of Account, 1973/74. Lagos: NBC Publications: 1975.

Nigerian Broadcasting Corporation. Annual Report and Statement of Account, 1975/76. Lagos : NBC Publications : 1976.

Nigerian Broadcasting Corporation Staff Training Department: Programme of Courses. Lagos: NBC Publications 1977.

Nigerian Broadcasting Corporation Growing up with the Nation: The First Twenty Years, 1957-1977. Lagos: NBC Publications 1977.

Nigerian Yearbook, 1975. Lagos: *Daily Times* Publication. 1975.

Niven, Rex. *The War of Nigerian Unity 1967-1970.* Totowa, New Jersey: Rowman and Littlefield. 1970.

Nkrumah, Kwame. *The African Journalist.* Dar es Salaam: The Tanzania Publishers. 1965.

Nordenstreng, Kaarle and Schiller, Herbert I. (editors) *National Sovereignty and International Communication.* Norwood, New Jersey: Ablex Publishing Corporation. 1979.

Nwankwo, Arthur Agwuncha and Ifejika, Samuel Udochukwu. *Biafra: The Making of a Nation.* New York: Praeger Publishers. 1970.

O'Brien, Cruise Rita. "Domination and Dependence in Mass Communication: Implications for the use of Broadcasting in Developing Countries." *Institute of Development Studies Bulletin.* Vol. 6 No. 4. March, 1975.

Offiong, Daniel A. *Imperialism and Dependency.* Enugu: Fourth Dimension Publishing Company Limited. 1980.

Paxton, John, ed. *The Stateman's Year-Book: Statistical and Historical Annual of the States of the World for the Year 1976-1977.* New York: St. Martin's Press. 1976.

Pye, Lucian W. *Aspects of Political Development.* Boston: Little, Brown and Company. 1966.

Pye, Lucian W. ed. *Communication and Political Development.* Princeton, New Jersey: Princeton University Press. 1963.

Roger, Penn. "Broadcasting in Nigeria." Unpublished Master's Thesis. American University. Washington, D.C. 1960.

Ruben, Brent D. editor. *Communication Yearbook I.* New Brunswick, New Jersey: Transaction Books, 1977.

Schramm, Wilbur. *Mass Media and National Development: The Role of Information in the Developing Countries.* Stanford: Stanford University Press. 1964.

Schramm, Wilbur. "Communication Development and the Development Process." In *Communications and Political Development.* Edited by Lucian W. Pye. Princeton, New Jersey: Princeton University Press. 1963.

Sharp, Mary Margaret. "Two Nigerian Coups - A Comparative Study." Unpublished Master's Thesis. The Ohio State University. Columbus, Ohio. 1967.

Sklar, Richard L. and Whitaker, Jr., C.S. "Nigeria." In *Political Parties and National Integration in Tropical Africa.* James S. Coleman and Carl G. Rosberg, Jr. eds. Berkeley & Los Angeles: University of California Press. 1964.

Sklar, Richard L. and Whitaker, Jr. C.S. "The Federal Republic of Nigeria." In *National Unity and Regionalism in Eight African States.* Gwendolen M. Carter, ed. Ithaca, New York: Cornell University Press. 1966.

Sommerlad, Lloyd E. *The Press in Developing Countries.* Sydney: Sydney University Press. 1966.

Taylor, Sidney, ed. *The New Africans: A Guide to the Contemporary History of Emergent Africa and Its Leaders.* New York: G.P. Putnam's Sons. 1967.

Third National Development Plan 1975-1980. Revised Edition. Lagos: The Central Planning Office, Federal Ministry of Economics Development. 1977.

Uche, Ukaonu W. *Education in Nigeria Today: A Critical Analysis and a proposal for change.* Greensboro, North Carolina: Piedmont Press. 1975.

Ugboajah, Frank Okwu (editor). *Mass Communication, Culture and Society in West Africa.* K.G. Saur Munchen. New York. London. Paris: Hans Zell Publishers. 1985.

UNESCO. Developing Information Media in Africa. Reports and Papers on Mass Communication. No. 37. 1962.

UNESCO. Mass Media in Developing Countries. Reports and Papers on Mass Communication. No. 33 1961.

UNESCO. Television: A World Survey. New York: Arno Press. 1972.

UNESCO. Television Traffic - A One-Way Street? A Survey and Analysis of the International Flow of Television Programme Material. Paris: Boudin. 1974.

UNESCO. World Communications: Press, Radio, Television, Film. Paris: UNESCO. 1964.

U.S. Army Area Handbook: NIGERIA. Prepared by Foreign Studies Division, American University, Washington, D.C. Government Printing Office. 1972.

Voice of Nigeria. Lagos: An NBC Publication. 1977.

Waugh, Auberon and Cronje, Suzanne, *Biafra: Britain's Shame.* London: Michael Joseph Ltd. 1969.

Wilcox, Dennis L. *Mass Media in Black Africa: Philosophy and Control.* New York: Praeger Publishers. 1975.

Wilcox, Dennis L. "Press Controls in Black Africa." *Freedom of Information Center Report No. 322.* School of Journalism, University of Missouri, Columbia. June 1974.

Worldmark Encyclopaedia of the Nations: AFRICA. New York: Worldmark Press, Harper and Row. 1967.

Worsley, Peter. *The Third World.* Chicago: The University of Chicago Press. 1964, 1967.

Zolberg, Aristide R. *Creating Political Order: The Party States of West Africa.* Chicago: Rand McNally& Company. 1966.

Scholarly Journals and Papers

Ayo-Vaughan, Sam F."Africa's First TV." *The Journalist's World.* Vol. V. Nos. 3-4. 1967.

Babatunde, Jose. "Press Freedom in Africa." *African Affairs.* Vol. 74. No. 296. July 1975.

Bass, Abraham A. "Promoting Nationhood Through Television in Africa." *Journal of Broadcasting.* Vol. 12. No. 2 (Spring 1970).

Bower, Roger. "In Nigeria Talent is Easiest Problem." *Broadcasting.* May 25, 1964. p. 107.

Coltart, James M. "The Influence of Newspapers and Television in Africa". *African Affairs.* LXII. (July 1963).

Diamond, Leslie A.W. "Bringing Radio and Television to Northern Nigeria." *European Broadcasting Union Review,* 93B. September 1965. p. 27.

Edeani, David Omazo. "Ownership and Control of the Press in Africa." *Gazette.* Vol. XV No. I 1970.

Enahoro, Peter. "Africa's Besieged Press." *Africa.* No. 21 May, 1973.

Callagher, Wes. "Cdds Against Press Freedom in Africa." *Editor and Publisher.* (Aug. 4. 1962).

Garrison, Lloyd. "Biafra Revisited: Tears, Air Raids, Censorship, Despair." *Times Talk.* Vol. XII. (September 1968).

Mackay, Ian. "Concepts of Nigerian Broadcasting." *European Broadcasting Union Review.* No. 788. March, 1963.

McClung, James. "The Impact of Television on African Development." *Corona.* Part I. (February 1961). Part II. (March 1961).

Nixon, Raymond B. "Factors Related to Freedom in National Press Systems" *Journalism Quarterly.* Vol. 37. (March 1961).

Nixon Raymond B. "Freedom in the World's Press: A Fresh Appraisal with New Data." *Journalism Quarterly.* Vol. 42.No. 1 (Winter 1965).

Nord Bruce A. "Press Freedom and Political Structure." *Journalism Quarterly.* 43 (Autumn) 1966.

O'Brien, Rita Cruise. "Domination and Dependence in Mass Communications: Implications for the Use of Broadcasting in Developing Countries". *Institute of Development Studies Bulletin.* Vol. 6. No. 4 March 1975.

Rogers, Everett M. "New Perspectives on Communication and Development: Overview." *Communication Research.* Vol. 3. April 1976.

Schiller, Herbert I. "National Development Requires some Social Distance." *The Antioch Review.* Vol. XXVII. No. 1, (Spring) 1967.

Uche, Luke Uka. "Credibility Factor in Opinion Leaders' Media Preference: A case study of Foreign Broadcasts During Crisis Situations in Nigeria. *Communicatic Socialis Year-book.* Vol. IV. 1985.

Uche, Luke Uka. "The Politics of Nigeria's Radio Broadcast Industry: 1932 - 1983". *Gazette* (35), 1985.

Uche, Luke Uka. "Broadcasting in Nigeria and Cultural Identity in an Era of Media Imperialism." *The Third Channel: IBS Journal of International Communication* Vol. II No. 1 1986.

Uche, Luke Uka. "Government - Media Relations in Nigeria: Factors Influencing the Degree of Press Freedom." Forthcoming in the *Unilag Communication Review.*

Uche, Luke Uka. "The Press in Nigeria: Evolution and Roles in National Politics." Forthcoming in the *Zeszyty PRASOZNAWCZE.*

Ugboajah, Frank Okwu. "Nigerian Mass Media Behaviour on Development Issues of Conflict." *Instant Research on Peace and Violence* Vol. VI., No. 4, 1976.

Ugboajah, Frank Okwu "Nigerian Mass Communication Trends in the African Context." *Gazette.* Vol. XXXII. No. 3. 1976.

Ugboajah, Frank Okwu "Traditional-Urban Media Model: Stocktaking for African Development." *Gazette.* Vol. VXIII. No.W. 1972.

Uyo, O'Kevbe Adidi. "Here's the NBC News in full...!" Unilag *Communication Review.* Vol. I. No. 1 January/March 1977.

Newspapers and Magazines

"Sowemimo Awards 8,000 to Mr. Coker."*Daily Times.* December 6, 1969.

"Ohonbamu Faces Sedition Charge." *Daily Times.* November 8, 1975.

"All TV Stations Fall into Federal Hands." *Daily Times.* November 10, 1975.

"Government Take-Over of Radio-TV." *Daily Times.* November 13, 1975.

"Investigate the Airport Incident." *Daily Times.* December 4, 1975.

"Newspapers Take-Over Flayed." *Daily Times.* January 8, 1976.

"Open Letter to NTV Boss," *Daily Times.* February 19, 1977.

"Reporters are Timid." *Daily Times.* May 4, 1977.

"50,000 Copies of *Newbreed* Impounded." *Daily Times.* May 5, 1977.

"Ogunlade's Microphone." *Daily Times.* May 10, 1977.

"Attention, NTV." *Daily Times.* May 13. 1977.

"Programme Appraisal at the NBC." *Daily Times.* May 16, 1977.

"Good Start, NBC-2". *Daily Times,* May 17, 1977.

"Journalism-Invaluable Instrument in Nation-Building." *Daily Times.* May 27, 1977.

"NBC"s Newscasters." *Daily Times.* May 27, 1977.

"The Press Under Fire." *Daily Times.* May 27, 1977.

"The Press After 1979." *Daily Times.* May 28, 1977.

"The Journalist and the Return to Civil Rule." *Daily Times.* May 30, 1977.

"Guidelines for Journalistic Performance." *Daily Times.* May 31, 1977.

"The Press Under the Draft Constitution." *Daily Times.* June 4, 1977.

"Broadcasting Age in Nigeria." *Headlines.* May 1977.

"Government Sponsors the Competition."*IPI Report.* XVII (June 1968).

"The Press Under Pressure." *IPI Report.* June 1974.

"Press Freedom in Principle, On Paper, But in Reality..." *IPI Report* October 1974. No. 11.

"Bitter Police and Press Exchanges in Nigeria." *IPI Report*. December 1974. No. 12.

"The Press Under Pressure." *IPI Report*. January 1975.

"Black Africa - No Press Freedom Today." *IPI Report*. Vol. 24, **No. 6**. June 1975.

"Nigeria's Regime Seizes Two Editors." *New York Times*. November 20, 1965.

"Press and Regime Clash in Nigeria." *New York Times*. April 21, 1975.

"Structure of NBC Management." *Radio-TV Times*. April 1977. Lagos.

"Thank God I Am Now Free." *Sunday Times*. August 24, 1975.

"The Nation's Whispering Wires." *Sunday Times*. May 1, 1977.

"The Press Also Has a Stake." *Sunday Times*. May 1, 1977.

"Wake up Radio Nigeria." *Sunday Times*. May 1, 1977.

"Sweet are the Uses of Adversary Journalism." *Sunday Times*. May 15, 1977.

"Bloody Coup Crushed in Nigeria." *Washington Post*. February 14, 1976.

"Police Raid Sketch." *West Africa*. September 23, 1974.

"The Nigerian Press." *West Africa*. March 3, 1975.

"Jose on Press Freedom." *West Africa*. March 3, 1975.

"*New Nigerian* and *Daily Times*." *West Africa*. September 8, 1975.

APPENDICES

Appendix A

NEWSPAPERS (AMENDMENT) ACT, 1964

ARRANGEMENT OF SECTIONS

1964, No. V

AN ACT TO AMEND THE NEWSPAPERS ACT

[12th October, 1964]   Commencement.

BE IT ENACTED by the Legislature of the Federation of Nigeria in this present Parliament assembled and by the authority of the same as follows :—

1.—(1) The proprietor and every publisher of a newspaper printed or published as the case may be, in Nigeria elsewhere than in the Federal territory but circulating in the Federal territory shall, within two months from the commencement of this Act, or if the newspaper first circulates in the Federal territory after the said commencement then within two months of such first circulation, establish an office for such newspaper in the Federal territory and give notice in writing of the fact to the Minister. *(Marginal note: Nigerian newspapers to have offices in the Federal territory.)*

(2) Any other enactment to the contrary notwithstanding, it shall be sufficient service of any process or notice required to be served on the proprietor, publisher or editor of the newspaper if the process or notice is addressed to them or any particular one or more of them as the case may be, and is left at or sent by post to the office of the newspaper established in the Federal territory as prescribed by this section.

(3) The failure to comply with the requirement of subsection (1) of this section shall be an offence punishable on conviction by a fine of not less than ten pounds or more than twenty-five pounds, or by imprisonment for a term of three months.

Appointment
of editor to
be notified
to Minister.
Cap. 129.

2.—(1) The proprietor of a newspaper published in the Federal territory shall appoint an editor to have general superintendence and control over all matters intended and suitable for publication in the newspaper, and section three of the Newspapers Act (in this Act hereafter referred to as "the principal Act") shall be amended so as to require the like affidavit to be made, signed and sworn by the editor as is prescribed for proprietors and others, and such affidavit shall thereafter be registered in the office of the Minister. The affidavit shall disclose the correct name and address of the editor, and if the affidavit prescribed under the aforesaid section was filed before the commencement of this Act and does not disclose information as to the editor, it shall to any extent necessary be replaced by a fresh affidavit made, signed, sworn and so registered within one month after the date of such commencement.

(2) The provisions of the foregoing subsection shall extend and apply to any person acting as editor for the purposes of the principal Act and this Act in the absence of the editor, so however that if such absence is unlikely to exceed fourteen days, notice in writing of the correct name and address of the person acting may be given by the printer to the Minister, and such notice when given shall be deemed to be sufficient compliance with the requirements of section three of the principal Act.

(3) The failure to comply with the requirements of this section shall be an offence punishable on conviction by a fine of not less than ten pounds or more than twenty-five pounds, or by imprisonment for a term of three months.

Delivery of
signed copy
of newspaper
by the
editor.

3.—(1) In addition to any other provision of the principal Act directing the delivery of signed copies of a newspaper, the editor shall himself sign and deliver or send to the Minister a copy of every newspaper and every supplement edited under his general supervision and control.

(2) If the editor is absent the person who, under what designation soever, then edits the newspaper shall be acting editor for the purposes of the principal Act and this Act, and shall sign and deliver or send to the Minister all copies of the newspaper and supplements (if any) published during the absence of the editor.

Publication
of certain
statements,
etc., an
offence.

4.—(1) Any person who authorises for publication, publishes, reproduces or circulates for sale in a newspaper any statement, rumour or report knowing or having reason to believe that such statement, rumour or report is false shall be guilty of an offence and liable on conviction to a fine of two hundred pounds or to imprisonment for a term of one year.

(2) It shall be no defence to a charge under this section that he did not know or did not have reason to believe that the statement, rumour or report was false unless he proves that, prior to publication, he took reasonable measures to verify the accuracy of such statement, rumour or report.

Publication
of name, etc.
of editor in
newspaper.

5. Section thirteen of the principal Act is amended by the insertion in subsection (1) immediately after the word "publisher" of the words "and of the editor in chief or editor, as the case may be".

6. In any Act other than the principal Act or this Act affixing the responsibility of, or conferring immunity on editors, the fact that a newspaper is published in the Federal territory by or under the authority of the Government of the Federation or of a Region, as the case may be, shall be immaterial, and the definition of "newspaper" in section two of the principal Act shall be amended to the extent necessary to give effect to this section.

Application of Act to editor of a government newspaper.

7.—(1) This Act may be cited as the Newspapers (Amendment) Act, 1964 and shall be read as one with the Newspapers Act.

(2) This Act shall apply to the Federal territory.

Short title, application, etc.
Cap. 129.

Appendix B

NEWS AGENCY OF NIGERIA DECREE 1976

ARRANGEMENT OF SECTIONS

SCHEDULES

Decree No. 19

[*10th May 1976*]   Commencement.

THE FEDERAL MILITARY GOVERNMENT hereby decrees as follows :—

1.—(1) There is hereby established a body to be known as the News Agency of Nigeria (hereafter in this Decree referred to as "the Agency").   Establishment of News Agency of Nigeria.

(2) The Agency shall be a body corporate with perpetual succession and a common seal, and may sue and be sued in its corporate name.

2.—(1) The objects of the Agency shall be—   Objects, etc. of the Agency.

(*a*) to seek, obtain and otherwise receive through subscription, payment, exchange or other means, international, regional, local and other news, news material and news features ;

(*b*) to distribute such news, news material and news features to sub-scribers against payment either in the form of fees or news exchange or on such other terms as may be agreed ;

(*c*) to present complete, objective and impartial information, news or news material or features on any matter of public or national interest within and outside the Federation ; and

(*d*) to report truthfully and fairly, without prejudice to public and national interest, the views of all sections of the population of the Federation.

(2) Without prejudice to subsection (1) of this section, the Agency shall have the monopoly of collecting news in Nigeria for sale to foreign news agencies.

Board of Directors.

3.—(1) Subject to the provisions of this Decree, the management of the Agency and responsibility for carrying out the objects of the Agency shall be vested in a Board of Directors (hereinafter referred to as "the Board") consisting of—

(*a*) a chairman who shall be appointed by the Federal Executive Council on the recommendation of the Commissioner ;

(*b*) seven persons to be appointed by the Commissioner of whom at least three but not more than four shall be persons employed by the Ministry under his control, one shall be a person employed by the Ministry of Communications and the others shall be appointed by the Commissioner from amongst other interests in the field of journalism and public relations which in the opinion of the Commissioner ought to be adequately represented ;

(*c*) one representative of the broadcasting organizations in Nigeria ; and

(*d*) the person appointed General Manager under section 5 (1) of this Decree.

(2) The provisions of Schedule 1 to this Decree shall have effect with respect to the qualifications and tenure of office of members of the Board, powers and procedure of the Board and the other matters mentioned in that Schedule.

Directions by the Commissioner.

4.—(1) The Commissioner may give to the Board directions of a general character or relating to particular matters (but not to any individual person or case) with regard to the exercise by the Board of its functions, and it shall be the duty of the Board to comply with the directions.

(2) Before giving a direction under subsection (1) of this section, the Commissioner shall serve a copy of the proposed direction on the Board and shall afford the Board an opportunity of making representations to him with respect to the direction ; and after considering any representations made to him in pursuance of this subsection, the Commissioner may give the direction either without modification, or with such modifications as appear to him to be appropriate having regard to the representations.

General Manager.

5.—(1) There shall be a General Manager who shall be appointed by the Federal Executive Council on the recommendation of the Commissioner and shall be the chief executive officer and responsible for the execution of the Board's policies and the administration of its day to day business.

(2) The General Manager shall hold and vacate office in accordance with the terms of the instrument by which he is appointed and shall—

(*a*) receive such remuneration and allowances, and

(*b*) be eligible to receive such pension, gratuity or other retiring allowances (if any),

as may be determined by the Board with the approval of the Commissioner.

6.—(1) The Board shall appoint a Secretary, who shall be an officer but not a member of the Board and who shall keep the Board's records, conduct its correspondence and perform such other duties of a clerical and secretarial nature as the Board or the General Manager may from time to time direct and require.

Secretary and other staff.

(2) The Board may appoint such other employees and agents as it thinks fit.

(3) The terms and conditions of service (including terms and conditions as to remuneration, allowances and retiring and medical benefits) of the Secretary and other employees and agents of the Board shall be such as may be determined by the Board with the approval of the Commissioner.

7.—(1) The Board may by an instrument in writing under its common seal delegate to any person or body such of its duties as may be necessary to be performed in or outside the Federation :

Delegation by the Board.

Provided that any such person or body shall have no control over the money of the Agency and shall act in all respects in accordance with the direction of the Board.

(2) The Board may, from time to time, form committees to consider special questions as may be referred to them by the Board ; and any such committee shall perform its functions according to directions given to it by the Board.

8. There shall be established a Council of Trustees (hereinafter referred to as "the Council") whose duties shall be—

Establishment and duties of Council of Trustees.

(*a*) to ensure that the Board carries out its functions in accordance with the provisions of this Decree ;

(*b*) to consider any complaint from any subscriber to the Agency or any user of services provided by the Agency ; and

(*c*) to consider any matter referred to it by the Board or by the Commissioner.

9.—(1) The members of the Council shall be appointed by the Federal Executive Council on the recommendation of the Commissioner and shall consist of—

Membership of the Council.

(*a*) the Chief Trustee and Chairman ;

(*b*) a representative each of the following, that is to say—

(*i*) the Nigerian Bar Association,

(*ii*) the Newspaper Proprietors Association,

(*iii*) the Nigerian Union of Journalists,

(*iv*) the Nigerian Guild of Editors ; and

(*c*) three other persons.

(2) The provisions of Schedule 2 of this Decree shall apply in respect of the tenure of office of members of the Council and the other matters therein contained.

Inquiries by the Council.

10.—(1) The Council shall inquire into any complaint received by it under section 8 (*b*) of this Decree, or into any matter referred to it by the Board or the Commissioner.

(2) For the purposes of subsection (1) of this section, the Council may receive oral or written evidence and may require any person to give such information as may in its opinion be necessary for the purpose of the inquiry.

(3) As soon as may be after the conclusion of an inquiry, the Council shall in writing deliver its findings and make such recommendations thereon as it may deem fit to the Board or, as the case may be, the Commissioner, who shall take such action thereon as may be deemed appropriate.

(4) The findings and recommendations of the Council shall if so directed by the Commissioner be published in full by the Board.

Financial provisions.

11.—(1) The Agency shall establish and maintain a fund (in this section referred to as "the fund") from which shall be defrayed all expenditure incurred by the Agency.

(2) There shall be paid and credited to the fund—

(*a*) such moneys as may from time to time be granted to the Agency by the Federal Military Government ; and

(*b*) all other moneys which may from time to time accrue to the Agency.

(3) The fund shall be applied towards the promotion of the objects of the Agency under this Decree and the payment of remuneration (including provision for pension, gratuity, superannuation or other retirement benefits) to or in respect of any employee or agent of the Agency.

(4) The Board may, with the approval of the Federal Executive Council, borrow money in connection with the operations of the Agency, and invest part of the fund in such securities as the Commissioner may from time to time approve.

Accounts, audit, etc.

12.—(1) The Board shall prepare and submit to the Commissioner not later than 31st December each year an estimate of its expenditure and income during the next succeeding financial year.

(2) The Board shall keep proper accounts in respect of each financial year, and proper records in relation to those accounts and shall cause the accounts to be audited as soon as may be after the end of the financial year to which the accounts relate by a firm of auditors approved as respects that year by the Commissioner.

(3) The Board shall prepare and submit to the Commissioner not later than 30th June in each financial year a report in such form as the Commissioner may direct on the activities of the Agency during the last financial year, and shall include in the report a copy of the audited accounts of the Agency for that last financial year and of the auditor's report on those accounts.

(4) The Commissioner shall cause a copy of each report made to him under this section to be laid before the Federal Executive Council.

13. The Agency shall have power—

(*a*) to acquire and hold property whether movable or immovable ; and

(*b*) to enter into contracts.

Power to hold land, etc.

14. The seal of the Agency may from time to time be broken, changed, altered or made anew as seems fit :

Seal of the Agency.

Provided that until a seal is provided under this section a stamp bearing the inscription "News Agency of Nigeria" may be used as the common seal.

15. The Agency shall have a principal office in the Federation and may establish such other office or offices at such place or places in or outside the Federation as the Board with the approval of the Commissioner may from time to time determine.

Offices of the Agency.

16.—(1) Notwithstanding any arrangements which the Agency may enter into or make for the reception and distribution of international news, subscribers to the Agency may, on request and on terms in regard to payment to be decided by the Board, receive through the Agency the full service supplied to the Agency by any international news agency.

Guarantee of full service.

(2) Arrangements for news collection and distribution made by the Agency shall be without prejudice to the right of Nigerian newspaper and radio subscribers to make their own independent arrangements for news coverage by their own correspondents.

(3) The term "correspondents" in subsection (2) of this section, shall include the editorial staff of a newspaper or any person who writes or supplies news for a fee either as a part-time or whole-time occupation.

17. The Agency shall be exempt from all stamp duties payable under any law for the time being in force in Nigeria.

Exemption from stamp duty.

18. No member of the Board shall incur any personal liability for any loss or damage caused by any act or omission in the management or conduct of the affairs of the Agency unless such loss or damage was occasioned by an intentionally wrongful act or omission on his part.

Protection against personal liability by members of Board.

19. Upon the commencement of this Decree, all moneys or other assets, if any, in the custody, or control of any person by virtue of any authority whatsoever given to or received by such person for or on behalf of the Agency in anticipation of the commencement of this Decree together with interest, if any, accruing thereon shall be deemed to form part of the income of the Agency and shall be transferred to and be vested in the Board.

Vesting of certain assets in the Board.

20. In this Decree, unless the context otherwise requires—

Inter-pretation.

"the Agency" means the News Agency of Nigeria established under section 1 (1) of this Decree ;

"the Board" means the Board of Directors referred to in section 3 (1) of this Decree ;

"the Commissioner" means the Federal Commissioner charged with responsibility for Information ;

"principal office" means any office of the Agency in Nigeria so designated by the Agency.

Citation.   **21.** This Decree may be cited as the News Agency of Nigeria Decree 1976.

SCHEDULES

SCHEDULE 1   *Section 3*

SUPPLEMENTARY PROVISIONS RELATING TO THE BOARD

1.—(1) A person shall not be appointed a member of the Board unless—

(*a*) he is a citizen of Nigeria ;

(*b*) has not been convicted of any offence involving dishonesty or fraud ; and

(*c*) if he has, he has in each case been granted a pardon.

(2) Subject to the provisions of this paragraph, a member shall hold office for a period not exceeding three years beginning with the date of his appointment :

Provided that a member shall not hold office, for a term of less than two years unless the Commissioner after consultation with the Board otherwise directs.

(3) Any member may, by notice to the Board, resign his office.

(4) A person who has ceased to be a member of the Board shall be eligible for re-appointment for not more than one further term of three years.

(5) Sub-paragraphs (2) to (4) of this paragraph shall not apply in respect of a member of the Board who is holder of an office in the public service of the Federation.

2.—(1) Subject to the following sub-paragraph and to any direction of the Commissioner under this Decree, the Board shall have power to do anything which in its opinion is calculated to facilitate the promotion of the objects of the Agency.

(2) Members of the Board who are not public officers shall be paid out of the fund of the Agency such travelling and subsistence allowances in respect of any period spent on the business of the Agency as the Commissioner may determine, but no other remuneration shall be paid to any member of the Board.

Proceedings of the Board

3. Subject to the provisions of this Decree and of section 26 of the Interpretation Act 1964 (which provides for decisions of a body to be taken by a majority of the members of the body and for the chairman to have a second or casting vote) the Board may make standing orders regulating the proceedings of the Board or of any committee thereof.

4. The quorum of the Board shall be five and the quorum of any committee of the Board shall be determined by the Board.

5.—(1) The Commissioner shall appoint one of the members of the Board to be the Deputy Chairman of the Board for such period as the Commissioner may determine, so however that a Deputy Chairman who ceases to be a member shall also cease to be Deputy Chairman.

(2) At any time while the office of the Chairman is vacant or the Chairman is, in the opinion of the Board, permanently or temporarily unable to perform the functions of his office, the Deputy Chairman shall perform those functions, and references in this Schedule to the Chairman shall be construed accordingly.

6.—(1) Subject to the provision of any standing orders of the Board, the Board shall meet whenever it is summoned by the Chairman ; and if the Chairman is required so to do by notice given to him by not less than six other members he shall summon a meeting of the Board to be held within seven days from the date on which the notice is given.

(2) At any meeting of the Board, the Chairman or in his absence the Deputy Chairman shall preside, but if both are absent, the members present at the meeting shall appoint one of their number to preside at that meeting.

(3) Where the Board desires to obtain the advice of any person on a particular matter, the Board may co-opt him as a member for such period as it thinks fit ; but a person who is a member by virtue of this sub-paragraph shall not be entitled to vote at any meeting of the Board and shall not count towards a quorum.

(4) Notwithstanding anything in the foregoing provisions of this paragraph, the first meeting of the Board shall be summoned by the Commissioner who may give such directions as he thinks fit as to the member who shall preside and as to the procedure which shall be followed at the meeting.

Committees

7.—(1) The Board may appoint one or more committees to carry out, on behalf of the Board, such of its functions as the Board may determine.

(2) A committee appointed under this paragraph shall consist of the number of persons determined by the Board, and not more than one-third of those persons may be persons who are not members of the Board ; and a person other than a member of the Board shall hold office on the committee in accordance with the terms of the instrument by which he is appointed.

(3) A decision of a committee of the Board shall be of no effect until it is confirmed by the Board.

Supplemental

8.—(1) The fixing of the seal of the Board shall be authenticated by the signature of the Chairman or of some other member authorised generally or specially to act for that purpose by the Board.

(2) Any contract or instrument which, if made or executed by a person not being a body corporate, would not be required to be under seal may be made or executed on behalf of the Board by any person generally or specially authorised to act for that purpose by the Board.

(3) Any document purporting to be a document duly executed under the seal of the Board shall be received in evidence and shall, unless the contrary is proved, be deemed to be so executed.

9. The validity of any proceedings of the Board or of a committee thereof shall not be affected by any vacancy in the membership of the Board or committee, or by any defect in the appointment of a member of the Board or of a person to serve on the committee, or by a reason that a person not entitled to do so took part in the proceedings.

10. Any member of the Board, and any person holding office on a committee of the Board, who has a personal interest in any contract or arrangement entered into or proposed to be considered by the Board or a committee thereof shall forthwith disclose his interest to the Board and shall not vote on any question relating to the contract or arrangement.

11. A person shall not, by reason only of his membership of the Board, be treated as holding an office in the public service of the Federation or of any State thereof.

SCHEDULE 2   *Section 9*

Supplementary Provisions Relating to the Council of Trustees

1. The term of office of members of the Council (including the Chief Trustee and Chairman) shall be four years and members shall be eligible for re-appointment.

2. The term of office of a new member appointed to fill a vacancy shall be the remainder of the term of office of the other members.

3. Three members shall constitute a quorum for a meeting of the Council.

4. The Council shall meet within one month of its appointment and shall appoint a Secretary.

5. All expenses of the Council shall be met out of the funds of the Agency.

6. A meeting of the Council shall be convened within one month of any matter being formally referred to it by the Board or on receipt of any complaint from a newspaper, radio or television subscriber to the Agency.

7. The office of a member of the Council other than a member appointed by virtue of office shall be vacated—

(a) if he dies ;

(b) if he ceases to be qualified ;

(c) if he becomes bankrupt, lunatic or of unsound mind ;

(d) if he absents himself from three consecutive meetings without leave of the Council, and the Council passes a resolution declaring his office vacant ;

(e) in the event of his resignation being accepted by the Commissioner ;
or

(f) on the occasion of his seventieth birthday.

MADE at Lagos this 10th day of May 1976.

LT.-GENERAL O. OBASANJO,
Head of the Federal Military Government,
Commander-in-Chief of the Armed Forces,
Federal Republic of Nigeria

EXPLANATORY NOTE

(This note does not form part of the above Decree
but is intended to explain its purpose)

The Decree establishes the News Agency of Nigeria and charges it, among other things, with responsibility for obtaining news from all sources, both within and outside Nigeria, and supplying at a fee the news obtained to the Agency's subscribers. The affairs of the Agency are to be managed by a Board of Directors the composition of which is set out in the Decree.

Appendix C

Decree No. 24

Nigerian Television Authority Decree [1*st April* 1976]   Commencement.

THE FEDERAL MILITARY GOVERNMENT hereby decrees as
follows :—

Nigerian Television Authority

1.—(1) There is hereby established a body to be known as the Nigerian   Establish-
Television Authority (hereafter in this Decree referred to as "the Authority")   ment of the
which under that name shall be a body corporate with perpetual succession   Nigerian
and a common seal, and may sue and be sued in its corporate name.   Television
Authority.

(2) The supplementary provisions contained in Schedule 1 to this
Decree shall have effect with respect to the proceedings of the authority and
the other matters mentioned therein.

2.—(1) The Authority shall consist of the following members to be   Membership
appointed by the Federal Executive Council on the recommendation of the   of the
Commissioner, that is—   Authority.

(*a*) a Chairman ;

(*b*) the Chairman of each Zonal Board ;

(*c*) the Director-General of the Nigerian Television Authority ;

(*d*) one representative of the Federal Ministry of Information ;

(*e*) one person to represent women's organisations in Nigeria ; and

(*f*) six persons with requisite experience in—

　(*i*) the mass media,

　(*ii*) education,

　(*iii*) management,

　(*iv*) financial matters,

　(*v*) engineering, and

　(*vi*) arts and culture.

(2) The Federal Executive Council may by Order published in the
Gazette increase or reduce or otherwise vary the composition of membership
of the Authority.

3.—(1) Subject to the provisions of this Decree, a person appointed to   Tenure of
be a member of the Authority, not being a public officer, shall hold office   office.
for a period of three years from the date of his appointment and shall be
eligible for re-appointment for one further period of three years.

(2) Any member, not being a public officer, may resign his appointment
by a letter addressed to the Commissioner.

(3) Members of the Authority, not being public officers, shall be paid
such remuneration and allowances as the Federal Executive Council may
determine.

4.—(1) If it appears to the Commissioner that a member of the Authority   Removal
should be removed from office on the ground of misconduct or inability to   from
perform the functions of his office, the Commissioner shall after consultation   office of
with the interests, if any, represented by that member make a recommendation   members of
to that effect to the Federal Executive Council, and if the Federal Executive   the
Council approves the recommendation, the Commissioner may declare, in   Authority.
writing, the office of that member vacant.

(2) Without prejudice to subsection (1) above—

(*a*) any member who is absent from two consecutive ordinary meetings of the Authority shall file his explanation in writing with the Secretary for consideration by the Authority and if the explanation is not accepted by the Authority; or

(*b*) where the Authority is satisfied that the continued presence on the Authority of any member is not in the national interest or the interest of the Authority,

the Authority may recommend to the Commissioner that the member be removed, and the Commissioner may declare, in writing, the office of that member vacant.

Appointment, etc. of the Director-General and other staff of the Authority.

5.—(1) There shall be an official of the Authority to be known as the Director-General who shall be the chief executive officer of the Authority and shall be responsible for the execution of the policy of the Authority and of its day to day business.

(2) The Director-General shall be appointed by the Commissioner with the prior approval of the Federal Executive Council.

(3) Subject to section 16 of this Decree, the Authority may delegate to the Director-General such of its functions under this Decree as are necessary to enable him to transact effectively the day to day business of the Authority of every kind whatsoever.

(4) The Authority shall appoint a Secretary to the Authority who shall keep the records and conduct the correspondence of the Authority and perform such other duties as the Authority or the Director-General may from time to time direct.

(5) The Authority may appoint such other staff and agents as it may deem necessary for the efficient performance of the Authority's duties under this Decree.

Functions of the Authority

General duties of the Authority.

6.—(1) It shall be the duty of the Authority to provide as a public service in the interest of Nigeria, independent and impartial television broadcasting for general reception within Nigeria.

(2) The Authority shall ensure that the services which it provides, when considered as a whole reflect the unity of Nigeria as a Federation and at the same time give adequate expression to the culture, characteristics and affairs of each State, Zone or other part of the Federation.

Exclusive right of Authority for television broadcasting in Nigeria.

7.—(1) The Authority shall, to the exclusion of any other broadcasting authority or any person in Nigeria, be responsible for television broadcasting in Nigeria and, accordingly, the transitional and savings provisions in Schedule 2 to this Decree shall have effect notwithstanding the provisions of any law under which any other broadcasting authority is established; and every such law shall be construed with such modifications, amendments and omissions as would bring it into line with the general intendment of this Decree.

(2) In this section "broadcasting authority" means any authority (whether or not a statutory corporation and howsoever known or designated) set up by the Government of the Federation or by any State or group of States as a public body charged with responsibility, either wholly or partially, for television broadcasting.

8.—(1) The functions of the Authority shall be—

Particular functions of the Authority.

(*a*) to erect, maintain and operate television transmitting and receiving stations ;

(*b*) to plan and co-ordinate the activities of the entire television network ;

(*c*) to ensure the establishment and maintenance of standards and promote the efficient operation of the entire system in·accordance with national policy ;

(*d*) to establish and operate a formula for sharing funds among stations

(*e*) to act as liaison between the Federal Government and the zonal operations ;

(*f*) to establish such number of production centres as it may consider necessary from time to time ;

(*g*) to specify the types of programmes which should be transmitted by the whole network and the quantity, type and contents of foreign materials ;

(*h*) to enter into arrangements with any person or any authority for the purpose of obtaining concessions, licences, privileges and other rights ;

(*i*) to manufacture, produce, purchase, or otherwise acquire films, gramophone and other mechanical records and materials and apparatus for use in connection with the broadcasting services ;

(*j*) to provide other persons with, and receive from them, matters to be broadcast ;

(*k*) to organise, provide, and subsidise, for the purpose of broadcasting, educational activities and public entertainment ;

(*l*) to collect, in any part of the world and in any manner that may be thought fit, both news and information and to subscribe to news agencies ;

(*m*) to acquire copyrights ;

(*n*) to publish printed matter that may be conducive to the performance of any of the functions of the Authority ;

(*o*) to do anything for the purpose of advancing the skill of persons employed in the broadcasting services, or the efficiency of the equipment used in the broadcasting services, or the manner in which that equipment is operated, including the providing by the Authority or by others on its behalf of facilities for training, education and research ; and

(*p*) to carry out such other activities as are necessary or expedient for the full discharge of all or any of the functions conferred on it under or pursuant to this Decree.

Duty of
Authority
as to pro-
grammes and
publications.

9.—(1) The Authority shall satisfy itself that the programmes broadcast by the Authority or on its behalf comply with the following requirements—

(*a*) that nothing is included in the programmes which is likely to offend against good taste or decency or is likely to encourage or incite to crime or to lead to disorder or to be offensive to public feeling, or to contain any offensive representation of, or reference to, a living person ;

(*b*) that the programmes maintain a proper balance in their subject-matter and a generally high standard of quality ;

(*c*) that any news given in the programmes (in whatever form) is presented with accuracy, impartiality and objectivity ;

(*d*) that due impartiality is preserved in respect of matters of political or industrial controversy or relating to current public policy ; and

(*e*) that, subject to the provisions of subsection (2), no matter designed to serve the interests of any political party is included in the programmes.

(2) Nothing in paragraph (*e*) of subsection (1) shall prevent—

(*a*) the inclusion in the programmes of properly balanced discussion or debates in which the persons taking part express opinions and put forward arguments of a political character ; and

(*b*) the inclusion in the programmes of party political broadcasts which seek to explain the views and policies of the various political parties in accordance with a scheme of such broadcasts which apportions the facilities and time allowed between the representatives of the political parties in such a manner as appears to the Authority equitably to represent their respective claims to the interest of the public.

(3) The Authority shall secure the exclusion from any publication which may be issued by it, or on its behalf, and without prejudice to the generality of the provisions of this section, from the programmes broadcast by it or on its behalf, of all expressions of its own opinion as to the matters referred to in paragraph (*d*) of subsection (1), or of the opinion as to any such matters of any of its members or officers, or of the opinion as to any such matters of any director or officer or any agent of the Authority.

Broadcasting
of matters.

10. Without prejudice to the generality of section 6, the Authority shall provide such facilities as may appear to the Authority to be desirable in the public interest for the broadcasting of—

(*a*) ministerial speeches, that is any speeches of the members of the Supreme Military Council, the National Council of States, the Federal Executive Council or the Executive Council of any State in Nigeria which consist wholly of statements of fact or which explain the policy and actions of the Government concerned ; and

(*b*) matters of any kind (including religious services or ceremonies) relating to or representing the main streams of religious thought or belief in Nigeria.

Duty to
broadcast
Government
announce-
ments.

11.—(1) The Authority shall, whenever so requested by an authorised public officer, send in a Government programme, at the Authority's own expense, any announcement which such officer may request the Authority to broadcast and shall also, whenever so requested by any such officer in whose opinion an emergency has arisen or continues, at the like expense, send as aforesaid any other matter which the officer may request the Authority to broadcast ; and the Authority may in its discretion announce or refrain from announcing that such a notice has been given or has been varied or revoked.

(2) In this section "authorised public officer" means any officer in any of the public services in the Federation declared to be such by the Head of the Federal Military Government or, as the case may require, the Military Governor of a State.

12.—(1) Subject to the provisions of this section, the programmes broadcast by the Authority or on its behalf may be sponsored and may include advertisements and sponsored announcements broadcast in consideration of payment by persons requiring such sponsored programmes, advertisements and announcements to be broadcast.

(right margin: Advertisements.)

(2) A special programme shall not be interrupted by any advertisement or sponsored announcement, but advertisements or sponsored announcements may immediately precede, or immediately follow, a special programme.

(3) Where a programme is specially broadcast for schools, the Commissioner may designate the types or classes of advertisements or sponsored announcements that may immediately precede or immediately follow that programme.

(4) A special programme shall be broadcast if so directed by the Commissioner in any particular case.

13. The Commissioner may give the Authority directions of a general character or relating generally to particular matters with regard to the exercise by the Authority of its functions under this Decree, and it shall be the duty of the Authority to comply with such directions.

(right margin: Powers of the Commissioner to give directions to the Authority.)

Zonal Boards of the Authority

14.—(1) For the purposes of variety and better reception of its television programmes, the Authority shall divide Nigeria into six districts, each such district being designated as a Zone.

(right margin: Establishment of Zones and Zonal Boards)

(2) There shall be established for each Zone a board to be known as the Nigerian Television Zonal Board.

(3) Each Zonal Board shall consist of not less than six or more than eight members who shall be appointed by the Commissioner with the prior approval of the Federal Executive Council and shall include—

(*a*) one member to represent each State making up the Zone who shall be appointed after consultation with the Military Governor of the State in question and shall be a person appearing to the Commissioner to have wide knowledge of, and experience in at least one of the following fields—

(*i*) newspapers, broadcasting and other media of mass communication;

(*ii*) cultural, economic and religious affairs of the Zone;

(*iii*) the creative arts;

(*b*) two persons appearing to the Commissioner to have wide experience in education and financial matters, respectively;

(*c*) one person appearing to the Commissioner to represent the interests of business and industry; and

(*d*) the Zonal Managing Director.

(4) The Commissioner, with the prior approval of the Federal Executive Council, shall nominate one of the members of the Zonal Board approved by him to be the Chairman of the Board.

Terms of
service.

15.—(1) A member of the Board shall hold office for a period of three years and shall be eligible for re-appointment.

(2) There shall be paid to members of the Board (excluding the Zonal Managing Director) out of the moneys at the disposal of the Board such remuneration and such travelling and subsistence allowances in respect of any period of time spent on the business of the Board as the Federal Executive Council may determine.

Functions of
Zonal
Boards.

16. Subject to this Decree, each Zonal Board shall be responsible for—

(*a*) the operation of its main station and production centres ;

(*b*) the control of the general policy of the Zonal programmes in such a manner as to ensure that all Zonal programmes are selected with due regard to the distinctive culture, interests and tastes of the people of the Zone on the one hand and the fulfilment of national needs on the other, and conform to any standards laid down by the Authority ;

(*c*) the appointment of an advisory committee to advise the Board on any matter concerning television broadcasting in its Zone and any other business of the Board referred to it for advice ;

(*d*) the supervision and control over the acts of all employees of the Authority in its Zone in matters of executive administration in the whole field of television broadcasting and matters concerning the accounts and records of the Zone ;

(*e*) the disposition of all questions relating to the service of the employees of the Authority in its Zone and their pay, privileges and allowances subject to the approval of the Authority ; and

(*f*) the performance of such other functions as the Authority may from time to time delegate to it.

Appoint-
ment of
Zonal
Managing
Directors.

17.—(1) There shall be for each Zone an officer of the Authority to be known as the Zonal Managing Director who shall be appointed by the Authority.

(2) In each Zone, the Zonal Managing Director shall—

(*a*) subject to any direction given to him by the Director-General, be responsible for the execution of the policy of the Authority ; and

(*b*) shall be the chief executive of the Zonal Board in matters within the competence of the Zonal Board and be responsible for giving effect to the decisions of the Zonal Boards.

Establish-
ment of
news
department.

18.—(1) There shall be established a department of the Authority which shall be responsible for the gathering of items of news from all sources and for their editing and subsequent dissemination.

(2) There shall be an officer of the Authority, to be known as the Director of News, who shall be responsible for the news department and shall, subject to any directions given to him by the Director-General, be responsible for the execution of the policy of the Authority in so far as the news department is concerned and for the administration of the day to day business of the department.

Provisions as to Land

19.—(1) The Authority shall have power—

(a) to enter on any lands for the purpose of erecting, maintaining and inspecting any installations belonging to the Authority or of repairing, altering or removing any such installations and to remain there for such reasonable time and execute and do all such works as may be necessary for the purposes of this Decree ;

(b) to cut and remove on each side of any proposed or existing installation all such trees and underwood as may interfere or be likely to interfere with the construction or proper working of any installation.

(2) Except for the purpose of removing danger to life or property, this section shall not authorise the Authority—

(a) to enter on any land which is occupied by any burial ground or cemetery or which contains any grave, grotto, area, tree or thing held to be sacred or the object of veneration ; or

(b) to cut any tree or underwood held to be sacred or the object of veneration, unless the owners or occupiers or the persons in charge thereof have given their prior assent.

(3) If any doubt arises whether any land, tree or underwood falls within those described in subsection (2) or who the persons competent to give their assent under subsection (2) are, the decision of the Commissioner shall be final for the purposes of this section.

> Power to enter on land.

20.—(1) Subject to the provisions of this section, before entering on any lands for the purposes defined in section 19 of this Decree the Authority shall give notice to the occupier of the land.

(2) The notice may be served either personally or by delivery of same at the place of abode of the person to be served.

(3) Where the condition of any installation is such as to endanger life or property, the Authority may enter on the land on which it is situated for any of the purposes defined in section 19 without notice.

> Notice of entry on land.

21.—(1) In the exercise of the powers conferred by section 19 of this Decree the Authority shall do as little damage as may be, and the Authority shall pay compensation for any damage done to any buildings, crops or economic trees.

(2) In case of dispute as to the amount of the compensation payable under this section the amount of the compensation may be determined by a magistrate having jurisdiction in respect of the place where the land is situated.

> Compensation for damage.

22. The Authority shall not, without the approval in writing of the Commissioner, alienate, mortgage, charge or demise any immovable property which has been vested in the Authority under or pursuant to the provisions of this Decree or in respect of which a right of occupancy has been granted to it.

> Restriction on alienation.

Financial Provisions

23.—(1) Subject to subsection (2) below, the Authority may from time to time borrow such sums as it may require in the exercise of its functions under this Decree.

> Borrowing powers.

(2) Subject to the following provisions of this section, the Authority shall not, without the approval of the Federal Executive Council, borrow any sum of money whereby the amount in aggregate outstanding on any loan or on all loans at any time exceeds ₦500,000 or such other limit as the Federal Executive Council may specify from time to time.

(3) A person lending to the Authority shall not be bound to enquire whether the borrowing is within the power of the Authority or not.

Funds of the Authority.

24. The Authority shall establish a fund which shall consist of—

(*a*) such sums as may be provided to it by the Federal Military Government for the running expenses of the Authority and all other assets from time to time accruing to the Authority ;

(*b*) such sums as may from time to time be lent to the Authority by any person ; and

(*c*) such sums as may be collected or received by the Authority from other sources either in the execution of its functions or in respect of any property vested in the Authority or otherwise howsoever.

Expenditure of the Authority.

25. The Authority may from time to time apply the proceeds of the fund established in pursuance of section 24 above—

(*a*) to the cost of administration of the Authority ;

(*b*) for reimbursing members of the Authority or of any committee set up by the Authority for such expenses as may be expressly authorised by the Authority in accordance with the rates approved by the Federal Executive Council ;

(*c*) to the payment of salaries, fees or other remuneration or allowances and pensions, superannuation allowances and gratuities payable to the officers and servants of the Authority, so however that no payment of any kind under this paragraph (except such as may be expressly authorised as aforesaid) shall be made to any person who is in receipt of emoluments from the Government of the Federation or the Government of a State ;

(*d*) for the maintenance of any property acquired or vested in the Authority ; and

(*e*) for and in connection with all or any of the functions of the Authority under this Decree.

Annual estimates, accounts and audit.

26.—(1) The Authority shall submit to the Commissioner not later than 31st December in each financial year an estimate of its expenditure and income during the next succeeding financial year.

(2) The Authority shall keep proper accounts and proper records in relation thereto and shall prepare in respect of each financial year a statement of accounts in such form as the Commissioner may direct.

(3) The Authority shall as soon as may be after the end of the financial year to which the accounts relate cause its accounts to be audited by qualified auditors approved by the Federal Commissioner for Finance.

(4) The auditors shall on completion of the audit of the accounts of the authority for each financial year prepare and submit to the Authority the following two reports, that is to say—

(*a*) a general report setting out the observations and recommendations of the auditors on the financial affairs of the Authority generally for that year and on any important matters which the auditors may consider necessary to bring to the notice of the Authority ; and (*b*) a detailed report containing the observations and recommendations of the auditors on all aspects of the operations of the Authority for that year.

Legal Proceedings

27.—(1) Notwithstanding anything in any other enactment, no suit against the Authority, a member or any staff of the Authority for any act done in pursuance or execution of any enactment or law, or of any public duties or authority, or in respect of any alleged neglect or default in the execution of such enactment or law, duties or authority, shall lie or be instituted in any court unless it is commenced within twelve months next after the act, neglect or default complained of or, in the case of a continuance of damage or injury, within twelve months next after the ceasing thereof.

(2) No suit shall be commenced against the Authority before the expiration of a period of one month after written notice of intention to commence the suit shall have been served upon the Authority by the intending plaintiff or his agent ; and the notice shall clearly and explicity state the cause of action, the particulars of the claim, the name and place of abode of the intending plaintiff and the relief which he claims.

28. The notice referred to in section 27 (2) above and any summons, notice or other document required or authorised to be served upon the Authority under the provisions of this Decree or any other enactment or law may be served by delivering the same to the Chairman or the Director-General of the Authority, or by sending it by registered post addressed to the Director-General at the principal office of the Authority or the relevant zonal office.

29. In any action or suit against the Authority no execution or attachment or process in the nature thereof shall be issued against the Authority, but any sums of money which may by the judgment of the court be awarded against the Authority shall, subject to any directions given by the court where notice of appeal has been given by the Authority in respect of the said judgment, be paid by the Authority from the funds of the Authority.

30. Every member, agent, auditor or staff for the time being of the Authority shall be indemnified out of the assets of the Authority against any liability incurred by him in defending any proceedings whether civil or criminal, in which judgment is given in his favour or in which he is acquitted, if any such proceeding is brought against him in his capacity as such member, agent, auditor or staff as aforesaid.

Miscellaneous and Supplementary

31. The Authority shall prepare and submit to the Federal Executive Council, through the Commissioner, not later than 30th June in each financial year a report in such form as he may direct on the activities of the Authority during the immediately preceding financial year, and shall include in such report a copy of the audited accounts of the Authority for that year and the auditor's report thereon.

32. The Federal Executive Council may by regulations published in the *Gazette* prescribe anything falling to be prescribed generally for the purposes of this Decree.

Limitation of suits against the Authority, etc.

Service of documents

Restriction on execution against the property of the Authority.

Indemnity of members and staff of the Authority.

Annual reports.

Regulations.

By-laws as
to conditions
of service
of staff.

33.—(1) The Authority may, with the approval of the Commissioner, make by-laws relating generally to the conditions of service of the officers and servants of the Authority ; and without prejudice to the generality of the foregoing, such by-laws may provide for—

(*a*) the appointment and disciplinary control of all employees of the Authority ; and

(*b*) appeals by such employees against dismissal or other disciplinary measures.

(2) By-laws made under subsection (1) above need not be published in the *Gazette* but the Authority shall bring them to the notice of all affected persons in such manner as it may from time to time determine.

Restricted
application
of the
Telegraphs
Act.
Cap. 195.

34. Nothing in section 4 of the Telegraphs Act shall apply to the broadcasting services provided by the Authority in accordance with the provisions of this Decree, so however that this subsection shall not exempt the Authority—

(*a*) from the provisions of section 4 of that Act in relation to any other telecommunication services, including telecommunication services ancillary to the broadcasting services which the Authority may desire to operate for the purpose of the efficient discharge of its functions under this Decree ; or

(*b*) from operating all broadcasting services provided by it in accordance with the terms, conditions and restrictions of a licence or licences granted under or pursuant to that Act or any other enactment to the Authority or to any affected authority referred to in Schedule 2 to this Decree.

Interpre-
tation.

35. In this Decree, unless the context otherwise requires—

"the Authority" means the Nigerian Television Authority established under section 1 of this Decree ;

"broadcasting" means television broadcasting ;

"the Chairman" means the person appointed as Chairman of the Nigerian Television Authority pursuant to section 2 (1) of this Decree ;

"the Commissioner" means the Federal Commissioner charged with responsibility for television broadcasting ;

"the Director-General" means the Director-General of the Nigerian Television Authority appointed pursuant to section 5 (1) of this Decree ;

"member" means a member of the Authority and includes the Chairman ;

"television broadcasting" means the transmission by wireless telegraphy of images of objects in movement or at rest ;

"Zone" means any one of the six zones into which Nigeria is divided for the purposes of section 14 (1) of this Decree ;

"Zonal Board" means the Nigerian Television Zonal Board established for each Zone.

Citation and
commence-
ment.

36. This Decree may be cited as the Nigerian Television Authority Decree 1977 and shall be deemed to have come into operation on 1st April 1976.

SCHEDULES

SCHEDULE 1

Section 1

SUPPLEMENTARY PROVISIONS RELATING TO THE AUTHORITY

Proceedings

1. Subject to this Decree and section 26 of the Interpretation Act 1964   1964 No. 1.
(which provides for decisions of a statutory body to be taken by a majority of
its members and for the chairman to have a second or casting vote), the
Authority may make standing orders regulating the proceedings of the
Authority or any committee thereof.

2. Every meeting of the Authority shall be presided over by the Chairman or, if the Chairman is unable to attend a particular meeting, the members
present at the meeting shall elect one of their number to preside at the
meeting.

3. The quorum at a meeting of the Authority shall consist of the
Chairman (or, in an appropriate case, the person presiding at the meeting
pursuant to paragraph 2 above) and five other members of whom at least two
shall be members appointed pursuant to paragraphs (*b*) and (*d*) of section 2
(1) of this Decree.

4. Where upon any special occasion the Authority desires to obtain the
advice of any person on any particular matter, the Authority may co-opt
that person to be a member for as many meetings as may be necessary, and
that person while so co-opted shall have all the rights and privileges of a
member except that he shall not be entitled to vote.

Committees

5.—(1) Subject to its standing orders, the Authority may appoint such
number of standing and *ad hoc* committees as it thinks fit to consider and
report on any matter with which the Authority is concerned.

(2) Every committee appointed under the foregoing provisions of this
paragraph shall be presided over by a member of the Authority and shall be
made up of such number of persons, not necessarily members of the
Authority, as the Authority may determine in each case.

(3) The quorum of any committee set up by the Authority shall be as
may be determined by the Authority.

6. Where standing orders made pursuant to paragraph 1 above provide
for a committee of the Authority to consist of or co-opt persons who are not
members of the Authority, the committee may advise the Authority on any
matter referred to it by the Authority.

Miscellaneous

7. The fixing of the seal of the Authority shall be authenticated by the
signature of the Chairman or of the Director-General of the Authority.

8. Any contract or instrument which, if made by a person not being a body corporate, would not be required to be under seal may be made or executed on behalf of the Authority by the Director-General or by any other person generally or specially authorised to act for that purpose by the Authority.

9. Any document purporting to be a contract, instrument or other document duly signed or sealed on behalf of the Authority shall be received in evidence and shall, unless the contrary is proved, be presumed without further proof to have been so signed or sealed.

10. The validity of any proceedings of the Authority or of a committee thereof shall not be affected —

(a) by any vacancy in the membership of the Authority, or any committee thereof, or

(b) by any defect in the appointment of a member of the Authority or any committee thereof.

11. Any member of the Authority or a committee thereof who has a personal interest in any contract or arrangement entered into or proposed to be considered by the Authority or committee thereof shall forthwith disclose his interest to the Authority or the committee and shall not vote on any question relating to the contract or arrangement.

12. No member of the Authority shall be personally liable for any act or omission done or made in good faith while engaged on the business of the Authority.

SCHEDULE 2

Section 7

Transitional Provisions relating to take-over of Staff and Television Facilities from other Broadcasting Organisations

1. Pursuant to section 7 of this Decree the functions conferred on, and being discharged by, any broadcasting authority affected by this Decree (hereinafter referred to as the "affected authority") and in so far as they relate to television broadcasting shall, as from the commencement of this Decree be disposed of in accordance with the following provisions of this Schedule and accordingly—

(a) the Authority shall so soon as may be after the commencement of this Decree but not later than the next twelve months following the making of this Decree, enter into such contract, agreement or other arrangement, as the Commissioner may approve, with every affected authority for the acquisition of such of its television equipment and facilities as may be necessary for the full discharge of the functions conferred on the Authority by or pursuant to this Decree ;

(*b*) within the next twelve months following the making of this Decree, the Commissioner, if he thinks fit, may by Order published in the *Gazette* make transitional or saving provisions relating to such of the employees of the affected authorities as may be required by the Authority for the full discharge of its functions as aforesaid ; and without prejudice to the generality of the foregoing, any such Order may provide for service under the aforementioned affected authorities to be regarded as service under the Authority for pensions purposes.

2. So soon as the provisions of paragraph 1 of this Schedule are complied with and, in any case, not later than the next twelve months following the making of this Decree (in either case hereinafter referred to as the "vesting day")—

(*a*) the rights, interests, obligations and liabilities in respect of television equipment and facilities of any affected authority existing immediately before the relevant vesting day, under any contract or instrument, shall by virtue of this Decree be assigned to and vested in the Authority ;

(*b*) any such contract or instrument as is mentioned in paragraph (*a*) above shall be of the same force and effect against or in favour of the Authority and shall be enforceable as fully and effectively as if instead of the affected authority, the Authority had been named therein or had been a party thereto ; and

(*c*) the Authority shall be subject to all the obligations and liabilities to which the affected authority was subject immediately before the relevant vesting day, and all other persons shall as from the aforesaid vesting day have the same rights, powers and remedies against the Authority as they had against the relevant affected authority before that day.

3. Any proceeding or cause of action pending or existing immediately before the relevant vesting day by or against an affected authority in respect of any right, interest, obligation or liability acquired pursuant to this Decree of such affected authority may be commenced, continued or enforced by or against the Authority as it might have been by or against an affected authority if this Decree had not been made.

4. In this Schedule—

"affected authority" means any authority (whether or not a statutory corporation and howsoever known or designated) set up by the Government of the Federation or by any State or group of States in Nigeria as a public body charged with responsibility, either wholly or partially, for television broadcasting which, pursuant to this Decree, is to divest itself of such responsibility ;

"vesting day" means the day (not being later than twelve months from the making of this Decree) on which television equipment and facilities of a particular affected authority are assigned to or vested in the Authority pursuant to paragraph 2 above.

MADE at Lagos this 23rd day of March 1977.

LT.-GENERAL O. OBASANJO,
Head of the Federal Military Government,
Commander-in-Chief of the Armed Forces,
Federal Republic of Nigeria

Explanatory Note

*(This note does not form part of the above Decree
but is intended to explain its purport)*

The Decree establishes the Nigerian Television Authority to be the body charged with exclusive responsibility for the provision of television broadcasting in Nigeria. Accordingly, provision is made by the Decree for the completion of the take-over by the Authority, within the next twelve months, of television broadcasting facilities from all other broadcasting organisations in Nigeria.

Other provisions relate to the division of Nigeria into six zones (each zone being under the supervision of a Zonal Board and each being capable of transmitting television broadcasts for reception anywhere in Nigeria) the establishment of a news department by the Authority and supplemental matters.

Appendix D

FEDERAL RADIO CORPORATION OF NIGERIA
DECREE 1979

ARRANGEMENT OF SECTIONS

Decree No. 8

[1st *April* 1978] Commencement.

THE FEDERAL MILITARY GOVERNMENT hereby decrees as follows :—

Establishment of the Corporation

1.—(1) There is hereby established a body to be known as the Federal Radio Corporation of Nigeria (hereinafter in this Decree referred to as "the Corporation") which under that name shall be a body corporate with perpetual succession and a common seal, and may sue and be sued in its corporate name

Establishment of the Federal Radio Corporation of Nigeria.

(2) The supplementary provisions contained in Schedule 1 to this Decree shall have effect with respect to the proceedings of the Corporation and the other matters mentioned therein.

2 —(1) The Corporation shall consist of a Chairman and the following other members to be appointed by the Commissioner with the prior approval of the Federal Executive Council, that is—

Membership of the Corporation and tenure of office.

(*a*) the Chairman of each Zonal Board ;

(*b*) the Director-General of the Corporation ;

(*c*) one representative of the Federal Ministry of Information ;

(*d*) one representative of the Ministry of External Affairs ;

(*e*) one person to represent women's interests in Nigeria ; and

(*f*) six persons with requisite experience in—

    (*i*) the mass media,

    (*ii*) education,

    (*iii*) management,

    (*iv*) financial matters,

    (*v*) engineering, and

    (*vi*) arts and culture.

(2) Subject to the provisions of this Decree, a person appointed to be a member of the Corporation, not being a public officer, shall hold office for a period of three years from the date of his appointment and shall be eligible for re-appointment for one further period of three years.

(3) Any member, not being a public officer, may resign his appointment by a letter addressed to the Commissioner.

(4) Members of the Corporation, not being public officers, shall be paid such remuneration and allowances as may be determined from time to time by the Federal Executive Council.

Removal
from office
of members
of the
Corporation.

3.—(1) If it appears to the Commissioner that a member of the Corporation should be removed from office on the grounds of misconduct or inability to perform the functions of his office, the Commissioner shall after consultation with the interests, if any, represented by that member make a recommendation to that effect to the Federal Executive Council, and if the Federal Executive Council approves the recommendation, the Commissioner may declare, in writing, the office of that member vacant.

(2) Without prejudice to subsection (1) above—

(*a*) any member who is absent from two consecutive ordinary meetings of the Corporation shall file his explanation in writing with the Secretary for consideration by the Corporation and if the explanation is not accepted by the Corporation ; or

(*b*) where the Corporation is satisfied that the continued presence on the Corporation of any member is not in the national interest or the interest of the Corporation,

the Corporation may recommend to the Commissioner that the member be removed and the Commissioner may declare, in writing, the office of that member vacant

Appointment
etc. of the
Director-
General and
other
employees
of the
Corporation.

4.—(1) There shall be an official of the Corporation to be known as the Director-General who shall be the chief executive officer of the Corporation and shall, subject to section 17 of this Decree, be responsible for the execution of the policy of the Corporation and its day to day business.

(2) The Director-General shall be appointed by the Commissioner with the prior approval of the Federal Executive Council.

(3) The Corporation shall appoint a Secretary to the Corporation who shall keep the records and conduct the correspondence of the Corporation and perform such other duties as the Corporation or the Director-General may from time to time direct.

(4) The Corporation may appoint such other employees and agents as it may deem necessary for the efficient performance of the functions of the Corporation under or pursuant to this Decree.

Functions of the Corporation

General
duties of the
Corporation.

5.—(1) It shall be the duty of the Corporation to provide as a public service in the interest of Nigeria, independent and impartial radio broadcasting services for general reception within Nigeria and to provide External Services for general reception in countries outside Nigeria.

(2) The Corporation shall ensure that the services which it provides, when considered as a whole, shall reflect the unity of Nigeria as a Federation and at the same time give adequate expression to the culture, characteristics and affairs and opinions of each State, Zone or other part of the Federation.

Exclusive
right of the
Corporation
to broadcast
in short-wave
or powerful
medium-
wave.

6.—(1) The Corporation shall, to the exclusion of any other broadcasting authority in Nigeria, be responsible for radio broadcasting in short-wave or powerful medium-wave for effective and simultaneous reception in more than one State at any one time and, accordingly, any other broadcasting authority in Nigeria shall be limited to transmission of radio broadcasts for effective reception in one State or part thereof and, in pursuance of this subsection, every radio broadcasting authority in Nigeria (other than those owned or controlled by the Government of the Federation) shall, as soon as may be after the making of this Decree, endeavour to transmit at such power as to ensure that the field strength, as measured at the State boundary, of which the transmitter is located, shall not be more than one millivolt per meter.

(2) In this section "broadcasting authority" means any authority (whether or not a statutory corporation and howsoever known or designated) set up by the Government of any State or group of States or by any other person or authority as a body charged with responsibility, either wholly or partially, for radio broadcasting.

7. The functions of the Corporation shall be—

(*a*) to erect, maintain and operate radio transmitting and receiving stations ;

(*b*) to install and operate wired radio distribution services ;

(*c*) to enter into arrangements with the Federal or a State Government or any other public body for the purpose of obtaining licences, rights, privileges and concessions ;

(*d*) to plan, regulate and co-ordinate the activities of the Zones and the entire Federal radio broadcasting system ;

(*e*) to ensure the establishment and maintenance of high standards and promote the efficient operation of the entire federal radio broadcasting system in accordance with national policy ;

(*f*) to establish and operate a formula for sharing funds amongst zonal stations.

(*g*) to organise, provide and subsidise for the purpose of broadcasting educational activities and public entertainment ;

(*h*) to collect from any part of the world and in any manner that may be thought fit news and information and, subject to the News Agency of Nigeria Decree 1976, to subscribe to news agencies ;

(*i*) subject to the News Agency of Nigeria Decree 1976, to provide and to receive from other persons matter to be broadcast ;

(*j*) to acquire copyrights ;

(*k*) to publish printed matter that may be conducive to the performance of any or all its functions ;

(*l*) to produce, manufacture, purchase or otherwise acquire gramophone and other mechanical records, tapes, and materials and apparatus for use in connection with records and tapes and to use them in connection with the broadcasting services ;

(*m*) to provide facilities for training and advancing the skill of persons employed in its services and for enhancing the efficiency of the equipment used in its services including provision by the Corporation or by others on its behalf of facilities for training, education and research ; and

(*n*) to carry out such other activities as are necessary or expedient for the full discharge of all or any of the functions conferred on it under or pursuant to this Decree.

(margin notes)

Particular functions of the Corporation.

1976 No. 19

Duty of the
Corporation
as to pro-
grammes and
publications.

8.—(1) The Corporation shall satisfy itself that the programmes broadcast by the Corporation and the Zones comply with the following requirements, that is to say—

(*a*) that nothing is included in the programmes which is likely to offend against good taste or decency or is likely to encourage or incite to crime or to lead to disorder or to be offensive to public feeling, or to contain an offensive reference to any person, alive or dead ;

(*b*) that the programmes maintain a proper balance in their subject matter and a generally high standard of quality ;

(*c*) that any news given in the programmes is presented with accuracy, impartiality and objectivity ;

(*d*) that due impartiality is preserved in respect of matters of political, or industrial controversy or relating to current public policy ; and

(*e*) that subject to subsection (2) above, no matter designed to serve the interests of any particular political party is included in the programmes ; and for the purposes of this subsection, the Corporation may set up a committee, which shall consist of the Director-General as the Chairman and all the Zonal Directors, to draw up guidelines and advise the Corporation on such other matters connected with the foregoing as the Corporation may from time to time refer to the committee.

(2) Nothing in paragraph (*e*) of subsection (1) above shall prevent—

(*a*) the inclusion in the programmes of properly balanced discussions or debates in which the persons taking part express opinions and put forward arguments of a political character ; and

(*b*) the inclusion in the programmes of party political broadcasts which seek to explain the views and policies of the various political parties in accordance with the scheme of such broadcasts which apportions the facilities and time allowed between the representatives of the political parties in such a manner as appears to the Corporation equitably to represent their respective claims to the interest of the public.

(3) The Corporation shall secure the exclusion from any publication which may be issued by it or on its behalf, and without prejudice to the generality of the provisions of this section, from the programmes broadcast by it or on its behalf, of its own opinion as to the matters referred to in paragraph (*d*) of subsection (1) above, or of the opinion as to any such matters of any of its members or employees or of the opinion as in such matter of any member or employee or any agent of the Corporation.

Broadcasting
of certain
matters.

9. Without prejudice to the generality of section 5 of this Decree, the Corporation shall provide such facilities as may appear to the Corporation to be desirable in the public interest for the broadcasting of—

(*a*) ministerial speeches, that is any speeches of the members of the Supreme Military Council, the National Council of States and the Federal Executive Council which consist wholly of statements of fact or which explain the policy and actions of the Government concerned ; and

(*b*) matters of any kind (including religious services or ceremonies) relating to or representing the main streams of religious thought or belief in Nigeria.

10.—(1) The Corporation shall, whenever so requested by an authorised public officer, broadcast a Government programme, at the Corporation's own expense, which such officer may request the Corporation to broadcast and shall also, whenever so requested by any such officer in whose opinion an emergency has arisen or continues, at the like expense, broadcast as aforesaid any other matter which the officer may request the Corporation to broadcast and the Corporation may in its descretion announce or refrain from announcing that such a notice has been given or has been varied or revoked.

Duty to broadcast government announce-ments.

(2) In this section "authorised public officer" means any officer in any of the public services in the Federation declared to be such by the Head of the Federal Military Government.

11. Without prejudice to sections 9 and 10 of this Decree, the Corporation shall not, for money or other valuable consideration received from any person, broadcast or refrain from broadcasting, any matter whatsoever or broadcast any commercial advertisement or sponsored programme :

Restriction on commercial or sponsored broadcasting.

Provided that nothing in this section shall be construed as precluding the Corporation from using for broadcasting purposes without payment or for a reduced payment any concert, theatrical entertainment or any other performance whatsoever given in public, or as precluding the Corporation from announcing the place of performance thereof or the name and description of the performers or from announcing the number and description of any record broadcast (including the name of the artist or names of the artists responsible therefor) or from acknowledging any permission granted for so using such matter.

12.—(1) News bulletins broadcast from the Federal headquarters therein referred to as a "Federal programme") in English and in any other language in common use in Nigeria as the Corporation may specify for the purpose (not being more than three) shall be relayed from transmitting stations of the Corporation not more than three times each day, but without prejudice to the right of the Zonal Boards of each Zone to cause items of news of zonal interest to be broadcast in English or any such language in common use in Nigeria in the zonal programme, or to cause a translation into any language aforesaid of a news bulletin broadcast in a Federal programme to be broadcast in a zonal programme.

Items to be relayed by all stations of the Corpora-tion.

(2) When any of the following items is broadcast in a Federal programme it shall be relayed by all the Corporation's transmitting stations, that is—

(*a*) speeches made by the Head of the Federal Military Government ;

(*b*) other matters of national interest or importance which the Corporation requires to be so relayed.

13.—(1) There shall be established a department of the Corporation which shall be responsible for External Services.

Matters to be broadcast in External Services.

(2) There shall be an officer of the Corporation to be known as Director of External Services who shall be responsible for the External Services department and shall, subject to any directions given to him by the Director-General, be responsible for the execution of the policy of the Corporation in so far as the External Services department is concerned and for the administration of the day to day business of the department.

(3) With respect to the External Services of the Corporation, the following provisions shall have effect, that is—

(*a*) the Corporation shall broadcast programmes in the External Services to such countries, in such languages and at such times as the Head of the Federal Military Government may prescribe from time to time ;

(*b*) the Corporation shall consult and collaborate with such ministries, departments and agencies of the Government of the Federation as may be specified by the Head of the Federal Military Government and shall obtain and accept from them such information regarding conditions in, and the policy of the Government of the Federation towards, the countries so prescribed and other countries as will enable the Corporation to plan and prepare its programmes in the External Services in the interest of the Federation.

Power of the Commissioner to issue directions to the Corporation.

14. Subject to section 13 of this Decree, the Commissioner may give the Corporation directions of a general character or relating generally to particular matters (but not to any individual or case) with regard to the exercise by the Corporation of its functions under this Decree, and it shall be the duty of the Corporation to comply with such directions.

Zonal Boards of the Corporation

Establishment of zones and Zonal Boards.

15.—(1) For the purposes of variety and better coverage, the Corporation shall have four zones which shall be responsible for broadcasting in the languages specified in respect of each such zone in Schedule 2 to this Decree.

(2) There shall be established for each zone, a Zonal Board which shall consist of not less than six or more than ten members, which members shall be broadly representative of the zone concerned and who shall be appointed by the Commissioner with the prior approval of the Federal Executive Council and shall include :—

(*a*) one member with wide knowledge of and experience in one of the following fields—

(*i*) newspapers, broadcasting and other media of mass communication,

(*ii*) cultural, economic and religious affairs of the zone, and

(*iii*) the creative arts ;

(*b*) two persons appearing to the Commissioner to have wide experience in education and finance respectively ;

(*c*) one person appearing to the Commissioner to represent the interests of business and industry ; and

(*d*) the Zonal Director.

(3) The Commissioner, with the prior approval of the Federal Executive Council, shall nominate one of the members of the Zonal Board approved by him to be the Chairman of the Board.

Tenure of Office.

16.—(1) Subject to section 3 of this Decree, a member of a Zonal Board (not being a public officer) shall hold office for a period of three years and shall be eligible for re-appointment for one further period of three years.

(2) There shall be paid to members of the Board (not being public officers) out of the money at the disposal of the Board such remuneration and allowances in respect of any period of time spent on the business of the Board as the Federal Executive Council may determine from time to time.

17. Subject to this Decree, each Zonal Board shall be responsible for— Functions of Zonal Boards

(*a*) the operation of its zonal stations and control of the general policy of the zonal programmes in such a manner as to ensure that all zonal programmes are selected with due regard to the distinctive culture, interests and tastes of the people of the Zone on the one hand, and the fulfilment of national needs on the other, and conform to any standards laid down by the Corporation ;

(*b*) the appointment of a Programme Advisory Committee to advise the Board on public reaction to its programmes and any other business of the Board referred to the Committee for advice ;

(*c*) the supervision and control over the acts of all employees of the Corporation in its zone subject to the approval of the Corporation ; and

(*d*) the performance of such other functions as the Corporation may delegate to it from time to time.

18.—(1) There shall be for each zone, an officer of the Corporation to be known as the Zonal Director who shall be appointed by the Corporation. Appointment of Zonal Directors.

(2) In each Zone, the Zonal Director shall—

(*a*) subject to any direction given to him by the Director-General, be responsible for the execution of the policy of the Corporation and the administration of its day to day business ; and

(*b*) be the chief executive of the Zonal Board in matters within the competence of the Zonal Board and be responsible for giving effect to the decisions of the Zonal Board.

Provisions as to Entry on Land

19.—(1) The Corporation shall have power— power to enter on land.

(*a*) to enter on any lands for the purpose of erecting, maintaining and inspecting any installations belonging to the Corporation or of repairing, altering or removing any such installations and to remain there for such reasonable time and execute and do all such works as may be necessary for the purposes of this Decree ; and

(*b*) to cut and remove on each side of any proposed or existing installation all such trees and underwood as may interfere or be likely to interfere with the construction or proper working of any installation.

(2) Except for the purpose of removing danger to life or property, nothing in this section shall be construed as authorising the Corporation—

(*a*) to enter on any land which is occupied by any burial ground or cemetery or which contains any grave, grotto, area, tree or thing held to be sacred or the object of veneration ; or

(*b*) to cut any tree or underwood held to be sacred or the object of veneration, unless the owners or occupiers or the persons in charge thereof have given their prior assent.

(3) If any doubt arises whether any land, tree or underwood falls within those described in subsection (2) above or as to the persons competent to give their assent under the said subsection, the decision of the Commissioner shall be final for the purposes of this section.

Notice of
entry on
land.

20.—(1) Subject to the provisions of this section, before entering on any lands for the purposes defined in section 19 of this Decree the Corporation shall give notice to the occupier of the land and such notice may be served either personally or by delivery of same at the last known place of abode of the person to be served.

(2) Where the condition of any installation is such as to endanger life or property, the Corporation may enter on the land on which it is situated for any of the purposes mentioned in section 19 without notice.

Compensa-
tion for
damage.

21.—(1) In the exercise of the powers conferred by section 19 of this Decree the Corporation shall do as little damage as may be necessary and the Corporation shall pay compensation for any damage done to any buildings crops or economic trees.

1978 No. 6.

(2) In case of dispute as to the amount of compensation payable under this section, such dispute shall be referred to the appropriate Land Use and Allocation Committee set up under the Land Use Decree 1978.

Restriction
on alienation.

22. The Corporation shall not, without the approval in writing of the Commissioner, alienate, mortgage, charge or demise any immovable property which has been vested in the Corporation under or pursuant to the provisions of this Decree or in respect of which a right of occupancy has been granted to it.

Financial Provisions

Funds of the
Corporation.

23. The Corporation shall establish a fund which shall consist of—

(*a*) such sums as may be provided to it by the Government of the Federation for the running expenses of the Corporation and all other assets from time to time accruing to the Corporation ;

(*b*) such sums as may from time to time be lent to the Corporation by any person ; and

(*c*) such sums as may be collected or received by the Corporation from other sources either in the execution of its functions or in respect of any property vested in the Corporation or otherwise howsoever.

Expenditure
of the
Corporation.

24. The Corporation may from time to time apply the proceeds of the fund established in pursuance of section 23 of this Decree—

(*a*) to the cost of administration of the Corporation ;

(*b*) for reimbursing members of the Corporation or of any committees set up by the Corporation for such expenses as may be authorised by the Corporation in accordance with the rates approved by the Federal Executive Council ;

(*c*) to the payment of salaries, fees or other remuneration or allowances and pensions, gratuities and other retiring benefits payable to the employees of the Corporation, so however that no payment of any kind under this paragraph (except such as may be expressly authorised by the Corporation) shall be made to any person who is in receipt of emoluments from any Government in the Federation ;

(*d*) for the maintenance of any property acquired or vested in the Corporation ; and

(*e*) for and in connection with all or any of the functions of the Corporation under this Decree.

25.—(1) Subject to subsection (2) below, the Corporation may from time to time borrow such sums as it may require in the exercise of its functions under this Decree.

Borrowing powers.

(2) The Corporation shall not, without the approval of the Federal Executive Council, borrow any sum of money whereby the amount in aggregate outstanding on any loan or on all loans at any one time exceeds ₦500,000 or such other limit as the Federal Executive Council may specify from time to time.

(3) Notwithstanding subsection (2) above, a person lending to the Corporation shall not be bound to enquire whether the borrowing is within the power of the Corporation or not.

26.—(1) The Corporation shall submit to the Commissioner not later than 31st December in each financial year (or such other date as the Commissioner may appoint in respect of the first year of existence of the Corporation) an estimate of its expenditure and income during the next succeeding financial year.

Annual estimates, accounts and audit.

(2) The Corporation shall keep proper accounts and proper records relating thereto and shall prepare in respect of each financial year a statement of accounts in such form as the Commissioner may direct.

(3) The Corporation shall as soon as may be after the end of the financial year to which the accounts relate cause its accounts to be audited by qualified auditors approved in that behalf by the Federal Executive Council.

(4) The auditors shall on completion of the audit of the accounts of the Corporation for each financial year prepare and submit to the Corporation the following two reports, that is to say—

(*a*) a general report setting out the observations and recommendations of the auditors on the financial affairs of the Corporation generally for that year and on any important matters which the auditors may consider necessary to bring to the notice of the Corporation ; and

(*b*) a detailed report containing the observations and recommendations of the auditors on all aspects of the operations of the Corporation for that year.

Legal Proceedings

27.—(1) Notwithstanding anything to the contrary in any other enactment, no suit against the Corporation, a member or any employee of the Corporation for any act done in pursuance or execution of any enactment or law, or of any public duties or authority, or in respect of any alleged negligence or default in the execution of such enactment or law, duties or authority, shall lie or be instituted in any court unless it is commenced within 12 months next after the act, negligence or default complained of or, in the case of a continuance of damage or injury, within 12 months next after the ceasing thereof.

Limitation of suits against the Corporation, etc.

(2) No suit shall be commenced against the Corporation before the expiration of a period of one month after the written notice of intention to commence the suit shall have been served upon the Corporation by the intending plaintiff or his authorised agent ; and the notice shall clearly and explicitly state the cause of action, the particulars of the claim, the name and place of abode of the intending plaintiff and the relief which he claims.

Service of
documents.

28. The notice referred to in section 27 (2) of this Decree and any summons, notice or other document required or authorised to be served upon the Corporation under the provisions of this Decree or any other enactment or law may be served by delivering the same to the Chairman or the Director-General of the Corporation or by sending it by registered post addressed to the Director-General at the principal office of the Corporation or the appropriate zonal office.

Restriction
on execution
against the
property of
the
Corporation.

29. In any action or suit against the Corporation no execution or attachment or process in the nature thereof shall be issued against the Corporation. but any sums of money which may by the judgment of the court be awarded against the Corporation shall, subject to any directives given by the court where notice of appeal has been given by the Corporation in respect of the said judgment, be paid by the Corporation from the funds of the Corporation.

Indemnity
of members
and
employees of
the
Corporation.

30. Every member, agent, auditor or employee for the time being of the Corporation shall be indemnified out of the assets of the Corporation against any liability incurred by him in defending any proceedings whether civil or criminal in which judgment is given in his favour or in which he is acquitted, if any such proceeding has been brought against him in his capacity as such member, agent, auditor or employee as aforesaid.

Miscellaneous and Supplementary

Dissolution
of certain
bodies and
transfer of
assets and
liabilities
thereof to
the
Corporation;
repeals and
savings.
Cap. 133.

31.—(1) The Nigerian Broadcasting Corporation established under the Nigerian Broadcasting Corporation Act is hereby dissolved and the said Act is hereby repealed and the following enactments are hereby consequentially repealed, that is—

1959 No. 24.
1960 No. 39.
1961 No. 35.

(a) the Nigerian Broadcasting Corporation (Amendment) Act 1959 ;
(b) the Nigerian Broadcasting Corporation (Amendment) Act 1960 ; and
(c) the Nigerian Broadcasting Corporation (Amendment) Act 1961.

1968 No. 51.

(2) Notwithstanding the provisions of the Companies Decree 1968 or any instrument (including the articles of association of the Company) the company known as the Broadcasting Company of Northern Nigeria is hereby dissolved.

(3) The transitional and saving provisions in Schedule 3 to this Decree shall have effect in relation to the employees, assets and liabilities of the bodies dissolved under this section and the other broadcasting organisations mentioned therein notwithstanding any other provision of this Decree or any other enactment.

Staff
regulations
as to
conditions of
service of
employees.

32.—(1) The Corporation may, with the approval of the Commissioner. make staff regulations relating generally to the conditions of service of the employees of the Corporation ; and without prejudice to the generality of the foregoing, such regulations may provide for—

(a) the appointment, promotion and disciplinary control of all employees of the Corporation ; and (*b*) appeals by such employees against dismissal or other disciplinary measures ;

and until such regulations are made any instrument relating to the conditions of service of employees of any body dissolved or affected by this Decree immediately before the making of this Decree, shall continue in force and have the same effect as if made under this Decree.

(2) Regulations made under subsection (1) above need not be published in the *Gazette* but the Corporation shall bring them to the notice of all affected persons in such manner as it may from time to time determine.

33. Nothing in section 4 of the Telegraphs Act shall apply to the broadcasting services provided by the Corporation in accordance with the provisions of this Decree, so however that this subsection shall not exempt the Corporation—

(*a*) from the provisions of section 4 of that Act in relation to any other telecommunication services ancillary to the broadcasting services, including telecommunication services to the broadcasting services which the Corporation may desire to operate for the purpose of the efficient discharge of its functions under this Decree ; or

(*b*) from operating broadcasting services provided by it in accordance with the terms, conditions and restrictions of a licence or licences granted under that Act, the Wireless Telegraphy Act 1961, or any other enactment to the Corporation or to any dissolved or affected body referred to in Schedule 3 to this Decree.

Restricted application of the Telegraphs Act. Cap. 195.

1961 No. 31.

34. The Corporation shall prepare and submit to the Federal Executive Council, through the Commissioner, not later than 30th June in each year (or such other date as the Commissioner may appoint in respect of the first year of existence of the Corporation) a report in such form as he may direct on the activities of the Corporation during the immediately preceding financial year, and shall include in such report a copy of the audited accounts of the Corporation for that year and the auditor's report thereon.

Annual reports.

35. The Federal Executive Council may make regulations generally for the proper carrying into effect of the provisions of this Decree and the due administration thereof.

Regulations.

36. In this Decree, unless the context otherwise requires—

Interpretation.

"broadcasting services" or "radio broadcasting" means services by which matter is sent by wireless telegraphy for general reception or is distributed through radio distribution services in sound, but does not include television broadcasting within the meaning of the Nigerian Television Authority Decree 1977 ;

1977 No. 24.

"the Chairman" means the person appointed for the time being as Chairman of the Corporation pursuant to section 2 of this Decree or, as the case may require, of a Zonal Board under section 15 of this Decree :

"the Commissioner" means the Federal Commissioner for the time being charged with responsibility for radio broadcasting ;

"the Corporation" means the Federal Radio Corporation of Nigeria established under section 1 of this Decree and includes the Zonal Boards ;

"the Director-General" means the Director-General of the Corporation appointed pursuant to section 4 of this Decree ;

"member" means a member of the Corporation or, as the case may require, of a Zonal Board and in each case includes the appropriate Chairman ;

"Zone" means any of the four Zones established by section 15 of this Decree ;

"Zonal Board" means any of the Federal Radio Corporation of Nigeria Zonal Boards referred to in section 15 of this Decree.

Citation and commence-ment.

37. This Decree may be cited as the Federal Radio Corporation of **Nigeria** Decree 1979 and shall be deemed to have come into operation on 1st April 1978.

SCHEDULES

SCHEDULE 1   *Section* 1

Supplementary Provisions Relating to the Corporation and Zonal Boards

Proceedings

1964 No. 1.

1. Subject to this Decree and section 26 of the Interpretation Act 1964 (which provides for decisions of a statutory body to be taken by a majority of its members and for the person presiding to have a second or casting vote), the Corporation may make standing orders regulating the proceedings of the Corporation or any committee thereof.

2. Every meeting of the Corporation shall be presided over by the Chairman or, if the Chairman is unable to attend a particular meeting, the members present at the meeting shall elect one of their number to preside at the meeting.

3. The quorum at a meeting of the Corporation shall consist of the Chairman (or, in an appropriate case, the person presiding at the meeting pursuant to paragraph 2 above) and five other members of whom at least two shall be members appointed pursuant to paragraphs (*b*) and (*c*) of section 2 (1) of this Decree.

4. Where upon any special occasion the Corporation desires to obtain the advice of any person on any particular matter, the Corporation may co-opt that person to be a member for as many meetings as may be necessary, and that person while so co-opted shall have all the rights and privileges of a member except that he shall not be entitled to vote.

Committees

5.—(1) Subject to its standing orders, the Corporation may appoint such number or standing and *ad hoc* committees as it thinks fit to consider and report on any matter with which the Corporation is concerned.

(2) Every committee appointed under the foregoing provisions of this paragraph shall be presided over by a member of the Corporation and shall be made up of such number of persons, not necessarily members of the Corporation, as the Corporation may determine in each case.

(3) The quorum of any committee set up by the Corporation shall be as may be determined by the Corporation.

(4) The provisions of this paragraph shall not apply to any committee set up pursuant to section 8 (1) of this Decree.

6. Where standing orders made pursuant to paragraph 1 above provide for a committee of the Corporation to consist of or co-opt persons who are not members of the Corporation, the committee may advise the Coraportion on any matter referred to it by the Corporation.

Miscellaneous

7. The fixing of the seal of the Corporation shall be authenticated by the signature of the Chairman or of the Director-General of the Corporation.

8. Any contract or instrument which, if made by a person not being a body corporate, would not be required to be under seal may be made or executed on behalf of the Corporation by the Director-General or by any other person generally or specially authorised to act for that purpose by the Corporation.

9. Any document purporting to be a contract, instrument or other document duly signed or sealed on behalf of the Corporation shall be received in evidence and shall, unless the contrary is proved, be presumed without further proof to have been so signed or sealed.

10. The validity of any proceedings of the Corporation or of a committee thereof shall not be affected—

(*a*) by any vacancy in the membership of the Corporation, or any committee thereof ; or

(*b*) by any defect in the appointment of a member of the Corporation or any committee thereof.

11. Any member of the Corporation or a committee thereof who has a personal interest in any contract or arrangement entered into or proposed to be considered by the Corporation or committee thereof shall forthwith disclose his interest to the Corporation or the committee and shall not vote on any question relating to the contract or arrangement.

12. No member of the Corporation shall be personally liable for any act or omission done or made in good faith while engaged on the business of the Corporation.

Proceedings of Zonal Boards

13. The provisions of this Schedule shall apply *mutatis mutandis* to Zonal Boards, so however that with respect to the quorum at a meeting of any Zonal Board the provisions of the following paragraph shall apply.

14. The quorum at a meeting of a Zonal Board shall consist of the Chairman (or in his absence any member of the Board elected by members present to preside at a particular meeting) and—

(*a*) in the case of a Board with not more than six members, two other members ;

(*b*) in the case of a Board with more than six members, three other members.

SCHEDULE 2

Section 15 (1)

THE ZONES AND THEIR RESPONSIBILITIES

Name of Zone	*Linguistic and other Coverage*
1. F.R.C.N.—Lagos (Located in Lagos)	(a) English and three Nigerian Languages. (b) National Programmes. (c) Educational Service Programmes. (d) F.R.C.-2.
2. F.R.C.N.—Kaduna (Located in Kaduna)	English, Hausa, Kanuri, Fulfulde and Nupe.
3. F.R.C.N.—Ibadan (Located in Ibadan)	English, Yoruba, Edo, Igala and Urhobo.
4. F.R.C.N.—Enugu (Located in Enugu)	English, Igbo, Izon, Efik and Tiv.

SCHEDULE 3

Section 31

TRANSITIONAL AND SAVINGS PROVISIONS AS TO
TAKE-OVER, ETC., OF STAFF AND ASSETS
AND LIABILITIES OF CERTAIN BODIES

Part A—Nigerian Broadcasting Corporation

1. By virtue of this Decree, there shall be vested in the Federal Radio Corporation of Nigeria (referred to in this Schedule as "the new Corporation") on the appointed day, without further assurance but subject as hereinafter provided, all assets, funds, resources and other movable or immovable property which immediately before the appointed day were vested in the Nigerian Broadcasting Corporation dissolved by this Decree (referred to in this Schedule as "the old Corporation").

2. As from the appointed day—

(a) the rights, interests, obligations and liabilities of the old Corporation existing immediately before the appointed day under any contract or instrument, or at law or in equity apart from any contract or instrument, shall by virtue of this Decree be assigned to and vested in the new Corporation ;

(b) any such contract or instrument as is mentioned in sub-paragraph (a) above shall be of the same force and effect against or in favour of the new Corporation and shall be enforceable as fully and effectively as if instead of the old Corporation, the new Corporation had been named therein or had been a party thereto ; and

(c) the new Corporation shall be subject to all the obligations and liabilities to which the old Corporation was subject immediately before the appointed day, and all other persons shall, as from the appointed day, have the same rights, powers and remedies against the new Corporation as they had against the old Corporation immediately before the appointed day.

3. Any proceeding or cause of action pending or existing immediately before the appointed day by or against the old Corporation in respect of any right, interest, obligation or liability of the old Corporation may be continued or, as the case may be, commenced and any determination of a court of law, tribunal or other authority or person may be enforced, by or against the new Corporation to the same extent that any such proceeding, cause of action or determination might have been continued, commenced or enforced by or against the old Corporation if this Decree had not been made.

Part B—Broadcasting Company of Northern Nigeria Limited

4. By virtue of this Decree, there shall be vested in the new Corporation on the appointed day, without further assurance but subject as hereinafter provided, all assets, funds, resources and other movable or immovable property which immediately before the appointed day were vested in the Broadcasting Company of Northern Nigeria Limited dissolved by this Decree (referred to in this Schedule as "the Company").

5. As from the appointed day—

(a) the rights, interests, obligations and liabilities of the Company existing immediately before the appointed day under any contract or instrument, or at law or in equity apart from any contract or instrument shall by virtue of this Decree be deemed to have been assigned to and vested in the new Corporation ;

(b) any such contract or instrument as is mentioned in sub-paragraph (a) above shall be of the same force and effect against or in favour of the new Corporation and shall be enforceable as fully and effectively as if instead of the Company, the new Corporation had been named therein or had been a party thereto ; and

(c) the new Corporation shall be subject to all the obligations and liabilities to which the Company was subject immediately before the appointed day and all other persons shall, as from the appointed day, have the same rights, powers and remedies against the new Corporation as they had against the Company immediately before the appointed day.

6. Any proceeding or cause of action pending or existing immediately before the appointed day by or against the Company in respect of any right, interest, obligation or liability of the Company may be continued, or as the case may be, commenced and any determination of a court of law, tribunal or other authority or person may be enforced, by or against the new Corporation to the same extent that any such proceeding, cause of action or determination might have been continued, commenced or enforced by or against the Company if this Decree had not been made.

Part C—Certain States Broadcasting Organisations

7. By virtue of this Decree, there shall be vested in the new Corporation on the appointed day, without further assurance such of the transmitters, which do not comply with the specifications mentioned in section 6 of this Decree and which immediately before the appointed day were vested in any radio broadcasting organisation (other than the old Corporation and the Company), as may be necessary for the full discharge by the new Corporation of its functions under or pursuant to this Decree.

8.—(1) By virtue of this Decree, there shall be deemed to have been vested, on the appointed day, by the new Corporation in any broadcasting organisation (corporate or unincorporate) owned or controlled by any State Government mentioned in the first column of the Table to this Schedule, the State broadcasting station located at the place or places mentioned in the second column/thereof which, immediately before the appointed day, was vested in the old Corporation.

(2) For the purposes of this paragraph, "State broadcasting station" means the broadcasting complex comprising the studios, transmitting stations, buildings, structures and ancillary works and all equipment and other assets (movable or immovable) used for the purpose of radio broadcasting by the station concerned.

9. The provisions of paragraphs 2 and 3 of this Schedule shall apply *mutatis mutandis* between the new Corporation and any affected organisation under paragraph 7 of this Schedule or, as the case may require, between the new Corporation and any broadcasting organisation under paragraph 8 of this Schedule as they apply between the old Corporation and the new Corporation.

Part D—Disposition of Employees of Organisations Affected

10. Notwithstanding the dissolution of the old Corporation and the Company by section 31 of this Decree but subject as hereinafter provided, any person who immediately before the appointed day held office under the old Corporation or the Company shall, on the appointed day, be deemed to have been transferred to the new Corporation on terms and conditions not less favourable than those obtaining immediately before the appointed day ; and service under the old Corporation or the Company shall be deemed to be service under the new Corporation for pensions purposes.

11. Any broadcasting organisation mentioned in paragraph 8 of this Schedule shall, subject as hereinafter mentioned, employ such persons being persons on the established staff of the old Corporation as may have been deployed from the service of the old Corporation to the service of such organisation immediately before the appointed day and such persons shall be deemed to have been deployed, on the appointed day, to such organisation by the new Corporation.

12.—(1) Any broadcasting organisation mentioned in paragraph 8 of this Schedule shall, not later than 3 months after the making of this Decree, by notice in writing offer, to every person remaining deployed to the service of such organisation at that time, employment by the organisation upon such terms and conditions as are not less favourable than these enjoyed by that person immediately before the date of such offer.

(2) For the purposes of this Schedule, the terms and conditions comprised in any offer shall not be construed as being less favourable merely because they are not in all respects identical with or superior to the terms and conditions enjoyed by the person concerned immediately before the date of such offer, if the first-mentioned terms and conditions taken as a whole offer substantially equivalent or greater benefits.

13.—(1) Any person to whom an offer of employment is made pursuant to paragraph 12 of this Schedule and who fails within 30 days thereafter to give the organisation concerned an acceptance in writing of the offer shall be deemed to have refused the offer.

(2) If a person refuses an offer of employment made to him pursuant to the said paragraph 12 (either as provided in sub-paragraph (1) above or otherwise howsoever), the obligation imposed on the organisation concerned to employ that person shall thereupon determine :

Provided that nothing herein shall be construed as extinguishing the right of any such person to be re-deployed to the new Corporation if, immediately before the appointed day, he was holding office as provided in paragraph 10 of this Schedule.

14. When a person accepts an offer of employment made pursuant to paragraph 12 of this Schedule, such person shall be deemed to have been transferred to the service of the organisation concerned with effect from the appointed day.

Part E—Miscellaneous and Supplementary

15. Notwithstanding any other provision of this Decree, it is hereby declared that any contract or obligation (at law or in equity) entered into or incurred in good faith by any employee of the old Corporation or the Company (being an employee having power immediately before the appointed day to enter into contracts on behalf of either body) on behalf of the new Corporation or having such effect, after the date of dissolution of the old Corporation and the Company by this Decree but before the date of making this Decree, shall be deemed to have been validly entered into or incurred by the new Corporation notwithstanding—

(*a*) the dissolution, as at that date, of the old Corporation and the Company by this Decree ; or

(*b*) the establishment, as at that date, by this Decree of the new Corporation ;

and accordingly, the provisions of this Schedule shall be construed with all such modifications (including alteration, substitution or omission of any entry in any relevant instrument) as may be necessary to give full effect to such contract or obligation as if the new Corporation had itself entered into such contract or incurred such obligation in the first instance.

16. Within the 12 months next after the making of this Decree the National Council of States, if it thinks fit, may by order published in the *Gazette* make additional transitional or saving provisions for the better carrying out of the objectives of this Schedule and may, by any such order, vary all or any of the provisions of this Schedule.

17. In this Schedule—

"the appointed day" means the day of coming into operation of this Decree ;

"the Company" has the meaning assigned thereto by paragraph 4 of this Schedule :

"the new Corporation" has the meaning assigned thereto by paragraph 1 of this Schedule ;

"the old Corporation" has the meaning assigned thereto by paragraph 1 of this Schedule.

TABLE   *Paragraph* 8

State	Location or locations of State Broadcasting Station of the dissolved Nigerian Broadcasting Corporation handed over
(1) Bauchi	Bauchi
(2) Bendel	Benin and Warri
(3) Benue	Makurdi
(4) Borno	Maiduguri
(5) Cross River	Calabar
(6) Gongola	Yola
(7) Imo	Owerri
(8) Kaduna	Kaduna, Zaria and Katsina
(9) Kano	Kano
(10) Kwara	Ilorin
(11) Lagos	Ikeja
(12) Niger	Minna
(13) Ogun	Abeokuta
(14) Ondo	Akure
(15) Plateau	Jos
(16) Rivers	Port Harcourt
(17) Sokoto	Sokoto

MADE at Lagos this 28th day of February 1979.

LT-GENERAL O. OBASANJO,
Head of the Federal Military Government,
Commander-in-Chief of the Armed Forces,
Federal Republic of Nigeria

EXPLANATORY NOTE

(This note does not form part of the above Decree but
is intended to explain its effect)

The Decree establishes the Federal Radio Corporation of Nigeria which, in addition to providing effective radio broadcasting services on a national scale, will also be responsible for providing external broadcasting services.

For the purposes of effective coverage and variety, the Corporation is divided into Zones to be administered by Zonal Boards and each such authority would be principally responsible for radio coverage of the Zone although capable also of national coverage.

The Decree also provides that any radio broadcasting organisation owned by a State should confine itself to coverage of that State only and, for the achievement of that objective, would be precluded from transmissions at such power as to exceed those specified in the Decree.

Appendix E

FEDERAL REPUBLIC OF NIGERIA

PAPER PRESENTED

BY

THE FEDERAL MINISTRY OF INFORMATION AND CULTURE

ON

CONSIDERATIONS FOR THE FORMULATION AND IMPLEMENTATION OF PUBLIC POLICY ON MASS MEDIA HARDWARES

AT THE

NATIONAL COMMUNICATION POLICY SEMINAR

2ND-7TH FEBRUARY, 1987

CONSIDERATIONS FOR THE FORMULATION AND IMPLEMENTATION OF PUBLIC POLICY ON MASS MEDIA HARDWARES : THE CHALLENGES OF NEW COMMUNICATION TECHNOLOGIES

Presented by the Federal Ministry of Information and Culture

Introduction

The Federal Ministry of Information and Culture welcomes each and everyone of you, attending this seminar on Communication Policy, into the Age of Information Technologies (AIT). Mankind has demonstrated his capacity to invent and conquer natural barriers in a bid to achieve efficiency and reliability in information processing. The age of communication revolution is here. We now live in a global information society. However, Nigeria is yet to undergo the transformation to become a member of the much-talked-about information society.

Let us take a brief inventory of some of the new forms of the "new media". The Cable TV, unlike the conventional TV systems, comes with it the capability to transmit TV programmes through a cable installed between the station and a subscriber's home. It also has the in-built technology that offers information such as home-banking, home-shopping and telemetering. The videotex and Teletext systems make it possible for information, stored in the form of characters and diagrams in data bases to be decoded on television screens when needed, by pushing the appropriate button. Videotex provides information on stock trading, the weather, shopping, travel, etc. On the other hand, Teletext provides a TV set with the appropriate gadget to call up information whenever needed. However, the information is transmitted along with TV programmes. The Direct Satellite Broadcasting System allows a television household to receive TV programmes directly from a satellite. The Still Picture Broadcasting provides lecture programmes on any subject. The Video Response System relies on wide-band lines of either co-axial cables or fibre optics to provide the same function as Videotex, in addition to voice-overs and moving pictures.[1] It is the amalgamation, or rather integration of the communication, postal communication, broadcasting and the print media that we refer to as the "new media". Formerly, each of the four was independent of the other. But modern technological advances have made it possible to merge them.[2] This has resulted in the advent of another media–electronic mail and electronic newspaper. The consequence of the "new media" is that there is no longer any defined demarcation between mass communication and telecommunication, as used to be the case in the past. Telecommunication system has constructed Integrated Services Digital Networks (ISDN). The implication of this is that in the past, such individual networks as telegraph, telephone, telex existed and functioned independent of one another. The advent of ISDN now makes it possible for all these once independent communication media systems to be merged into one single network.

Social Functions of Advanced Communication/Technology

In our selection and adoption of the "new media", our choice is usually influenced by the following technical characteristics they posses: promptness, effective bit rate, cheapness, reliability, accessibility, storage retrieval capacity and confidentially.[3] We are also influenced by the following technical functions they also posses: specific instruction, marketing information, news and weather services, entertainment, opinion formation and personal correspondence.[4] In a developing nation, such as ours, the new media technologies are being adopted because of the expected services they promise: that of raising the overall quality of life of rural residents in our numerous villages. The overall quality of life they are expected to enable us achieve is determined by the degree of the fulfillment of the following human goals: individual group, material and spiritual.[5] These goals are expected to lead in the formulation of communication policy, based on the new technology, that would lead to the provision of basic human needs, such as food, shelter, clothing, health, etc.[6]

The Political Realities of the "New Media" Technologies

Ordinarily, mankind, in all the countries of the world, irrespective of political leanings and ideologies, would have thought that the advent of the new communication/information technologies would lead to accelerated development in the Third Word. This is not to be the case. It is a false expectation to think that the new communication technologies are independent phenomena that would create new societies and new human conditions. A Third World critic of the new media, Dongshin Lee, is convinced that "advanced communication technologies such as computer networks and satellite broadcasting systems were introduced to many Third World countries only to worsen the cultural and financial dependency upon the advanced nations".[7] The new communication technologies do not only have extensive potentials to widen the North-South information gap, but also have the capability of promoting and consolidating Western cultural and economic dominance. Since the debate on the New World Information and Communication Order (NWICO) began, there has been very little change, if any, in the flow of information and media contents along the North-South information axis.[8]

Communication and information experts have identified two dimensions to the debate on new world information and communication order. One aspect of the debate is concerned with fairness (objectivity) in the media contents (bad news coverage) that give negative picture of African and other Third World nations by the mass media of the industrial world. The other area of the debate deals with the uneven flow of information that virtually gives monopoly of dissemination of media products that assault and threaten to submerge and subdue the cultures of the developing countries.[9]

While academics seem to be concerned with both media contents and information flow and balance between the North and the South, bureaucrats and other administrators in Governments and related parastatals and agencies are not only concerned with the research orientations and problems the academics have identified by the contents of the news channels that also gave rise to the debate, but rather, they (administrators and bureaucrats) are also much more concerned with the economic data that are transmitted daily across national borders for the benefit of transnational corporation.[10] Also implicit in the latter's concern is the identification of the potential for direct satellite broadcasting and the use of earth-scanning satellites. All these pose a great deal, of problem in the national security of the politically and economically weak nations in Africa, Latin America, Asia, etc. etc. In this regard, the following fair and honest evaluation of this aspect of the new broadcast technology by a former director of the United States Information Agency, buttresses our point:

"Long before a direct broadcast satellite....there will be electronic networks—some of them already in operation—which will pose realistic questions about information flow and cultural integrity....These networks will move massive amounts of information through high-speed circuits across national boundaries. Moreover, they will be effectively beyond the reach of the traditional forms of censorhip and control. The only way to "censor" on electronic network moving..648 million bits per set and is literally to pull the plug. The international extension of electronic mail transmission, data packet networks, and information-bank retrieval systems in future years will have considerably more effect on national cultures than any direct broadcast systems..."[11]

Also, the transmission of economic data that will enrich the multinational corporations, to the disadvantage of the developing nations, through the new technologies, is perceptively summarised by Herbert I. Schiller, an acclaimed American communications scholar thus:

"It requires little imagination to predict who will have control of and access to these (new) electronic networks....IBM now sits astride the global computer market. Poor nations and voiceless subgroups within countries, developed and non-developed, are and will probably be shut out from these powerful new capabilities of administration and governance. Unless there is social mobilization and awareness not now apparent, further domination and dependency will be the likely accompaniments of the extension of the new information technology.[12]"

That the new information technology is synonymous with domination and dependency is also attested to by the following account that Schiller has presented:

"....a minority report of a Brazillian government inquiry on the impact of the multinational corporations in Brazil, found that 'the multinationals have concentrated on producing expensive goods, such as automobiles and colour television sets, that demand a concentration of income....so more debts have been built up to finance the consumption of luxury goods instead of satisfying the minimum necessities of nutrition, health, housing and employment.[13]"

It is now quite obvious that the coming of new communication and information technologies has come along with them new systems of governance; systems that are quite technologically sophisticated. Nigeria's national interest and security are the guiding factors in our selection and adoption of the new information and communication technologies. The advent of new technologies makes information gathering and dissemination no longer the exclusive preserve of governments and their agencies because the technologies are making information easily accessible to those multinational corporation that are richer than most governments of the developing world. The following insight Schiller provides on the political and economic involvements of the multi-national corporations (MNCs) is quite revealing:

"....in the workings of a worldwide market econo.y..certain centres dominate for a variety of economic and socio-historical reasons. The normal operation of the system pre-supposes that capital is exported to places where the return is attractive, industrial facilities are created in new locations, workers are recruited, and production is expanded (or contrasted) according to market demand. New social classes emerge, and old social formations are absorbed or decay. All of these developments....occur without central direction or political intentionality once the underlying model of capitalistic enterprise has been established and set on its course....Transnational (and local) media participate vigorously in the process, both as profit-making businesses with products to sell and as promotional and marketing agents in the system overall. However, if the basic patterns of capitalistic enterprise in a country seem threatened, a development that occurs with increasing frequency, intentionality replaces the less delineate processes of conventional system maintenance. When this does in fact occur, the role assigned to the media is large indeed. For it is to be expected that the transnational media will do everything they can to rally support for the political "climate" that they find hospitable.[14]"

Finally, Schiller concludes his litany of offences of the multinational corporations with the following shocking insights:

"Accompanying the corruption of political life is the political infiltration and utilization of the local media beyond the "normal" penetration effected through commercial arrangements. In addition to the flooding of foreign economies with commercial TV programmes, films, published materials, and tourists, foreign-based news organizations and publishing companies are infiltrated. This accomplishment has the neat effect of controlling the flow of international information in all directions.[15]"

The Call for Government Divestiture of Media Ownership

In view of these numerous revelations of how the international economic market systems that invent, manufacture and sell the media hardwares, work very hard to exist for the economic and political control of the less powerful and weak nations, is the call by the privileged, elitist Nigerian, intellectuals and financiers for the government to divest itself of media ownership, and to hand them over to a few opportuned and privileged Nigerians, in order? The Federal Ministry of Information and Culture thinks that the timing of this demand is presently not propitious. The constant explosions in new communication technologies for the dissemination of information, most of which threaten the sovereignties of the weak and less powerful nations, make it imperative for a more dynamic communication policy that guarantees Nigeria's national security, defence purposes, and her sovereignty and integrity. Modern communication hardwares make it imperative for the governments of the developing countries (including those in Africa) not to get isolated by allowing big multi-nationals, through their local fronts, take over the mouldering and control of their nationals' public opinion, thus leading to mortgaging of their hard won independence.

The development of modern communication media hardwares is equally leading to formulation and implementation of appropriate communication policies in all the nations of the world; appropriate communication policies that are in consonance with their respective ideological leanings and national interests. Modern systems of mass communication are no longer the simple paraphenalia they used to be for dissemination of information. They are increasingly getting extremely sophisticated and economically and politically allied to the military power of the powerful nations that have invested heavily on nuclear weapons. It is doubtful if any nation can, at this stage in modern warfare and development of communication technology, win any of its battles without integrating the most advanced modern communication technologies. We are all aware of the jamming of radars in military confrontations of recent times. We are also aware of similar jamming of radio stations to subjugate public opinions of weaker nations.

If the Federal and State Governments are stampeded to handing over the most vital and sensitive information systems in this country to private enterprises, what then becomes our fate when a saboteur acquires any of the sophisticated communication technologies? An example will suffice: when the United States spaceship, The Challenger, crashed immediately it was blasted its space mission, initial news reports suggested that amateur radio operators had interferred with The Challenger's communication systems, thus leading to the shortcircuiting of its systems. Even though official probe findings blamed top officials for negligence, resulting from over-used system that failed to function when the Challenger was blasted, the possibility of an amateur radio operator using his electronics gadget to shortcircuit the Challenger's system remains a possibility. The question this US experience raises is: if Nigeria does get technologically advanced, can she afford privatization of the media at this time of its development to the extent that national security is endangered? One is not ruling out private initiative in this regard but should it not start with manufacturing of spare parts other than ultimate ownership of electronic media?

It is instructive, at this juncture, to say that even in the United States, there is a Federal Government Agency, known as the Federal Communications Commission (FCC) that exists to allocate frequencies, to supervise and license radio AM, FM and TV Stations. Licenses are granted for a period of three years and are renewed for another three-year period provided stations show evidence of having met the *needs, interests* and *necessities* of the countries in which they are located. Once any citizenship group petitions the FCC, accusing a particular station of violating any of the numerous guidelines for which it is licensed, the FCC institutes a fair hearing. If, at the end of such a hearing, a station is found guilty, its license is either witndrawn and the station sold to another competitor, or its liconse is renewed for a period less than the normal three years, or it gets a very serious warning.

It is also interesting to note that in a capitalistic country like the United States with a laissez-faire economic practice, individuals and groups are restricted as to the number of radio and TV stations to be owned. It was not until August, 1984 that the FCC revoked the Seven Station Rule that placed ceiling on multiple station ownership from 7 television, 7 FM and 7 AM stations to 12 radio stations in each case.[16"]

It is then a surprise that despite its capitalistically-based economy, the United States governments created a regularly agency that controls and supervises the broadcast industry. The FCC law also forbids any foreign participation in ownership of any radio or TV stations. If a nation that was founded on a free enterprise, a nation as old as 210 years, is still carefully controlling and regulating its broadcast media industry, is it really to Nigeria's national interest to hastely privatize her electronic media industry? In such a policy in the interest of a nation of more than 250 autonomous ethnic groups and about 970,000 communities where national loyalty can, as at now, be best described as an aspiration of the political leadership?

It is also instructive to remind ourselves that as old as the Western European nations that colonised Africa are, the broadcast media are still public utilities, under direct government supervision and control. It was only a couple of years ago that independent broadcasting authority was allowed to operate in Britain and compete with the publicy-owned BBC. In France, the government owns and controls the broadcasting industry. A recent suggestion on privatization triggered off hostile reactions from the French public.

At this stage in our development process, it will be too deer a price to pay as a nation, if, for purely economic reasons, we formulate a public communication policy that allows ultimate private ownership of the electronic media. The policy of the Federal and State Governments is that of making sure that the media they own are operated in the manner that would justify their existence as public utilities. Consequently, members of board of directors are appointed to reflect every spectrum of our society. No government dictates to editors and reporters what to publish. Our democracy is reflected in our media contents. It is therefore the view of this paper that privatization of broadcasting industry in this country at this stage of its development should not be rushed. If we must privatize, we should not start with ownership of electronic media but begin privatization with the manufacturing of components like transmitters, integrated circuits, TV picture tubes, stereo sets, cassette sets, stereo amplifiers, loudspeakers, capacitors, etc. all of which are prerequisites for self-reliance and final ownership of the electronic media by the private sector. An ultimate immediate drive towards privatization of everything in Nigeria at this time of low development in technology is spearheaded by those who want power and not orderly development.

Federal Ministry of Information and Public Policy Objectives

First and foremost, Nigeria's national interests from the bedrock of the services of the Federal Ministry of Information and Culture. Nigeria's domestic and foreign policy objectives are reflected in the contents of what the Ministry disseminates to our national and external audiences. The bold steps Nigeria normally takes on sensitive issues, whose international ramifications affect the nation and the rest of Africa, coupled with the accelerated rate of development in every sector of our society led to the establishment of a very virile *External Publicity Department* in the Ministry in 1986. The goal was (and still is) to effectively and efficiently assist in publicizing and executing Nigeria's domestic and foreign policy objectives, and their attainment, as well as the accomplishments of Nigeria's goals and to generate international respect for the Nigerian personality.

When we realised that the constant technological break-throughs in communication hardwares, being invented in the western societies, are increasingly widening the information imbalance between the industrialised and developing world, thereby putting multinational corporations at extremely privileged and advantageous positions in economic and political enslavement of the less privileged societies, our External Publicity outfit was established as our only viable option to protect our values and present our side of the case in any international issue. The well orchestrated adverse publicity and campaign of calumny and falsehood the Western media frequently unleash on Nigeria leaves us with no other option but to fashion out an aggressively subtle propaganda machinery, possessing efficient retaliatory strike capability to any hostile press outside our borders.

However, just as it is bad for South African paid agents and our adversaries and their secret services to plant imaginary, damaging and false news items in the media houses abroad, to misinform foreigners and bias them about Nigeria, so also it is unpatriotic for some of our national press, particularly the newspapers and magazines, to cull such adverse publications for circulation and readership by their national audience. Let us hope that by the time the present seminar comes to an end, all those charged with dissemination of information must come to the realisation that information policy is not isolated from national interest. Also, our economic, political and social values based on our national philosophy of constructing a fair, just and humane society, should influence the direction of communication policy formulation and decisions. The trend in modern mass communication practices is to impose the cultural, economic and political values and preferences of the societies with the most advanced communication technologies and the media bases from which news sources originate. Our national needs, commitments, interest and obligations should constitute the framework of our communication policy.

It is in furtherance of these objectives that the Federal Public Enlightenment Department has been created in the Ministry to bridge the information gap between the urban and rural communities. The Information Ministry discovered that our print and electronic media are increasingly being concentrated in the urban centres. This amounted to negligence of the rural areas where almost 80 per cent of our people live and produce the food for the entire nation. Public Enlightenment came to bridge the urban-rural communication gap. The Department restored to using all the traditional forms of communication such as local singers using the gong, the drum, flute, etc. to inform, educate, entertain and transmit our cultural values to those in the rural areas. The culmination was the founding of the newspaper, *Town Crier* and numerous traditional systems of communication, news and information on national issues, activities of the government, major events and developments in the nation, government programmes, are communicated to the rural dwellers. The Division evolves public campaign strategies for mobilization of public awareness on development issues of the moment.

Each of the 19 States and the Federal Capital Territory, Abuja, and each of the former senatorial districts, has a station. The Ministry developed this strategy of grassroot information to the rural population and that of developing a vernacular newspaper ever before UNESCO started popularising rural press in the developing nations. As of today, the Ministry disseminates news in over thirteen major languages spoken by Nigerians.

The Domestic Publicity and Film Production Department forms a major power house of the Ministry. In addition to handling all publications of the Ministry, the Department has also Resident Information Officers (RIOs) posted to all the Federal Ministries and Parastatals. The rationale was to publicize the activities of the Ministries and parastatals and to assist journalists and researchers to gain easy access to information they need. This Department administers the National Institute of Public Information, Kaduna, where Information Officers with divergent academic backgrounds and serving officers are trained and updated on journalism and public information practices. Mention must also be made of the crucial role being played by the Departments of Culture and Archives in the propagation of our cultural heritage and the preservation of records, vital for effective communication. With these and its eleven parastatals, the (FMIC) is the pivot of public enlightenment in the country.

In this paper, the Federal Ministry of Information and Culture has not only identified some of the new media, but has also detailed the national and international ramifications of their selection and adoption. If privatised, their owners could be fronting for the multinational corporations. The thesis of the paper is that our national interests, especially economic self-sufficiency in food production and industrialization, political stability that guarantees our nation's territorial integrity and its indivisibility, and preservation of our culture, make it imperative for a careful examination, assessment and the development of our present media structure and ownership.

If the audio cassettes that contained the revolutionary instigations of Ayatola Khomeni in exile in France that were smuggled into Iran triggered off the revolt against the Shah and his eventual overthrow; and spliced-up tape of events at the Manila International Airport on the day Benigno Aquino was assassinated and his funeral, as captured by video cassette recorder (VCR), could provoke a democratic revolution in the Phillipines that led to the toppling of a dictator, it means that the "new media" in the predictions of Nora C. Quebral, "could potentially be used to forment revolution of another kind in politically unstable countries ...."[17] It therefore suggests that constant technological break-throughs in the communication field make public policy formulation to be adopted to *risk* and *uncertainty*, especially in the developing countries that depend on advanced communication technologies that come from outside their political spheres of jurisdiction.

Ideally, a technologically developed or developing country would naturally have no problem deciding what public communication policy to choose, among available options, after a thorough analysis, examination and appraisal of "all possible courses of action and their possible consequences and after an evaluation of those consequences"[18] in the light of its values. But presently, our rate of technological development has not synchronised with our society's values as none of our communication hardwares is locally-produced. One fact that obviously surfaces from this brain-storming seminar on conceptualising and determining as well as defining the parameter of Nigeria's communication policy, is indeed that there are segregated communication/information policies which need to be streamlined. New ideas and changes with scholars and experts in the field will go a long way to reinforce our communication policy. In most instances, accomplishments of communication policy objectives cannot be quantified. But failures are easily identifiable. Our package of communication policy involves the totality of the Nigerian experience in all spheres of human endeavour. Major developments and accomplishments in all sectors of our society form the basis of our communication policy, as predicated by our national interest.

In the absence of a Nigerian developed technology in the communication field, it will not be appropriate to identify policy-making, policy analysis and decision-making with problem solving in the field of communication—a field that is witnessing an explosion of new discoveries, with each new invention rendering obsolete a previously acquired hardware. Perhaps in the future, our scientists in the relevant technologies in communication processing, could be the most influential actors in our "new media" policy options.

REFERENCES

1. Oh Myung. "New Media and The Third World: Broadcasting in the Future. The Third Channel. Vol. 1, No. 2. 1985 pp. 174-175.
2. *Ibid*
3. Susanna Eun. "Telecommunications Planning for Social Development: Application of Socio-Technical Assessment Model (A Case Study in South Korea)." Paper presented at the 35th Annual Conference of International Communication Association to the Intercultural/Development Communication Division, in May, 1986 in Honolulu, Hawaii, USA.
4. *Ibid*
5. *Ibid*
6. *Ibid*
7. Dongshin Lee: "Deffusion or Imperialism...A View of Communication, Culture, Mass Media and Technology." Paper presented at the Joint Session of Korean Society for Journalism and Mass Communication and Korean American Communication Association at the 35th Annual Conference of International Communication Association, held in May, 1985, in Honolulu, Hawaii.
8. Luke Uka Uche. "The New World Information and Communication Order: Towards a Conceptual Model for Understanding the Debate." *The Third Channel.* Vol. 1, No. 2 1985. pp. 283-289.
9. *Ibid*
10. *Ibid*
11. Herbert I. Schiller. "Transnational Media and National Development." In *National Sovereignty and International Communication—A Reader*

Edited by Kaarle Norden Streng and Herbert I. Schiller, Norwood, New Jersey: Ablex Publishing Corporation 1979. p. 30

12. *Ibid*
13. *Ibid*
14. *Ibid*
15. *Ibid*
16. Harvey J. Levin. "US Broadcast Dereguletin : A Case of Dubious Evidence." *Journal of Communication (Winter)* 1986. Vol. 36, No. 1, pp. 25-28.
17. Nora C. Quebral. "The Video Recorder in Developing Countries." *Communication Socialis*. Vol. IV. 1985 p. 199.
18. David Braybrooke & Charles E. Lindblom. A Strategy of Decision. New York: The Tree press 1970 pp. 140-142.

Appendix F

Supplement to Official Gazette Extraordinary No. 18, Vol. 71, 4th April, 1984—Part—A

PUBLIC OFFICERS (PROTECTION AGAINST FALSE ACCUSATION) DECREE 1984

ARRANGEMENT OF SECTIONS

Decree No. 4

[*29th March* 1984]

Commencement.

THE FEDERAL MILITARY GOVERNMENT hereby decrees as follows :—

Publication or transmission of rumours, etc.

1.—(1) Any person who publishes in any form, whether written or otherwise, any message, rumour, report or statement, being a message, rumour, statement or report which is false in any material particular or which brings or is calculated to bring the Federal Military Government or the Government of a State or a public officer to ridicule or disrepute, shall be guilty of an offence under this Decree.

(2) Any station for wireless telegraphy which conveys or transmits any sound or visual message, rumour, report or statement, being a message, rumour, report or statement which is false in any material particular or which brings or is calculated to bring the Federal Military Government or the Government of a State or a public officer to ridicule or disrepute, shall be guilty of an offence under this Decree.

(3) It shall be an offence under this Decree for a newspaper or wireless telegraphy station in Nigeria to publish or transmit any message, rumour, report or statement which is false in any material particular stating that any public officer has in any manner been engaged in corrupt practices or has in any manner corruptly enriched himself or any other person.

Power to
prohibit the
circulation of
newspapers,
etc.

2.—(1) Where the Head of the Federal Military Government is satisfied that the unrestricted circulation in Nigeria of a newspaper is or may be detrimental to the interest of the Federation or of any part thereof, he may by order published in the *Gazette*, prohibit the circulation in the Federation or in any part thereof, as the case may require, of that newspaper ; and, unless any other period is prescribed in the order, the prohibition shall continue for a period of twelve months unless sooner revoked or extended, as the case may require.

(2) Where the Head of the Federal Military Government is satisfied that the unrestricted existence in Nigeria of any wireless telegraphy station is detrimental to the interest of the Federation or any part thereof, he may by an order published in the *Gazette*—

1961 No. 31.

(*a*) revoke the licence granted to such wireless telegraphy station under the provisions of the Wireless Telegraphy Act 1961 ; or

(*b*) order the closure or forfeiture to the Federal Military Government as the case may be, of the wireless telegraphy station concerned.

Trial of
offences
under this
Decree.

3.—(1) In any prosecution for an offence under this Decree, the burden of proving that the message, rumour, report or statement which is the subject-matter of the charge is true in every material particular shall, notwithstanding anything to the contrary in any enactment or rule of law, lie on the person charged.

(2) Prosecutions under this Decree may be commenced and proceeded within the tribunal set up pursuant to this Decree.

1964 No. 1.

(3) Section 24 of the Interpretation Act 1964 (which among other things provides that a person shall not be punished twice where he is guilty of an offence under more than one enactment) shall, subject to the provisions of sections 7 and 10 of this Decree, apply in respect of an offence under this Decree.

(4) A tribunal appointed under subsection (1) of this section shall consist of—

(*a*) a Chairman who shall be a serving or retired judge of a High Court or of any court of like jurisdiction ; and

(*b*) three members of the Armed Forces not below the rank of major or its equivalent.

Jurisdiction
and powers
of
tribunal, etc.

4.—(1) A tribunal shall have jurisdiction to try any person and award any of the penalties specified in section 8 of this Decree.

(2) For the purposes of subsection (1) of this section, where in respect of any act which is an offence under this Decree a tribunal is satisfied that any other person acted in concert with the person charged or knowingly took part to any extent whatsoever in the commission of the act constituting an offence under this Decree, the tribunal shall have power to treat that other person in the same manner as the person charged under this Decree and shall proceed against him accordingly, notwithstanding anything to the contrary in any other enactment.

Rules of
procedure
and
institution of
proceedings.

5.—(1) The rules of procedure to be adopted in prosecutions for offences under this Decree before a tribunal and the forms to be used in such proceedings shall be as set out in the Schedule to this Decree.

(2) Prosecutions for offences under this Decree shall be instituted before a tribunal in the name of the Federal Republic of Nigeria by the Attorney-General of the Federation or such officer in the Federal Ministry of Justice as he may authorise so to do and, in addition thereto, he may—

(a) after consultation with the Attorney-General of any State in the Federation, authorise any officer in the Ministry of Justice of that State to undertake any such prosecutions directly or assist therein ;

(b) if a tribunal so requests, or if contingencies so dictate, authorise any other legal practitioner in Nigeria to undertake any such prosecution directly or assist therein :

Provided that the question whether any or what authority has been given in pursuance of this subsection shall not be inquired into by any person other than the Attorney-General of the Federation.

(3) Any person accused of any offence under this Decree shall be entitled to defend himself in person or by a person of his own choice who is a legal practitioner resident in Nigeria.

(4) Where the rules of procedure contained in the Schedule to this Decree contain no provisions in respect of any matter relating to or connected with the trial of offences under this Decree, the provisions of the Criminal Procedure Code or, depending on the venue, the Criminal Procedure Act shall, with such modifications as the circumstances may require, apply in respect of such matter to the same extent as they apply to the trial of offences generally.

6. Notwithstanding the provisions of any other enactment conferring power to search, if the Chairman of a tribunal is satisfied that there is reasonable ground to suspect that there are or may be found in any building or other place whatsoever, any money or other property or any books, records, accounts statements or information in any other form whatsoever he may issue a warrant under his hand authorising any police officer or any member of the armed forces or security agencies to enter, if necessary by force, the said building or other place and every part thereof, and to search for, seize and remove any such thing as aforesaid found therein.

Power to issue search warrants.

7. Nothing in this Decree shall be construed as affecting the right of any person to institute civil proceedings in respect of the publication of any false message, rumour, report or statement which is the subject-matter of proceedings under this Decree.

Prosecution not to be a bar to civil proceedings.

8.—(1) Any person found guilty of an offence under this Decree shall be liable on conviction to be sentenced to imprisonment for a term not exceeding two years, without the option of a fine and, in the case of a body corporate, to a fine of not less than ₦10,000.

Penalty and forfeiture.

(2) Where an offence under this Decree has been committed by a body corporate, every person who at the time of the commission of the offence was a proprietor, publisher, director, general manager, editor, secretary or other similar officer of the body corporate, or was purporting to act in any such capacity, shall be deemed to be guilty of that offence unless he proves that the offence was committed without his consent or connivance, and that he exercised all such diligence to prevent the commission of the offence as he ought to have exercised, having regard to the nature of his functions in that capacity and in all the circumstances.

(3) Where a body corporate is convicted of an offence under this Decree, the tribunal may, in addition to any other penalty, order all or any of the equipment of the newpaper or wireless telegraphy station, with which the offence was committed, to be forfeited to the Federal Military Government.

(4) No appeal shall lie from a decision of any tribunal established under this Decree.

Exclusion of proceedings.

9. The validity of any direction, notice or order given or made or, as the case may be, of any other thing whatsoever done under this Decree shall not be inquired into in any court of law, and accordingly, nothing in Chapter IV of the Constitution of the Federal Republic of Nigeria 1979 shall apply in relation to any matter arising out of this Decree.

Offences continued after conviction.

10. Without prejudice to the right to bring separate proceedings for contraventions of this Decree taking place on separate occasions, a person who is convicted of an offence under this Decree consisting in repeated publication or transmission of the message, rumour, report or statement which is the subject-matter of proceedings under this Decree, shall be deemed to have committed a separate offence in respect of every day or occasion on which the publication or transmission is so repeated or continued.

Interpretation.

11. In this Decree, unless the context otherwise requires—

"circulation" includes the sale, offering for sale or distribution or possession of, with a view to selling, offering or distributing, a newspaper ;

"newspaper" includes any paper containing public news, intelligence or occurrences or any remarks or observations therein printed anywhere and circulating in Nigeria for sale and published in Nigeria, or periodically, or in parts, or in numbers at intervals, and includes any paper printed in order to be dispersed and made public (in numbers at periodic intervals) or containing only or principally advertisements ;

1961 No. 31.

"wireless telegraphy stations" has the same meaning assigned to it in the Wireless Telegraphy Act 1961 ;

"public officer" means any person who holds any office in the public service of the Federation or of a State as defined in the Constitution of the Federal Republic of Nigeria 1979, as affected by the Constitution (Suspension and Modification) Decree 1984.

1984 No. 1.

Citation and repeal.

12.—(1) This Decree may be cited as the Public Officers (Protection Against False Accusation) Decree 1984.

1976 No. 11.

(2) The Public Officers (Protection Against False Accusation) Decree 1976 is hereby repealed.

SCHEDULE   *Section* 5 (1)

RULES OF PROCEDURE

Commencement and Conduct of Trial

1. The trial of offences under this Decree shall commence by way of an application, supported by a summary of evidence, made to the tribunal by the prosecutor.

Institution of proceedings.

2. Where after perusal of the application and the summary of evidence or any further evidence in such form as the tribunal may consider necessary, the tribunal is satisfied that any person appears to have committed any offence under this Decree, it shall cause that person to be brought before the tribunal on such date and at such time as it may direct.

Order on an accused to appear.

3.—(1) When the tribunal is ready to commence the trial, the accused shall be brought before it and the tribunal shall read or cause to be read to him the substance of the complaint against him and he shall be asked whether he is guilty of the offence or offences charged.

Commencement of trial.

(2) If the accused pleads guilty the plea shall be recorded and he may in the discretion of the tribunal be convicted thereon.

Plea of not guilty or no plea.

4. If the accused pleads not guilty or makes no plea or refuses to plead or if the tribunal enters a plea of not guilty on behalf of the accused, the tribunal shall proceed to try the case.

5.—(1) After a plea of not guilty has been taken or no plea has been made the prosecutor may open the case against the accused, stating shortly by what evidence he intends to prove the guilt of the accused.

Presentation of case for prosecution.

(2) The prosecutor shall then examine the witness for the prosecution who may be cross-examined by the accused or his counsel and may thereafter be re-examined by the prosecutor.

6.—(1) After the conclusion of the presentation of evidence by the prosecutor, the tribunal shall ask the accused—

Procedure after presentation of evidence by the prosecution.

(*a*) whether he wishes to give evidence on his own behalf ; and

(*b*) whether he intends to call witnesses other than witnesses to character.

(2) If the accused says that he does not intend to call any witnesses other than witnesses to character, the prosecutor may sum up his case against the accused and the tribunal shall then call upon the accused to enter upon the defence.

(3) Notwithstanding the provisions of paragraph (2) of this rule, the tribunal may, after hearing the evidence for the prosecution, if it considers that the evidence against the accused or any of several accused is not sufficient to justify the continuation of the trial, record a finding of not guilty in respect of such accused without calling upon him or them to enter upon the defence and such accused shall thereupon be discharged and acquitted and the tribunal shall then call upon the remaining accused, if any, to enter upon the defence.

(4) If the accused or any one of several accused says that he intends to call any witness, other than a witness to character, the tribunal shall call upon the accused to enter upon the defence.

(5) Notwithstanding the provisions of paragraph (4) of this rule, the tribunal may, before calling upon the accused to enter upon the defence, call upon the prosecutor to sum up his case against any one or more of the accused against whom it considers that the evidence is not sufficient to justify the continuation of the trial and, after hearing the summing up, if any, may in its discretion record a finding of not guilty in respect of any such accused or call upon any of them to enter upon his or their defence.

Defence.

7. When the tribunal calls upon the accused to enter upon the defence the accused or his counsel may open his case stating the facts or law on which he intends to rely and making such comments as he thinks necessary on the evidence for the prosecution, and the accused may then give evidence on his own behalf, examine his witnesses, if any, and, after their cross-examination and re-examination, if any, the accused or his counsel may sum up his case.

Right of prosecutor to reply.

8.—(1) If the accused or any of the accused calls any witness, other than a witness to character, or any document, other than a document relating to character, is put in evidence for the defence, the prosecutor shall be entitled to reply.

(2) If the accused has called only evidence as to character, the prosecutor may at the close of the case for the defence adduce evidence of previous convictions of the accused, if any, as to corruption, abuse of office or any other offence as to dishonesty.

(3) Notwithstanding the provisions of paragraphs (1) and (2) of this rule, in any case, with the leave of the tribunal, the prosecutor may be heard in reply on a point of law or, where none of the accused has adduced evidence other than as to character but any of them has introduced new matter in his statement to the tribunal, on such new matter.

Consideration of finding.

9. When the case for the defence and the reply of the prosecutor, if any, are concluded and the tribunal does not desire to put any further question to the accused, the tribunal shall retire or adjourn to consider its finding.

Announcement of finding.

10. After the tribunal has made its finding the Chairman shall announce that finding and, where the accused is found guilty, it shall impose the appropriate penalty prescribed by this Decree and issue a commital warrant accordingly.

Notes of evidence to be taken.

11.—(1) The Chairman or any other member of the tribunal authorised by the Chairman in that behalf shall in every case take notes in writing of the oral evidence, or so much thereof as he considers is material, in a book to be kept for that purpose and such book shall be signed by the Chairman at the conclusion of each day's proceeding and not less than two other members of the tribunal including the person who took down the notes.

(2) The record so kept as aforesaid or a copy thereof purporting to be signed and certified as a true copy by the Chairman shall, without further proof, be admitted as evidence of such proceedings and of the statements made by the witnesses.

Supplemental

Issue of summons for witness.

12. If the tribunal is satisfied that any person is likely to give material evidence for the prosecution or for the defence the tribunal may issue a summons to such person requiring him to attend, at a time and place to be mentioned therein, before the tribunal to give evidence respecting the case

and to bring with him any specified documents or things and any other documents or things relating thereto which may be in his possession or power or under his control.

13. If the person to whom any such summons is directed does not attend before the tribunal at the time and place mentioned therein, and there does not appear to the tribunal on inquiry to be any reasonable excuse for such non-attendance, then after proof to the satisfaction of the tribunal that the summons was duly served or that the person to whom the summons is directed wilfully avoided service, the tribunal, on being satisfied that such person is likely to give material evidence may issue a warrant to apprehend him and to bring him, at the time and place to be mentioned in the warrant before the tribunal in order to testify as aforesaid.

Warrant of witness after summons.

14. It shall be the duty of the tribunal to make or cause to be made such local inspection as the circumstances of the case may require.

Local inspection.

15. Subject to the express provisions, of this Decree, the forms contained in the Annex to this Schedule may, in accordance with any instruction contained in the said forms, and with such variations as the circumstances of the particular case may require be used in the cases to which they apply, and, when so used, shall be good and sufficient in law.

Forms.

16. In these rules, "the prosecutor" means the Attorney-General of the Federation or any other person authorised by him pursuant to section 5 (2) of this Decree to conduct the prosecution of an offence before the tribunal or to assist therein.

Definition.

ANNEX 1 (*Rule* 15)

[FORMS

FORM 1

APPLICATION TO COMMENCE TRIAL FOR AN OFFENCE UNDER THE PUBLIC OFFICERS (PROTECTION AGAINST FALSE ACCUSATION) DECREE 1984

To : The Chairman,
Tribunal for the trial of offences under the Public Officers (Protection Against False Accusation) Decree 1984.

....

....

....

Pursuant to section 5 (2) of the Public Officers (Protection Against False Accusation) Decree 1984, I hereby apply for the commencement of a trial for

the offence of...under section

....of the aforesaid Decree against the undermentioned persons :—

(*i*)..

(*ii*)..

2. In support of this application I attach hereto.................................
....copies of the summary of evidence for the consideration of the Tribunal.

3. If this application is granted, I shall be relying on the facts disclosed in the summary of evidence and any further evidence the Tribunal may consider necessary at the trial. I attach hereto four copies of the charge against the accused. A list of the deponents and their addresses is also attached for the purpose of issuing witness summons on them.

....
Prosecutor

FORM 2

Public Officers (Protection against False Accusation)
Decree 1984

SUMMONS TO ACCUSED

In the Tribunal for the trial of offences under the Public Officers (Protection Against False Accusation) Decree 1984.

To A.B. of...

Complaint has been made this day by (*iii*)..

for that you on the..................day of..

at...in the...

aforesaid did*...

....

....

....

You are therefore summoned to appear before the Tribunal mentioned above sitting at..

....

on...............................to answer the said complaint.................................

DATED the..day of......................................19..........

....
Chairman of the Tribunal

_____

(*i*), (*ii*) *Insert name of accused persons.*
(*iii*) *State name of prosecutor*

FORM 3

Public Officers (Protection Against False Accusation)
Decree 1984

WARRANT FOR APPREHENSION OF ACCUSED

In the Tribunal for the trial of offences under the Public Officers (Protection Against False Accusation) Decree 1984

Between

The Federal Republic of Nigeria

and

.... Accused

To..Police   Officer.

Complaint has been made on.....................................of...........................by

.... that...

(hereinafter called the accused) on the..day of

....did*

....

You are hereby commanded to bring the accused before the Tribunal mentioned above sitting at...on.....................to answer the said complaint and be dealt with according to law.

DATED the..day of...........................19.................

....
Chairman of the Tribunal

—————
State concisely the substance of the offence.

FORM 4

Public Officers (Protection False Against Accusation) .
Decree 1984

SUMMONS TO WITNESS

In the Tribunal for the trial of offences under the Public Officers
(Protection Against False Accusation) Decree 1984.

Between

The Federal Republic of Nigeria

and

.... Accused

To (*i*)..

(*ii*)...has been

charged by (*iii*)..at................

....in...

that he did (*iv*)..

....

and it appearing to me on the application of (*iii*)...

....that you are likely to give material evidence
therein on behalf of the prosecutor (or accused).

You are therefore summoned to appear before the Tribunal named above
sitting at...on the...............................day of

....19....................at the hour of.................................

....in the.......................................noon,
to testify what you know in such matter.

DATED the................day of.................................19........

....
Chairman of the Tribunal

---

*State concisely the substance of the offence.

(*i*)   *Insert name of witness.*
(*ii*)   *Insert name of accused.*
(*iii*) *Insert the name of prosecutor or, if applicable, the accused.*
(*iv*) *State concisely the substance of the offence.*

FORM 5

Public Officers (Protection Against False Accusation)
Decree 1984

WARRANT FOR APPREHENSION OF WITNESS IN THE FIRST INSTANCE

In the Tribunal for the trial of offences under the Public Officers (Protection Against False Accusation) Decree 1984.

To..

A.B. has been charged by...

for that he on the...

day of...at...

in the...State aforesaid

did*..

....

....

And it appearing to me by the oath of..
that E.F. is likely to give material evidence concerning the said matter, and that it is probable he will not attend to give evidence unless compelled to do so.

You are therefore hereby commanded to bring him before the Tribunal

named above sitting at..forthwith
to testify what he knows concerning the said matter.

DATED the.................day of.................................19.........

....
Chairman of the Tribunal

—————

*State concisely the substance of the offence.

A 64   **1984 No. 4**   *Public Officers (Protection against False Accusation)*

FORM 6

Public Officers (Protection Against False Accusation)
Decree 1984

WARRANT FOR APPREHENSION OF A WITNESS

In the Tribunal for the trial of offences under the Public Officers (Protection Against False Accusation) Decree 1984.

Between

The Federal Republic of Nigeria

and

.... Accused

To ....Police Constable or to each and all the Constables of..

(*i*)...was duly summoned to appear before the Tribunal named above sitting at ....

on .... at the hour of...

in the...noon, to testify what he knows concerning a certain complaint against...

....

And he has neither appeared thereto, nor offered any just excuse for his neglect.

And it has been proved on oath that the summons has been duly served on him (and that a reasonable sum has been paid (or tendered) to him for his costs and expenses in that behalf).

You are therefore hereby commanded to bring him before the tribunal named above sitting at...forthwith to testify what he knows concerning the said matter.

DATED the...of day...19......

....

Chairman of the Tribunal

(*i*) *Insert name of witness.*

Public Officers (Protection against False Accusation) **1984 No. 4** **A 65**

FORM 7

Public Officers (Protection Against False Accusation)
Decree 1984

WARRANT FOR COMMITMENT OF WITNESS

In the Tribunal for the trial of offences under the Public Officers (Protection Against False Accusation) Decree 1984.

Between

The Federal Republic of Nigeria

and

....Accused

To .... and to the

Superintendent of..Prison

(*i*) ....having appeared
or been brought before the Tribunal named above sitting at...............................
....on the...........................day of.........................19.........
to testify what he knows concerning a certain matter against

(*ii*) ....refused to take an oath
(or having taken an oath) refused to answer any (or a certain) question put to him concerning the matter and did not offer any just excuse for his refusal.

You the said Police Officer are hereby commanded to convey the said

....safely to the prison
and deliver him to the Superintendent thereof, together with this Warrant and you, the Superintendent of the said prison, to receive him into your custody and keep him for the period of...unless he in the meantime consents to be examined and to answer concerning the matter.

DATED the..................................day of.................................19.........

....
Chairman of the Tribunal

(*i*) Insert name of witness.
(*ii*) Insert name of accused.

FORM 8

Public Officers (Protection Against False Accusation)
Decree 1984

COMMITMENT ON REMAND

In the Tribunal for the trial of offences under the Public Officers (Protection Against False Accusation) **Decree 1984.**

Between

The Federal Republic of Nigeria

and

.... Accused

To...and Officer-in-charge

of...Police Station and to

the Superintendent of...Prison.

(*i*) ....(hereinafter called the accused) being brought before the Tribunal named above, sitting at............ ....

....charged with having

(*ii*) ....

The hearing of the case being adjourned :

You the said Police Officer are hereby commanded to convey the accused from police custody at...*to the said prison and there to deliver him to the Officer-in-charge*/Superintendent thereof, together with this Warrant, and you, the Officer-in-charge*/the Superintendent of the said prison to receive him into your custody, and keep him until the..........

.... day of...................19...............and

on that day to convey him before the said tribunal at the hour of...........................

in the..noon to be further dealt with according to law.

DATED the..day of..................19.............

....

Chairman of the Tribunal

(*i*)   *Insert name of accused.*
(*ii*) *State the Offence or Offences.*
  * *Delete whichever does not apply.*

FORM No. 9

Public Officers (Protection Against False Accusation) Decree 1984

In the Tribunal for the trial of offences under the Public Officers (Protection Against False Accusation) Decree 1984.

WARRANT OF CONVICTION

Between

The Federal Republic of Nigeria

and

.... *Accused*

(*i*) ....having appeared before

the tribunal named above sitting at...................................is this day convicted

for that he, on the...day of..................................

19..............at..within the..........................did

(*ii*) ....

And it is adjudged that the accused, for his said offence, be sentenced to

(*iii*) ....

....

DATED the...........................day of.................................19..............

....

Chairman of the Tribunal

(*i*) *Insert name of accused.*
(*ii*) *State concisely the substance of offence.*
(*iii*) *State sentence imposed on accused.*

MADE at Lagos this 29th day ot March 1984.

MAJOR-GENERAL M. BUHARI,
Head of the Federal Military Government,
Commander-in-Chief of the Armed Forces,
Federal Republic of Nigeria

A 68   **1984 No. 4**   *Public Officers (Protection against False Accusation)*

EXPLANATORY NOTE

(This note does not form part of the above-mentioned Decree but is merely intended to explain its purpose)

The Decree makes it an offence for any of the print or electronic media to print or transmit without justification any false message, rumour, report or statement calculated to bring to ridicule or disrepute the Federal or any State Government or any public officer, as defined in the Decree. Penalties are imposed for any contravention of the provisions of the Decree and such penalties include—

(*a*) in the case of an individual such as a proprietor, publisher, manager, editor or such similar officer, a term of imprisonment for 2 years without the option of a fine ;

(*b*) in the case of a body corporate, the imposition of a fine of not less than ₦10,000 and, in an appropriate case, the forfeiture to the Federal Military Government of any equipment of the print or electronic media concerned or the proscription of the newspaper or periodical.

Offences under the Decree are triable by a Military Tribunal constituted under the Decree for that purpose.

Index